W9-BQX-160

Praise for Kate Christensen's

## *Blue Plate Special*

"A fine case for life's simplest pleasures—soul-satisfying sustenance shared with a soul mate."
—*The Washington Post*

"Picking up *Blue Plate Special* is a little like having Kate Christensen sit down next to you in a bar and hearing her life story. . . . In a bar, you wouldn't get her recipes, however. They appear in the book and are built for comfort, from the Bachelorette Puttanesca to the Dark Night of the Soul Soup."
—*Los Angeles Times*

"An inspiring and refreshing memoir that should whet the reader's appetite to seek out the rest of [Christensen's] oeuvre."
—*The Miami Herald*

"The memoir of an utterly original thinker, a free-spirited gourmand, and a great American writer. [*Blue Plate Special*] is an expert guide on inspiration, ingenuity, heartbreak, buoyancy, home, love, family, screwing up, bouncing back, and perfecting the bacon-cheddar biscuit."
—Gillian Flynn,
author of *Gone Girl*, *Dark Places*, and *Sharp Objects*

"[A] poignant, delicious first memoir. . . . A delightful book that leaves you hungering for more."
—*People*

"Christensen . . . brings a real sense of enchantment to her food writing. . . . She is both sensual and wickedly observant, a hard combination to pull off."
—NPR

"A breathtaking book, sensuously written, emotionally generous, and decadent as a bowl of macaroni and cheese."
—Jami Attenberg, author of *The Middlesteins*

"A banquet of sorts, with a surfeit of flavors. Christensen eats for all of us, and writes about food at the intersection of everything that matters. . . . [A] fierce, bighearted memoir."
—*Portland Press Herald*

"A moving feast of memory, a repast of the past. . . . [Christensen's] clean prose is sprinkled with witty phrases and wry observations. . . . An honest portrayal of the forces that have shaped her: love and loss; joy and pain; trust and despondency."
—*The Christian Science Monitor*

"Warm, wise, earthy, funny, honest, haunting, and big-hearted. . . . If you're crazy about M. F. K. Fisher and Laurie Colwin, you will be crazy for this book, too. There's not a single empty calorie here: every morsel is both delicious and nourishing."
—Rosie Schaap, author of *Drinking With Men*

"Christensen lifts her story toward something bigger, something signifying. She looks up and glances across her page. 'I see you,' she says. And we feel seen."
—*The Millions*

"A banquet of a book about eating, loving, and overcoming, to be devoured as fast as one's fingers can turn the pages." —Cathi Hanauer, author of *Gone* and *Sweet Ruin*, and editor of *The Bitch in the House*

Kate Christensen

*Blue Plate Special*

Kate Christensen is the author of six novels, including *The Astral*. *The Great Man* won the 2008 PEN/Faulkner Award. She has published reviews and essays in numerous publications, such as *The New York Times Book Review*, *Bookforum*, *O, The Oprah Magazine*, *Elle*, and *Gilt Taste*. She writes an occasional drinks column called With a Twist for *The Wall Street Journal*. She lives in Portland, Maine.

http://katechristensen.wordpress.com

*Also by Kate Christensen*

# Blue Plate Special

AN AUTOBIOGRAPHY OF MY
APPETITES

## Kate Christensen

ANCHOR BOOKS
A Division of Random House LLC
New York

FIRST ANCHOR BOOKS EDITION, APRIL 2014

All of the events and incidents in this book have been written exactly as I remember them. In addition, I have corroborated many of the facts with the people involved. All dialogue has been reconstructed to conform as closely as possible to my memories. Nonetheless, I have changed many names and identifying characteristics of the individuals involved.

Portions of this work were previously published in different form, in the following publications: *Heavy Rotation* edited by Peter Terzian (New York: Harper Perennial, 2009); *The Bitch in the House* edited by Cathi Hanauer (New York: William Morrow & Company, 2002); *Love Is a Four-Letter Word* edited by Michael Taeckens (New York: Plume, 2009); *Elle* magazine (May 26, 2011); *Largehearted Boy* (http://blog.largeheartedboy.com/); *The Days of Yore* (http://www.thedaysofyore.com/); *Don't Let It Bring You Down* (http://katechristensen.wordpress.com/)

The Library of Congress has cataloged the Doubleday edition as follows:
Christensen, Kate.
Blue plate special : an autobiography of my appetites / Kate Christensen. — First edition.
pages cm
1. Christensen, Kate. 2. Women authors, American—21st century—Biography.
3. Authors, American—21st century—Biography.
4. Mothers and daughters—United States. 5. Appetite—Psychological aspects.
6. Food—Psychological aspects. I. Title.
PS3553.H716Z46 2013
818'.5403—dc23
[B]    2012048556

**Anchor Trade Paperback ISBN: 978-0-307-95110-6**
**eBook ISBN: 978-0-385-53627-1**

Book design by Maria Carella

www.anchorbooks.com

Printed in the United States of America
10  9  8  7  6  5  4  3  2  1

*For Liz, Susan, and Emily*

Often the place and time help make a food what it becomes, even more than the food itself.

M. F. K. FISHER

If we could just have the kitchen and the bedroom, that would be all we need.

JULIA CHILD

# CONTENTS

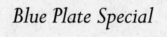

*Blue Plate Special*

## Prologue

—— Often, whenever I come up against anything painful or difficult, my mind escapes to food. I am sure I am far from alone in this. Even if I'm too upset to eat, just the thought of a grilled cheese sandwich and a bowl of tomato soup is warm and cozy and savory and comforting. Unlike memories, emotions, experiences, food is an irrefutable fact, a bit of physical nourishment, and when it's gone, it's gone.

During the worst dark nights of the soul, my smaller failings rise up one by one in a chorus of metallic voices: that unwritten, obligatory important letter; my tipsy, laughing, unintentional, klutzy faux pas booming into a sudden silence; the failure to speak when speaking would have helped someone. . . .

These things are much worse to recall than any of my gigantic, life-changing mistakes. Those are boulders too big to see all at once, hulking, unmoving, and strangely safe, whereas the little things generate a cascade that turns into an avalanche. They're all attached to one another somehow, neurochemically, so that remembering just one of them sets off a chain reaction sparking all the way back through the decades with increasing urgency until I've looped through my entire life, all the way back to the first one, which now seems worse than ever in light of all the others.

Evidently, my mind wants to whirl and foment and obsess in those dark little hours when there's nothing to distract it from its own petty storms. But sometimes, if I start to picture what's downstairs in the kitchen cupboards and fridge and those bowls on the counter, and try to piece everything together in a series of interesting meals and fill in any gaps with a mental grocery list, it turns into a fun, riveting game so engaging I forget what a horrible person I am and fixate instead on the far more relevant question of what I plan to cook and eat in the near future. Let's say hypothetically that there's some goat cheese downstairs plus a butternut squash, some red onions, ginger, garlic. Also, there are some apples . . . a box of chicken broth . . . pine nuts. . . .

Before I know it, I'm asleep again.

My love of food was slow to ignite, but when it did, the year I turned eight, it exploded into one of the great passions of my life, along with writing (alcohol and sex came later, of course). This was exciting, but it also brought the usual perils that threaten any avid eater.

Food can be dangerous. For the unintegrated person—someone hiding a deep, essential truth from herself or someone in the grip of emotions almost too strong to tolerate (both of which have been me at various times)—it can cause trouble, and I don't just mean indigestion. Food is not a means toward resolution. It can't cure heartbreak or solve untenable dilemmas. Maybe for this reason, food often feels meaningless in times of true emotional duress. When I'm in some sort of extreme state—depression, mania, heartbreak, crisis—I can't eat. When I'm so full of yearning I think I might implode, or when there's so much trouble in my life I can't see a way out, food overwhelms me—my soul has become so splayed open that to eat might be to disintegrate from overload.

Food is a subterranean conduit to sensuality, memory, desire, but it opens the eater to all of it without changing anything. If carnality is what you're after, there's a danger of increased frustration in the seductive, savory earthiness of a plate of spinach ravioli with sage butter: food can do many things, but it can't substitute for sex. If you're seized with terrible, unprintable rage toward someone you love, a ripe, velvety avocado can send you over the edge with its innocent bystander meekness.

To taste fully is to live fully. And to live fully is to be awake and responsive to complexities and truths—good and terrible, overwhelming and minuscule. To eat passionately is to allow the world in; there can be no hiding or sublimation when you're chewing a mouthful of food so good it makes you swoon.

I began with eating and moved on to cooking just as I began with reading and moved on to writing. I was very lonely for most of my life until the past few years, and this loneliness was assuaged, as it so often is, with reading and writing, cooking and eating. These were most often solitary pleasures for me. The company of other people, the vicissitudes of romantic relationships, or just being out in the world, have often made me feel anxious, uncomfortable, judged, shy, or misunderstood, and fundamentally unconnected to myself, the truest cause of loneliness. Eating a good meal, like reading a satisfying novel, has returned me to myself during times when this disconnect was a profound internal chasm.

Through the years, I've published six novels, all of which engage in some way with the same themes—struggling, loneliness, floundering, and excess, as well as food, love, art, marriage, and family. All my novels are about, in one way or another, people whose lives are changing whether they like it or not, people who are faced with some degree of external crisis and have to scramble to deal with it. My protagonists are men and women, young and old, but they all share this. The older I get, the more my own life feels implicated in my own novels, and the clearer it is to me that all my characters' concerns come directly from my own experiences.

In recent years, my life has started to intrude on my writing. It first announced itself as a subject quietly but insistently, as subjects will if you let them, the way a cat might sit on a book you're trying to read. Finally, a year ago, as my fiftieth birthday approached, I gave in, put aside the novel I was working on, and out of nowhere for the first time started to write short essays about my life—ostensibly centered on food as a lifelong passion and favorite pastime but, in a deeper way, addressing my own experiences and memories. These essays emerged naturally, almost as if I were transcribing rather than writing them. Not for many years had my work felt so urgent, effortless, and fun. I posted them online, one by one, as a blog, in order to connect with readers, even if they were just my mother and a few friends. To my happy surprise, more and more people began reading these essays, until I became aware of a growing readership and understood from their responses that I was offering comfort, somehow, simply by revealing certain truths about my own life.

It finally dawned on me, after a few months, that this of course was my next book. And so I set about writing down my own chronology, a sort of autobiography, through which run the currents that have preoccupied me all my life. I wanted to account for them, to trace them back all the way to the beginning, and watch them twist together through time all the way to the present. I wrote out of a feeling of "emotion recollected in tranquility," as Wordsworth famously described his own writing.

Writing this book has felt in some way like an offering of thanks, the way I might cook a meal in gratitude for having been nourished. During dark, lonely periods in my life, of which there have been many, I have derived a great deal of solace from books by the likes of M. F. K. Fisher, Julia Child, Nicolas Freeling, and Laurie Colwin. I've been as nourished by their warm generosity on the page, their revelations about food and their own lives, as I would have been if they'd cooked me feasts.

The impulse to write comes for me directly from reading good books, just as the urge to cook comes from eating good food. And the coincidence of food and language is as excellent and reassuring a combination as any other I've ever found. My favorite writing about food, like my favorite food, is plain and unfussy: clear, declarative sentences with a strong undercurrent of feeling, a soulful, hearty meal, nothing fancy, nothing pretentious, nothing but a blue plate special.

---

## DARK NIGHT OF THE SOUL SOUP

Peel, core, and chop a small butternut squash and 3 apples into bite-size pieces. Peel and cut up a red onion. Coarsely chop a knob of ginger and peel 8 cloves of garlic. Coat everything in peanut oil and roast on a cookie sheet for 40 minutes or so at 375 degrees, or until everything softens and caramelizes. Puree with enough chicken broth to make a thick soup, adding half-and-half as desired. Salt and pepper to taste. Heat in a saucepan. Serve in large shallow soup bowls with goat cheese and toasted pine nuts on top.

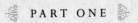

PART ONE

*Berkeley*

## CHAPTER 1

## Breakfast at McGee

When I was a kid, on what passed for chilly mornings in Berkeley, my mother used to make my sisters and me soft-boiled eggs with pieces of buttered toast broken into them. We had eggcups, but we never used them. These soft-boiled eggs were so good, we'd lick the bowls clean.

One such morning, when I was about two years old, my parents sat at the breakfast table with my baby sister, Susan, and me. The table was littered with cups and plates and bowls, eggshells and toast crumbs. The sun shone in the windows of the kitchen in our small bungalow on McGee Avenue in Berkeley. My father was about to walk out the front door to go somewhere, work probably.

My mother said in a high, plaintive voice, "Please stay and help me, Ralph. I just need some help. Don't leave yet."

My father paused in the kitchen doorway, looking back at us all at the table. Something seemed to snap in his head. Instead of either walking out or staying to help my mother, he leaped at her and began punching her in a silent knot of rage. It went on for a while. He slammed his fist into her chest and stomach. He pulled her hair. He seemed to want to hurt her badly. She gasped with shock and tried to stop him, but he was much stronger than she was. Then he let her go abruptly and slammed out the door and left us there, the three of us. My baby sister was wailing. My mother picked her up out of her high chair and held her, weeping slow, silent tears, rocking back and forth. I remember being paralyzed with an inward, panicky terror, but I didn't cry, I'm sure of it. I just stared at the table, at the eggshells and toast crumbs, and then I looked at my mother.

There we sat, a young family around a breakfast table on a sunny morning, surrounded by the shells of soft-boiled eggs, such a cozy and nourishing breakfast. The air jangled with the wrongness of what had just happened, vibrated with the disjunction between this sweet scene, mother and children, and the terrible thing my father had just done.

There were many later violent incidents like this one, according to my mother, but that is the only one from those early years that has stayed near the surface of my memory. Maybe this was the first time it happened, the first time my father beat up my mother in front of me. Maybe I had learned by the next time to shield myself by blinding myself, by blocking my memory.

Whatever the case may be, this particular wrecked breakfast is imprinted on my soul like a big boot mark. It became a kind of primordial scene, the incident around which my lifelong fundamental identity and understanding of the dynamic between women and men was shaped, whether I liked it or not.

In that moment, as a helpless child, I had two choices of people to identify with. In that moment, I split in half. As part of me stared at the eggshells, the toast crumbs, the empty, yolk-streaked bowls, that other part allied itself with my father, the person with the strength and force and power.

And so, from then on, I denied that part of me that was female. I tried to be like some idealized version of a guy: tough, impermeable, ambitious, sexually aggressive, and intolerant of weakness and vulnerability, in myself and everyone else.

My self-protective urge to be masculine, remove myself from all things female—myself, my mother, my baby sister—

let me get through my childhood and early adulthood believing, because I told myself so, that I was unaffected and unscathed by any of it. My father didn't hit me. He hit my mother. She was the one who was hurt. I was okay. And it had nothing to do with my own relationships with men. I wasn't my mother. This last was key: I was not my mother, I wasn't vulnerable, I wasn't feminine, and I wasn't ever going to be beaten up by anyone. I would do the beating up, if it came to that.

And so internally I absorbed my father, beating up his wife, a young, exhausted, vulnerable girl, punching her in the breasts, pulling her hair, seized by a rage that had nothing, really, to do with her at all, a rage that went all the way back to his childhood and was now caused by his own sense of failure, his disappointment in himself.

I absorbed my mother's perspective, too, even as I refused to identify with it. She was attacked and punished for being needy, for daring to ask for something, for revealing her weakness. Her withstanding of this punishment without fighting back or leaving went back to her own childhood and was caused by a deep sense of unworthiness and a fundamental unlovableness.

When I understood this, I believed that by understanding, I was free of it. That was, of course, not true at all.

## CHAPTER 2

## Liz and Ralph

—— Despite her treatment at the hands of my father, my mother never seemed like a victim to me, no doubt because she refused to see herself as one.

She was born Marie Elisabeth Pusch in July 1936 in Dornach, Switzerland, to Hans and Ruth Pusch. Her parents were anthroposophists, devoted followers of Rudolf Steiner, the philosopher and clairvoyant who started the first Waldorf School in a Stuttgart cigarette factory for the children of its workers. Hans was an actor and theater director at the Goetheanum, where he worked with Marie Steiner, Rudolf's widow. Ruth was a eurythmist, a kind of dancer, who performed all over Europe with a troupe of other young sylphs in purple gowns and veils, waving their arms while overenunciating vowels and diphthongs in wobbling, dramatic voices.

Hitler's rise to power put my grandparents on edge; they weren't sure what would happen to anthroposophists at the hands of the Third Reich, since they didn't take kindly to weird spiritual/artistic types. So Hans and Ruth began to consider fleeing Germany for New York City; my grandmother was American, my grandfather German.

When Hans was drafted into the SS, they immediately booked passage on an ocean liner to New York City, set to sail the following month. But something intervened, so they had to postpone their trip another month. The ship they would have taken sank, and everyone on board drowned. When they finally did set sail on another, later boat, three SS U-boats stopped the ship at midnight, as it was passing the Rock of Gibraltar. All the German passengers were called up on deck as a list of names was read, Hans Pusch's among them.

My grandfather went down below to say good-bye to his wife and tiny daughters. My grandmother, crying, insisted that they sit and share an orange before he went. So they sat on the bunk, all four of them, and shared the orange that Ruth had peeled as slowly as she could. By the time Hans arrived back up on deck, the U-boats had pulled away and left him behind. And so they all came to America, saved by a piece of fruit.

Hans and Ruth immediately sent their daughters to Lossing, Ruth's older sister Gladys's boarding school for mentally handicapped children. My mother was three. She spoke only Swiss German and had to learn English as quickly as she could. At the farm school were a group of mentally handicapped children, including my aunt Aillinn, my mother's older sister, who had been born deaf and mentally handicapped. With no one else to compare herself to, my mother didn't realize she herself wasn't "retarded," as they called it back then, until she was five.

Gladys herself had gone deaf in her mid-twenties, while she was touring Europe as a concert pianist, and, suddenly bereft of her dreamed-of brilliant musical career—and with a gaping hole in her life to fill—she discovered the trendy, radical teachings of Steiner. She convinced her baby sister Ruth to join her in Europe, where she met Hans Pusch. Meanwhile, Gladys came back to America with a head full of pedagogical steam and single-handedly started the school, whose underlying philosophy was based on Steiner's teachings.

Gladys was a mean little troll of a woman, and she beat my mother for her childish infractions and impish curiosity. My mother was expected to do chores even though she was only three. After Gladys took her by the hair one day and slammed her head against the wall over her little bed, then left her crying, Lizzie, as my mother was called when a child, ran off into the fields alone. She stayed outside for hours. She ate ears of corn, raw and warm from the stalks, lay between the rows, looking at the sky, feeling untethered to anything on earth, as if she could float away and no one would miss her or notice. But she also taught herself something important—that she could distance herself from whatever was going on by narrating her life to herself as if she were a character in a book. And that was how she got through her time there.

At five, she was sent to a "normal" Waldorf boarding school, in Pennsylvania. She didn't live with her parents again until she was ten, when she moved in with them in New York City and was sent to the Steiner school there. Her father, Hans, a childish, rather stupid man given to tantrums, ignored her. Her clever, literary mother, Ruth (who had told my mother that she'd given birth to her solely as a companion and caretaker for Aillinn), made it clear to Lizzie that she could expect no affection, since her husband and older daughter demanded all the energy she had.

My mother refused to be the pliable, respectful, spiritual daughter her parents expected and wanted her to be. Instead, she rebelled against her upbringing, rejected the teachings of Steiner, got into trouble constantly, and excelled at everything she did. She was sent away once more. She graduated from High Mowing, another Waldorf boarding school, this one in New Hampshire, at the top of her high school class with straight A's, having been the captain of the basketball team and student body president. That summer, she took her cello to the Accademia Musicale Chigiana in Siena, Italy, to take a master class with Pablo Casals. After that, she went to Swarthmore for one year, then studied cello at the Yale music conservatory for another year, and then she went to Juilliard as a cellist, all on full scholarships. Then, with one semester to go before she would have graduated from Juilliard, my mother decided she wasn't cut out for the life of a concert cellist, so she quit and bought a train ticket to Berkeley and moved there in June 1960.

She was exotic and beautiful, with olive skin, long dark wavy hair, deep-set brown eyes, broad shoulders, long legs, and a figure both slender and curvaceous. She had been a model in New Haven as a student in the 1950s; her photograph adorned the sides of buses in a milk ad. In Berkeley, when I was little, she was never a hippie, or even particularly bohemian; she was just sexy. She wore cropped peg-leg jeans with wide belts, ribbed cotton turtlenecks, big sunglasses, pendant necklaces, dangly earrings.

Before she met my father, she had heard about him from mutual friends, who raved about their handsome, dynamic, politically aware, funny, interesting friend Ralph Johansen. She knew instantly somehow that he'd be her husband and the father of her children. When they were finally introduced, in the summer of 1961, she was twenty-five and he was thirty-seven; she saw right away that her friends had been right about him. He was not tall, but he was athletic, well-knit, and charismatic. And he was ridiculously handsome: he had black hair and piercing blue eyes, an expressive, intelligent face, and a strong jaw.

They stayed up all night talking under the stars. They became an inseparable couple right away: Liz and Ralph, good-looking as movie stars, cool, smart, and fun. They were great pals, extremely well matched, even though he was twelve years older than she was. They hung out with a pack of interesting friends. They went to parties. They ate in Chinatown at a hole-in-the-wall restaurant where a famous waiter named Edsel Ford Fong screamed at the customers and told them what to order. They went camping in Aspen and Arizona and the Tetons with two other couples, a pair of musicians nicknamed Oboe Bob and Oboe Molly who rode motorcycles, and my mother's old

Juilliard friends, Peter Schickele, the composer who would later invent P. D. Q. Bach, and his wife, a dancer. They laughed a lot, sang together, bantered in fake accents, and cracked each other up.

But my mother was pregnant with me by the time of their Carson City wedding the following winter, and in her last months of pregnancy, as they settled into a cheap, tiny shack of a bungalow on McGee Avenue in Berkeley together—and then for several months after I was born—she stopped feeling sexual. This was a normal enough occurrence, of course, but it greatly upset my father. He called her frigid and gave her books to read about this so-called unnatural condition, books that had been written, naturally, by men. My mother sensed that something was wrong with my father's interpretation of things, but had no idea, in those days, what it could be.

## CHAPTER 3

## The Johansens

My mother wanted to name me Katherine, but my father, who had some unpleasant association with the name from some ex-girlfriend in his distant past, refused to let her. He agreed to compromise on Kate as a middle name. My mother's mother suggested Laurie for my first name, possibly because she'd always liked the boy in *Little Women*; and my father, who had no associations with the name, agreed to it.

As soon as I was born, my mother became instantly vapor-locked on me. Most mothers tend to be somewhat obsessed with their firstborns, but her fixation on me was a little more intense than usual. Photographs taken shortly after my birth show her staring down at me, clutching me, engrossed, mesmerized, as if she could not believe I existed, as if she were afraid that if she took her eyes off me for a split second, I might disappear.

I was a frustrating baby for her in many ways. I had no interest in breast-feeding, or in solid food either, when that came along. I had likewise no interest in lap sitting or cuddling. My mother yearned to enfold me in her arms and rock me as much as I would let her, which was not at all. Possibly I sensed her extreme focus on me and tried to shield myself from it. I was and am by nature averse to being stared at, solitary, and fierce about my autonomy. My poor mother, who wanted a chubby little lap child to suckle and dandle, a sweet-tempered baby who would coo and gurgle with cuddly placidity, had given birth to me instead.

I didn't want to be looked at; I wanted to do the watching myself. As long as my baby seat was turned toward whatever conversation was going on, and I was left alone to watch and listen, I was perfectly happy. If I couldn't hear the grown-ups talking, I fussed. If my mother tried to hold me too long on her lap, I made an impatient grunting sound to be put down and left alone. I was too busy eavesdropping to eat. A little suck on the nipple, a bit of tapioca or Cream of Wheat, and that was that, time to get back to business.

Consequently, and not surprisingly, I was a very skinny baby. Old ladies stopped my mother in the Berkeley Co-op, to her chagrin, to poke at my sticklike little arms and instruct her on what I should be eating and how she should be feeding me. It got worse. When my hair grew in, it did so in white-blond wispy tufts that stood up on my small head. I had huge staring green eyes set into a small, pale face. In photos, I look like an elf or an alien. I was never babyish in any way. It was probably a bit eerie for someone else to be watched so intently by those gleaming, saucerlike eyes.

When I was nine months old, well before I could walk, I looked up at my mother from my baby seat on the table and said very clearly, without a trace of baby talk, "I want more Cheerios." My mother was naturally startled to have her incontinent, tiny infant not only speak but address her in a complete sentence. I'd never said anything before, never babbled or baby talked.

From the get-go, I felt a nervous, headlong urge to catapult myself into life, to start realizing the desires I seem to have been born with: to learn as much as I could about people, to figure out how words worked, and to collect as many of them as I could. I wanted words the way other kids wanted fun experiences or toys or friends: intensely, greedily, as many as I could get. I stood between my parents in the McGee Avenue house when I was about two, raising my arms toward them. I had just learned that there was such a verb as "comfort," and I was pretty sure I knew what it meant, but I wanted it demonstrated.

"Comfort me," I said to them, feeling deeply and totally focused on this. They looked down at me, puzzled; was I upset? I was not. I was calm but insistent. "Comfort me," I repeated, shaking my upstretched hands for emphasis.

They must have figured out what I was after, because they picked me up and theatrically pretended to give me soothing, reassuring affection—first one of them, then the other—while I watched them closely. There they were, my parents, comforting me. This memory is one of the nicest ones I have of my father. There he was, being a father, just for a moment. I had to ask him to, in the spirit of curiosity about a word, but he complied. I have always kept this memory in the mental equivalent of a velvet box at the back of a top shelf in a closet, where rare things are hidden so no one steals or breaks them.

As if to compensate for me, my sister Susan was a fat, cute, cuddly, sweet baby who laughed as early as I had stared fixedly at people, hard peals of merry laughter even while she nursed, milk running down her chin, until my mother had to laugh, too. Right away, Susan sent me into fits of hysterics; I lay gasping feebly on the floor like an exhausted beetle. She was a pretty baby and a pretty little girl. She was hilarious with her family but quiet and meek and shy with strangers. And she was given to explosions, wordless fits of emotion during which she could only cry, kick, scream, and howl. She was unable to talk, to tell my mother what the matter was. There was something vulnerable and tender about Susan that made me fiercely protective of her from the start. She was my sweet companion throughout childhood, always stalwartly by my side. She came running up to my classroom, crying, when she wet her pants in kindergarten so I could help her get home to change. She came to me on the playground at recess when her jacket zipper was stuck so I could fix it. We bolstered each other. I got as much from her as she got from me—her absolute trust in me gave me confidence, made me feel tough and strong.

We never fought as children. We were both docile peacemakers by nature, but we were also terrified of the possible repercussions of overt conflict, having seen it firsthand from our father.

And then, when I was four and a half, Emily arrived—a placid baby with a big round head, fat kissable cheeks, button brown eyes, and a button nose. Her arms and legs and stomach were all dimples and pudge. As soon as she was born, I decided that she was mine and claimed her. She was born with thrush, a yeast infection in her mouth; the pediatrician treated it with gentian violet, so my mother's shirts all turned purple around the nipples. In her early months, Emily had several very high fevers and had to be rushed to the ER and packed in ice; if she had been born with a docile personality, it was burned out of her, and a headstrong, willful, oddly singular bent took its place. She became increasingly eccentric and stubborn as she got older, but the fevers didn't affect her warm sweetness or her deep, thoughtful intelligence.

Having babies more than made up for the years of yearning and loneliness my mother had endured. She had been in a fog before she became a mother, she told my sisters and me repeatedly: we were the sun breaking through, the one real thing. And so everything my sisters and I did—any triumph we brought to her attention, no matter how small—was lauded, praised, applauded, exclaimed over.

My mother had been engrossed in my father before I was born. Now he must have felt that he had been supplanted, in classic style, by a manifestly unworthy rival: a female baby, and then another and another. And it wasn't the first time this had happened. He'd left his first wife, Nancy, a decade before I was born, after twin daughters had wrecked his fun with her. Nancy had grown up just down the lake from him, and their parents had all known one another for years. She and Ralph had had a lot of fun together, partying, playing bridge, and going to big band dances at ballrooms and clubs around the Twin Cities in the late forties. They were a glamorous couple, and music was a huge part of their romance: Artie Shaw, Benny Goodman, Ella Fitzgerald, Rosemary Clooney, Anita O'Day. But when he was around twenty-seven, the age of life-defining decisions, he got her pregnant, and then they'd married, and then came the twin babies. Maybe he missed the fun life after that, or maybe he didn't really want children, or maybe he'd never planned to stick around for long in the first place. Whatever the reason, in 1952, Ralph abruptly quit his new wife and their one-year-old twin daughters and left Minnesota behind forever.

He'd moved out to California, where he became a social worker. After he met my mother, he passed the bar exam with her adamant encouragement and became a lawyer. And all was well until more babies came. Now here we were, first me, then my sisters—more daughters—wrecking his fun with his second wife.

His perplexing (possibly to him, as well) tantrums of violence toward my mother came out of nowhere and then they were over, and both my parents acted as if they'd never happened. Although he all but ignored us kids, Ralph gave every impression, to those outside the family, of being a devoted husband and father. He was a Marxist lawyer, defender of and hero to Black Panthers, rabble-rousing politicos, and draft dodgers. In court, he was a low-key, articulate, persuasive advocate, often pitted against more bellicose, ham-fisted lawyers, and so he won more of his cases than he lost.

He loved music. He was a jazz lover, a guy's guy; he and his

Marxist lawyer pals regularly went to hear live shows in San Francisco together. At night sometimes, he stood in his blue plaid bathrobe over the forced-air heating vent in the hallway floor and snapped his fingers with unself-conscious enthusiasm to a Mingus or Monk record. And he loved to sing, songs with a lot of words, fast. As I got older, it turned out that I could quickly memorize any lyrics he threw at me and sing them right along with him in my high, fluty voice, and I used this talent to get his attention whenever I could, since, regardless of his violence, I adored him.

Somehow, probably because it was obvious, I had picked up on his yearning for a son, and so I strove to be as boylike as I could—I was verbal like him, and I looked like him, with a long face, strong jaw, thin mouth, and flashing eyes, and I was the firstborn of this new clan, so I felt like a viable candidate. And my personality was very much like his, easygoing and affable on the surface and hotheaded and paranoid just below. In fact, whenever my father was around, I remember feeling almost manic with attention-getting wiles (which were no doubt highly irritating to him). He didn't say much to me as a general rule, but whenever he talked, I absorbed it all; when I asked what he did at work, he told me that he stole the jailers' keys when they were at lunch and let innocent people out of jail. Naturally, I believed him. I believed anything and everything he said.

I also wasn't afraid of him. His violent rages were between him and my mother. He never once threatened to explode at me. I understood that he was dangerous to her, and I feared him for her sake, but I felt safe enough with him. My greatest concern with my father was getting, and keeping, his attention, which was never easy, because I so clearly bored him most of the time, or maybe it was just that he had no idea what to do with such a small girl.

Still, I've always believed that he was born with this dark

side, the only son of a successful Minnesota businessman who owned an envelope company. Ralph Johansen, Sr.——broad shouldered, unsmiling, a full head taller than his son—is rumored to have said to my father, his last words before he left the Bay Area and choked on a chicken bone and died shortly afterward: "You are a big disappointment to me." My mother wonders whether Ralph's father regularly hit him; everything I know about my father suggests to me that he was probably an angry iconoclast from birth—that his rage and rebellious nature were as much a part of his makeup as his rich singing voice and roguish charm. When Ralph was a teenager, his father sent him to Shattuck, a military school, after he was caught stealing a bottle of Coca-Cola from the side of a truck. (Fittingly, Marlon Brando was his roommate there.) I imagine that my father hated his own father, and authority, and the system, and the man, for every second of his life afterward, and I suspect that he still does, wherever he is now.

## CHAPTER 4

## Acton Street

As it turned out, my father had been having an affair while my mother was pregnant with Emily, repeatedly punching my mother in the stomach to try, no doubt, to get rid of the fetus. When Emily was born, and he learned that he'd had another daughter, he turned around without a word to my mother and went out of the room.

Nonetheless, he was surprised and puzzled when my mother announced that she was leaving him. When Emily was still a baby, we moved out of our father's huge Victorian house on Regent Street in Oakland, which he'd bought recently with the money he'd inherited from his father, and into a small but beautiful, bright, airy stucco cottage on Acton Street in Berkeley.

Our new house had a fireplace in the living room, wood floors, a glassed-in front porch with a floor of red terra-cotta tiles; two cute little bedrooms and one bathroom; and a kitchen in back with a breakfast nook by a big window, where the four of us ate all our meals and spent much of our time. We would also invent things in that kitchen, make whatever concoctions we could come up with without interference. I remember putting flour, milk, eggs, and various other things I thought might be good together into a bowl, stirring madly, pouring the result into a greased pan, and pulling it out of the oven to find a flat, dense rectangle that tasted like Play-Doh, salty and gummy and bland.

All through my early childhood, I had had allergies to chocolate, peanuts, and strawberries, some of the cruelest things a kid can be allergic to; they gave me eczema and asthma, which we called "itchies and wheezies." I'd been taking allergy shots for months. As soon as we moved out of my father's house, and the bouts of violence toward my mother stopped altogether, my food allergies went away: the correlations between these allergies and the unacknowledged, internalized stress I felt, watching my father beat my mother, seem fairly clear to me now.

To supplement the small child-support checks from my father, which he sent every month according to their divorce agreement, my mother turned our Acton Street house into a day care center. I therefore became the tallest and oldest, and the de facto leader, of a gang of kids. There were Susan and Emily; and our neighbor from across the street Frieda, who was Emily's age; and my mother's charges: Norwegian Bjorn with his sweet blue eyes and curly rust-colored hair; Eduardo, a cute little boy with a throaty chuckle; Dhoti, a weird kid with bug eyes and permanent snot problems; and Dorothy and Eugene, a scrappy, sturdy, funny brother and sister duo who were always up for any game, any challenge. All their parents were just as poor as we were, and therefore they often couldn't pay my mother, and meanwhile, she fed and cared for their kids all day, but she never seemed to mind. Berkeley in the late sixties was a world in which people bartered, got by. Life was loose and easy. And we always had enough to eat, as I remember, thanks to food stamps during our last year there, and my mother always managed to pay the rent on time.

My mother seemed happy and carefree in those years, away from our father. She hung out with other cool, sexy young mothers, a cabal of hot chicks in their late twenties and early thirties. In my memories of her during this time, she was always surrounded by friends, always laughing, having fun, drinking Gallo, dancing to the Beatles and the Stones. And all the people she knew were part of the political and cultural movements going on in the Bay Area in the sixties. As a result, I thought all adults everywhere were long-haired activists and that most men had beards. I thought the whole world was politically charged, exciting, sometimes scary, and always left-leaning, radical, subversive. "Pigs" were bad and "the man" was the enemy and "the establishment" had to be overthrown. I thought everyone in the world knew that, as a matter of course. I thought "boycott" was a kind of grape.

At McGee Avenue, in the early years, my mother had cooked big pots of spaghetti for my father's political friends, and they all sat talking for hours. After my parents were divorced, my father was still a frequent presence in our lives. I rode on his shoulders high above the crowd at peace marches in San Francisco, looking down at a sea of headbands and beards, granny glasses and ponchos. We went to happenings and demonstrations in People's Park, to potlucks and parties. I remember when People's Park was built and destroyed and the protesters were teargassed; and I remember when it was rebuilt and destroyed again. We got clothes from the free box and protested its destruction, twice, and ate potluck food at long tables there under the trees.

On University Avenue—which smelled of pot, incense, and various hippie perfumes and oils, where electric guitar-and-sitar rock vibrated psychedelically in every window and doorway, where everybody was protesting something or looking for a high or trying to find peace and truth—the black dudes walked along like the panthers they'd named themselves after, lithe and feline, with rich, glossy Afros, in tight paisley or bright-hued bell-bottoms and billowy shirts unbuttoned to show their gleaming chests, their medallions and beads. They wore high-heeled boots and belted leather coats. They knew and loved my father, like everyone else back then.

I sat with my mother's friend Paul Opokam, a Nigerian writer, on a hillside at a happening in a San Francisco park when I was three or four. He ate grass to make me laugh and pretended to be a cow on all fours. We hung out together like pals, little white me and tall black Paul. I loved him; he was one of my favorite people as a very small kid. And then Paul disappeared suddenly; for many years, I remembered only that something terrible and sad had happened to him. My mother told me later that Paul had been there when the National Guard stormed the San Francisco State campus, where she was taking psychology classes. They seized Paul, took him down into a men's room, and, after planting some drugs on him, beat him up. Paul, a peaceful, sober man who had never done any drugs in his life, spent a number of years in San Quentin before being taken in handcuffs to the airport and deported back to Nigeria.

The Bay Area in the 1960s was, of course, a fortuitous time and place for a budding writer to grow up. But unfortunately, all the hot foment, the hullabaloo, the questioning of authority, the endless discussions everyone was having all around me, failed to turn me into a political creature of any stripe. In fact, it all made me squirm a little with the same detached embarrassment I felt watching a group of naked, hairy grown-ups getting stoned in a park: I was a prudish romantic, daydreamy and internal. I liked thinking about castles and princesses. It was all too noisy, too druggy, and too strident for me. I would have preferred the decorous strands of pearls, glamorous fedoras, cigarette holders, and gloves of a much earlier era, when grown-ups smoked only cigarettes.

In second grade, I went to Washington School on Bancroft and McKinley, and so did Susan, who was in kindergarten. We walked the three quarters of a mile to school by ourselves every morning and home again every afternoon. The two challenges of our daily commute were getting past Princess and Bumblebee, two snarling, lunging, enormous-seeming dogs who guarded a fenced-in yard about a block from our house, and then crossing Sacramento, which was tricky because the traffic was in four lanes rather than two, but there was an island in the middle where we could wait on the grass under the palm trees until the other lanes were clear.

Washington School had open classrooms, a pedagogical fad, which meant that there were older and younger kids in every classroom. A gang of glamorous third-grade black girls in my class somehow adopted me as their mascot. I wore thick glasses by then; I was skinny and reserved. They called me "White Patty" and teased me affectionately and kindly for being so shy, trying to draw me out. I worshipped them.

At recess on Fridays, the teachers played R&B records in the playground over a loudspeaker system, and the kids danced on the asphalt. I sat by the sidelines, too shy to shake my booty with the cool kids. I watched those older, bigger black girls with their hair in many ponytails clipped with bright plastic bobbles, wearing their mod dresses and polyester bell-bottoms, grooving to the music. All year, I was dying to get up and dance with them, and they always encouraged me to, but I didn't have the nerve until the last day of school, my last chance ever, when I flung myself into their midst and shook my bony little butt to the slinky beat of Sly and the Family Stone. My idols surrounded me, clapping, cheering, egging me on.

Birthdays in our family were the usual bacchanalian, delirious affairs with balloons, streamers, signs, paper crowns, heaps of presents, kids high to the gills on sugar games, and manic excitement permeating the whole day. On my seventh birthday, my father came over for the party. Afterward, my parents announced that they had a big present for me, but I had to go out to the garage to find it. The garage was a little wooden structure in back that we never used; I had no idea what I'd find out there. The door lifted, and I saw that they had turned it into a playroom for me, with a big rug, an old couch, a table and chairs my father had built himself, and a bookshelf. It was meant to be my own place, my own room, to go into and be alone in whenever I wanted, where I could read in peace without shushing my sisters every ten minutes, where I could close the door and do whatever I wanted. It was the best present they could have given me. I never got to be by myself; none of us had any solitude. I shared a room with both my sisters, and there were all those other kids around all the time. My mother could have taken the garage for herself, but she gave it to me instead. I was only seven, but I was a very serious kid, a bookworm, anxious and overly responsible; I felt the full weight of my status as the oldest kid and my mother's helper. Now the advantages of being the firstborn had never been clearer. I went into that garage and wrote stories. In my first completed story, "My Magic Carpet," the narrator and her sister went around the world and into outer space on a magic carpet and got home in time for "tea," as I called it.

On Christmas Eve in 1969, we went to a party at the house of my mother's friends Bobby and Christine in the North Berkeley Hills. They were rich, or, at least, they seemed rich to me. Bobby was a chemistry professor at Berkeley with curly dark hair who played the piano. His wife, Christine, was my mother's age, but she had long silver-gray hair, a smooth, pretty, oval face, and a high, fluty voice. I always thought of her as the Good Witch of the East. Their three daughters, Diana, Juliet, and Katherine, were all our same ages.

Christine and my mother had met on a bench, watching their kids on the swings at the local kiddie park, Totland. Their house on Indian Rock Road—so named because the Indians had carved bowl-like depressions into the boulders—had a grand piano and a curved staircase and huge leaded windows overlooking their deep, green, lush yard. Diana, who was my age, had her own room, which was actually two rooms, since there was a large sleeping porch attached to her bedroom. She lived like a princess, with a canopy bed, a window seat, and a Victorian dollhouse with real-looking furniture and a family of dolls with jointed limbs and painted porcelain heads. Driving to their house, we left behind our ordinary, familiar world on the Flats of little bungalows, straight wide streets, and palm trees and ascended in a swooping, steep trail to what seemed like a mountain castle.

When we arrived, all the grown-ups were dressed up, drinking wine. Music and conversations billowed on the warm, food-scented air. The six of us girls raced through the house shrieking, chasing each other in tutus and princess dresses and Christine's high-heeled shoes. Hungry, we crowded into the enormous kitchen, where Christine was setting out platters and dishes for the buffet help-yourself dinner. It smelled so good, so strange and new—I had never smelled food like that before. There was some sort of rice pilaf with golden sultana raisins and pine nuts and a thrilling spice that must have been cardamom, alongside chutneys and breads, a roast leg of lamb, vegetables, other things—an elaborate, exotic feast.

I distinctly remember the taste of those raisins with the

pine nuts and cardamom. It was a revelation—spiciness with sweet with nutty. I ate so much, I had to lie down on the big, soft, white couch afterward with my head in my mother's lap.

In May 1970, when she was almost thirty-four, my mother finally graduated from Mills College with a B.A. She had gone to a total of thirteen colleges over the course of almost half her life. For the graduation ceremony in early May, she wore a proper cap and gown over a minidress with strappy high heels. She walked in the procession with all the other students, most of whom were far younger than she was.

My mother had decided to go to graduate school to get her doctorate in psychology. She'd started taking psych classes after I was born, as a way to better understand her marriage to my father, and had ended up leaving the marriage and finding her calling. She applied to many graduate programs, but the only place that accepted her with enough money for us to live on was Arizona State University in Tempe. This was far from her first choice. Tempe was a politically conservative desert, wildly different from Berkeley, and we didn't know anyone there.

We're moving to Arizona!" our mother announced.

"Arizona!" we trilled, having no idea what that meant.

Our mother always made everything seem exciting. All changes, upheavals, and surprises, big or small, were occasions of adventure, to be met with optimism and courage.

In late August, just after my eighth birthday, we packed up our little Acton Street house and sent our things on ahead with movers, and then we left the Bay Area forever.

Our father stayed behind.

## SOFT-BOILED EGGS

With a spoon, into a saucepan of rapidly boiling water, gently place
4 eggs, one by one. Boil them for 6 minutes. Meanwhile, toast and
butter 2 slices of bread. Turn off the flame, run the eggs briefly under
cold water, then tap the hat off each one with a knife and carefully
slide the innards out of the shells with a spoon. The whites should be
firm, the yolks still runny enough to soak into the toast. Break one
piece of toast into each bowl. Salt and pepper generously. Serves 2.

## TAPIOCA PUDDING

There were two kinds of tapioca: the disgusting large-pearl slippery-
fish-egg kind that grown-ups ate and pretended to like, and the
smooth creamy puddinglike delicious kind that we kids loved. My
mother made the latter kind, adding 3 cups of milk, ½ cup of sugar,
and 2 beaten eggs to ½ cup of small tapioca pearls with a little salt
and vanilla extract, simmering it on the stove for 5 or 10 minutes. She
served the fluffy, warm pudding as a bedtime snack. It was just sweet
enough and rich tasting, but mild and fragrant with vanilla. We lapped
it up like kittens.

# PART TWO

# *Wildermuth*

## CHAPTER 5

## Neighbors

We landed in Sky Harbor Airport in Phoenix and walked out between the automatic sliding glass doors, my sisters and I all wearing matching purple-checked cotton dresses and sandals, carrying our little flowered zippered suitcases and inflatable inner tubes, out into the dry heat and intense sunlight that would be our "outside" for years to come. On the drive from the airport, there were saguaros, drab stucco buildings, billboards, and flat, baking, dun-colored land. After the cool, foggy, gentle Bay Area weather, it was a shock—an exciting one, like every new experience.

"Wow, girlie Qs!" my mother said. "Look at all the cacti!"

For $185 a month, she had rented a small cinder-block three-bedroom ranch house on East Wildermuth Drive, a semirural, pockmarked lane only a block from the busy commercial strip of Apache Boulevard, but somehow seeming to exist in its own enclosed world. The floors of our new house were concrete covered by a polyester moss-green wall-to-wall carpet. The swamp cooler ran with a constant whir and a trickling noise and made the whole house smell like a brackish pond. There was fake-wood paneling in the kitchen-living room and a sliding glass door out to the patio. The kitchen had an avocado-green electric stove, whose coiled burners clicked as they heated, and a matching fridge with slotted iron shelves and rickety crisper drawers in the bottom. There was a stiff, tall hedge in front of the picture window in the playroom that grew hard little blue inedible berries. At the back of the house was a covered concrete patio with a barbecue pit and a big, wild yard where we built forts and climbed trees and invented long, elaborate adventure games.

My mother had the so-called master bedroom, which was hardly bigger than the others, but it had its own separate bathroom. Thrillingly, I had my own room while Susan and Emily had to share a room with a bunk bed. This was hard for Susan, who was sensitive and keenly concerned with social protocol. Emily, by contrast, was a headstrong individualist, dramatic and loud. Their room was always full of activity and noise and the occasional fight.

Small and drab as our house was, it was a mansion compared to the other houses on Wildermuth. Next door to us lived the Tates, who'd moved to Tempe from West Texas, although they looked like they were from central casting. There was Mister Roy, the gun-toting, cowboy hat–wearing, potbellied father, and Miz Joyce, his slovenly, scattershot, enraged wife. Then there were the kids: Rusty, the oldest, who was eleven and blind and who was madly in love with me, although I couldn't imagine why; Shelly Renee, who was my age and who was banished from our house for a few days when my mother caught her stealing an apple from our fruit bowl; two other brothers whose names I don't remember; and Runt, the youngest, a wily little savage.

The Tates lived in one half of a run-down one-story duplex whose other half was occupied by Mister Bob (the Tate kids were raised to call all adults Miz or Mister with their first names; my mother was therefore Miz Liz), a mild-mannered geologist who always, on his way home from work, stopped by the rock stand I set up at the end of our driveway and picked out a couple of choice pieces of quartz for a quarter each; he was my best, and often only, customer.

On the other side of us, in a dark shabby little house all the way on the corner, lived my friend Beverly Begay, a Navajo princess, or so she said, with her vast, extended clan and many siblings. Her parents were always in the backyard on aluminum folding chairs, drinking beer with other adult family members, smoking cigarettes. They paid little attention to the wild gang of kids they'd spawned.

I had another Navajo friend named Debbie Shelltrack, who lived down in the trailer park at the end of Wildermuth with her mother, a nurse who always seemed to be at work, and her little brother. Debbie was in my third-grade class at Flora Thew School along with Shelly Renee and Beverly. After school, Debbie took care of her little brother, fed him his dinner, and put him to bed. She was a very intelligent, very unhappy girl with a big, splotchy face and stringy black hair. She was quick and funny and dark. She was skinny; we all were, back then, but she was especially so. When her mother didn't have time to buy groceries and there was nothing for her and her brother to eat for dinner, Debbie went to the dingy little trailer park market and begged for cans of chili or corn. She picked up cigarette butts from the gutters and smoked them because she was "hooked." She pretended to French-kiss big, flat leaves that fell from trees, claiming she was practicing for when she had a real boyfriend.

When these neighbor kids first came over to our house, they seemed amazed, entranced. My sisters and I had a lot of books and toys. Our mother was almost always in a good mood and laughing. She encouraged our games. We played together constantly, we three sisters, elaborate, dramatic games of make-believe. We sang together and put on plays and variety shows. The other kids just watched us at first, and then they figured out how to join in. We became a big gang, running through the huge cornfield across from our house, following the irrigation ditches far back into the tangle of desert between the big thoroughfares, roller-skating and riding our bikes along the wide, empty streets.

## CHAPTER 6

## Blue Plate Special

Summer lasted year-round in Arizona, and therefore, swimming pools were a big part of our regular life. Sometimes my mother's friend Carol would have her consciousness-raising group, which included my mother, over for pool parties, with all their kids. Carol was divorced and she lived with her four pretty, perfectly blond, blue-eyed girls, Marcia, Julie, Jeannie, and Janelle, in a huge air-conditioned stucco house. I remember spending the entire day in their pool, all of us kids shrieking and jumping into the blue water, playing Marco Polo and racing from end to end, pushing against the side and shooting off like launched rockets to the other side of the pool, throwing ourselves on and off rubber rafts and inner tubes, and taking turns running down the diving board and belly flopping or dive bombing into the pool.

Then Carol lit the grill and we had a cookout: hamburgers with melted cheese on toasted sesame buns with pickles and ketchup, potato salad, potato chips, Coke, and ice cream for dessert. I stood dripping and shivering a little in the sudden desert chill at sunset, a wet towel around my shoulders, my hair streaming water between my shoulder blades, eating a cheeseburger as fast as I could shove it into my mouth and chew and swallow it, and wondering how food could taste even better through the chlorine clouds on my tongue.

Before we moved to Arizona, I was largely indifferent to

food, except those few favorite things I loved best and requested constantly. But at Wildermuth, something ignited a passion for eating in me. Maybe my palate had developed enough finally to enable me to taste fully what I was eating for the first time. Maybe Tempe itself, this wild, strange new place that was so profoundly different from Berkeley, opened my senses to taste and texture, flavor and smell.

I was in no way a born gourmet, and my palate was not instinctively refined. Far from it. I was an omnivore, a glutton. I loved putting things in my mouth and chewing them and swallowing. I loved eating, and thinking about food, as much as I loved reading and writing, and somehow all these passions were connected for me, on a deep level.

The rest of my family liked food, but no one else felt as vehemently about it as I did. At mealtimes, my sisters and mother ate happily enough, but I devoured, exclaimed, crowed, exulted. When something tasted particularly good, I would say in a didactic, insistent voice, "Yum!" My sisters would look at me, knowing I wanted them to concur but unable to share my visceral intensity. Susan later told me that she felt a certain strong pressure to agree with me and quailed under the fierce unblinking certitude of my stare around the table.

My mother was (and still is) possibly the slowest eater in the world. At the beginning of the meal, as the rest of us were all attacking our plates of food, she took a bite very deliberately, chewed and swallowed, then took a sip of whatever was in her glass, wine or water or beer. A long time elapsed before the next bite, during which she would talk, laugh, lean back in her chair. She appeared to have forgotten she was eating, as if the ongoing flow of bites that make up a meal, start to finish, were of no consequence to her, as if she were oblivious to any gustatory narrative flow. Instead, for my mother, each new, successive mouthful of food seemed to have its own logic, its

own internal poetry. Every morsel was a world in itself, separate from all the others. She sat over her plate until long after
the rest of us were finished.

My mother could also do a neat trick: sometimes, when she
was eating corn, she could blow a kernel out her nose, much to
our astonishment. We had no idea how she did that. None of us
ever could. She was very mysterious about it. "Oh, you know,"
she told us. "It's just one of those things."

During most of our years as a family in Arizona, we were
flat-out poor. My mother clipped coupons, saved books of
Green Stamps, was very careful about her budget, and bought
all our clothes in thrift shops. But we didn't feel deprived. Every
night before bed, our mother read us stories or made them up.
In the mornings or afternoons, she sat with her cello in the living room and practiced the Bach suites, which she played with
fluid, soulful beauty. For her graduate school friends and their
spouses and kids, she threw barbecues, pumpkin-carving parties, and poker parties.

She also fed us very well with the little money she had—
before dinner, to stave off our immediate hunger while she
cooked, we got a plate of cut-up raw carrots and peppers and
jicama, which, not knowing any better, we gobbled up as fast as
she could dole them out—or a big bowl of frozen mixed vegetables, which we called frozies. She baked fresh whole-wheat
bread and handed us a piece of fruit or a graham cracker for
midafternoon snack. Sugary things were restricted; candy was
limited, and the only cereals we got were Cheerios, corn flakes,
and wholesome hot cereals. Pop (as we called it in Arizona) was
out of the question; we drank nothing but milk, water, and
juice in our house. Of course, out-and-out junk food like Chee-
tos and Pop-Tarts was never allowed.

My mother was a cook of the plain, simple, homey variety, which was perfect for our undeveloped palates. She wasn't

a puritan or a health nut, but she greatly cared what we ate and took pains to serve us good meals every night. Sometimes, when she dished up one of her typical home-cooked dinners, and we told her how good it was and asked for seconds, she would say half joking, "Aw, it's nothing but a blue plate special!" She told us this meant the kind of dinner you got in an old 1950s diner: a piece of fatty, salty meat or chicken or fish, usually fried, with or without gravy, plus a side of vegetables cooked to a gray pallor, plus something starchy, like mashed potatoes or baked beans. It was old-fashioned and filling, and also cheap, which was a big consideration for her back when she was a student and had to live on fried farina for most of the week.

My mother's own versions of those other, earlier blue plate specials from her past struck me as a lot more special than those meals she described to us. Her mashed potatoes were rich, lumpy, and buttery, and when she made fried chicken, she shook it in a paper bag of spiced flour before frying it in very hot oil, so it was always both juicy and crunchy. She thawed frozen cod or haddock fillets—firm, white, mild, kid-friendly fish—and baked them just till they were flaky and tender, then squeezed lemon juice on them. She made meat loaf with ketchup, eggs, chopped onions, and bread crumbs, then served us each a savory thick slice that melted on the tongue. Her vegetables were usually frozen French-cut string beans or peas brought to a boil, then drained when they were still bright green and tossed with salt and margarine. They were never gray or overcooked; we loved them.

Part of it might have been the romance of eating the food that had comforted and nourished my mother when she was very young and very poor, and part of it might have been how good these meals were, but the term "blue plate special" has always been one of the homiest, coziest, most sweetly nostalgic phrases in the English language for me. It brings me right back to Wildermuth, back to that time in my childhood when I had my mother and my sisters all to myself; we were a complete family then, just us four girls, living in a wild, strange place, making a home for ourselves.

## CHAPTER 7

## Food, Glorious Food

As if to counterbalance the charms of her blue plate specials, and perhaps to teach us a lesson about life, my mother had the occasional seemingly sadistic spell during which she dished up the most disgusting things on the planet: smooth but granular chunks of fried calves' liver that tasted the way cat poop smelled and had, I imagined, a similar texture; frozen okra that she boiled into sluglike tubes with creepily crunchy guts held together by strings of snot; brussels sprouts both soft and coarse that tasted bitter and gaseous; and wretched heaps of foul, mealy, slimy lima beans. I could tolerate broccoli and spinach, barely, in a stalwart mood, but otherwise they made me gag. Meat was expensive in the 1970s, so my mother sometimes bought cheap cuts of beef that came with pieces of gristle in them; these likewise caused me to retch and want to spit them out.

These rare but intensely memorable awful meals were the occasion of much subversive drama among my sisters and me, silent antics, because we weren't allowed to complain about our food. We were expected, like most kids, to eat it. So we mastered the near-universal childhood table arts of the wadded-up napkin containing half-chewed bites, the under-the-table palm off to the cat, the pushing-food-around-the-plate maneuver into patterns that minimized volume. We also all developed other means of avoiding hated food. Emily, who unlike Susan and me was given to histrionics and wild displays of rebellion, could always plausibly throw a tantrum and be sent to sit on the hamper in the bathroom (her usual punishment), thus escaping the horrible item in question. Susan, the most sly and resourceful of the three of us, would excuse herself to go to the bathroom and sneak an entire napkinful of liver or okra with her then flush the whole thing away.

As the oldest—or, in other words, as the people-pleasing rule follower, the obedient one, the mama's girl—I found ways to actually eat whatever food I couldn't feed to the cat or hide in my napkin. I taught myself to simultaneously disarm my gag reflex and block my sense of smell by lifting my palate up into my adenoids, or something like that. Then I'd fork a gigantic piece of liver or okra or gristly steak into my mouth, barely chew it, keep it off my tongue as much as possible, and take three big swallows of milk.

And so, while one sister got herself banished to the bathroom and the other one snuck there to throw her dinner into the toilet, I stayed behind and powered through the vile stuff under my own steam until my plate was clean, and I could have dessert. Revulsion gave me a certain shivery almost-pleasure similar to that of the most terrifying ghost stories. I was proud of my ability to overcome and control it.

But it wasn't all healthy, home-cooked, square meals every night. It was the 1970s, after all, the decade in which American food reached a magical synergy of convenience, animal deliciousness, and creative packaging; and we reveled in as many of its glories as our mother would let us. Sometimes we got hot dogs or baloney or chicken pot pies, those magical things that came from the freezer section of the supermarket in cardboard boxes and were put into the oven in their individual little aluminum pie pans to turn golden brown on top and bubbling and savory inside, with chunks of peas, carrots, and chicken suspended in hot, salty, ambrosial glue. We sometimes were allowed to have TV dinners. My favorite of these was Salisbury steak—a small rectangle of soft meat in gummy brown gravy, with suspiciously bright-colored vegetables—and what might originally have been fresh apple slices suspended in the same gummy cornstarchy stuff that was used to make the gravy (and no doubt the chicken pot pie filling), bound with sugar and topped with crunchy "oat" topping that might have been 2 percent oats and 98 percent sugar. It was stupefyingly delicious.

For a treat, my mother once bought Spam and fried slices of it for supper so we could see what it tasted like; we loved it, but she thought it was disgusting and nixed the stuff forevermore. Somehow fish sticks passed muster, however. God, how I loved fish sticks, those breaded, crunchy, tender oblongs, dredged in ketchup and tartar sauce. I don't know what the manufacturers put in them, but they were mildly addictive.

On special occasions, like birthdays, we got to eat at McDonald's, where I always ordered two McChicken sandwiches, medium fries, a hot apple pie, and a chocolate shake, and ate it all and wanted more every time. Or we went to the Chinese restaurant in a nearby strip mall; I had a hot romance back then with crunchy-slippery, luridly neon-red sweet-and-sour pork. Afterward, we generally had dessert at Baskin-Robbins, where I chose either mint chocolate chip or bubblegum ice cream in a sugar cone. Some nights we went to the thrillingly glamorous, or so it seemed at the time, local Mexican place, where I always ordered the deep-fried beef chimichanga with a deep-fried honey-soaked sopaipilla for dessert.

At school, I would pore over the weekly lunch calendar, looking for my favorites: fried chicken, chicken tostadas, sloppy joes, spaghetti with meatballs, and tamale pie, ladled out by smiling lunch ladies in hairnets. We also got little cartons of fresh-tasting, ice-cold whole milk. I always ate everything on my tray, even the (God forbid) brussels sprouts, and I passionately loved the fresh-baked white rolls with cold little pats of margarine; the warm, fudgy brownies; and Mississippi mud cake, which was dense and nutty and gooey.

Every Saturday at noon, if we'd cleaned and vacuumed our rooms and done our weekly chores, we all got an allowance of 50 cents. This we pocketed and, making a collective beeline for the 7-Eleven on Apache Boulevard, promptly blew on Jolly Ranchers, bubble gum, SweeTarts, and Snickers bars. When Pop Rocks were invented, we were right there to try them out. Grape Bubble Yum was a whole new world.

On days when our mother got home after we did because of graduate school classes, my sisters and I used to sneak into her room, lie on her bed in a row on our stomachs, and watch her little black-and-white TV with the rabbit ears antenna. We watched *Gilligan's Island* reruns and *Family Affair* and *Wallace and Ladmo* (a local comedy show) from the instant we came home from school until we heard our mother's car in the carport, when we turned it off and scrambled to our rooms to give the appearance of afternoon-long engagement in wholesome, sanctioned reading and drawing and playing with our toys.

While we watched, we ate graham crackers, the closest thing to junk food our cupboards could provide. One after another, we slid them from their tightly folded wax-paper wrapping and crammed them mindlessly into our mouths, crunching them to wet pulp. The dusty, sweet, innocuous taste of graham crackers is forever associated for me with the sound of cartoon music and the *Gilligan* theme song. After about five of these corrugated, mealy-flour biscuits, I staggered to the kitchen and opened the fridge and poured cold milk from the carton into my mouth and gulped it, open throated like a python swallowing a rabbit. Then I went back to my mother's bed, the TV, the graham crackers, to do it all again. This was my first experience of the catch-22 of mind-numbingly narcotic pleasures.

## CHAPTER 8

## I Am Woman

—— I still thought about my father. But now, living so far away from him—just us girls, free to coexist peacefully without fear of violence, without a presence among us of an indifferent, distant, unreachable man—we flourished as a family. Life in Tempe wasn't easy, not the way it had been in Berkeley, where everything had sort of flowed and people were all in it together. Here, we were more isolated. We were all we had. We didn't belong to any church or social organization or larger extended family. My mother's grad school friends were all transients, like us. We had no history here; our history was in Berkeley, and that was over.

The "we" of our family was something we clung to. We banded together, cultivated an identity as a group, defined ourselves out loud to one another—"We're gypsy WASPs," my mother told me when I asked what ethnicity we were, looking around at all my Mexican and Indian friends. I understood from my mother that we were different from a lot of the people around us in Tempe. We were Democrats. We listened to Bach and Joan Baez and Benny Goodman. We had Indian bedspreads on the walls. Our bookshelves were filled, overflowing, with novels and essay collections and poetry and literary classics. Our divorced mother smoked pot, had long hair, and wore chunky necklaces and hip-huggers. "We" were weird. And weird meant special, or, at least, that was how I interpreted it. I needed to feel that my family was special, so this was the story I told myself, instead of seeing us as isolated, poor, vulnerable. We were great, we were tough, even though we had no man around; we couldn't have the cool, fun junk food or the brand of track shoes Susan and I desperately wanted that all my friends got, but we could afford to pay for her ballet lessons and my violin lessons because "we" valued art more than fashion.

In many ways, my insistence that we were safe and happy and strong came out of a sense of protectiveness toward my mother and sisters—I was afraid to feel anything negative, afraid of opening that door even a crack, for fear of the entire thing crumbling. But while I had books and writing to shield me, imaginary worlds as a buffer, Susan was a realist, pragmatic and clear-eyed, and she was always afraid, always felt vulnerable. Although we were less than two years apart in age, Susan and I had almost completely different childhoods. In some ways, we grew up in two different families. We each adopted a different part of our mother's personality as if we had chosen our characteristics from birth and agreed not to trespass on the other's turf. I was the brainy, swashbuckling, tomboyish, overly anxious but adamantly positive one. Susan, on the other hand, was the visceral, emotional, feminine, worried one. She registered every tremor on our mother's face, every threat from the outside world, every cause for worry like a seismograph. And Emily co-opted another side of our mother entirely: her iconoclastic unorthodoxy, deliberate sureness of purpose, unswerving adherence to an internal truth, no matter what anyone else said or did or thought, an admirable, maddening, constitutional refusal to conform to expectations and social conventions. Sometimes it seemed to me that Susan and I clung to two sides of one life raft together while Emily swam alone.

Something was happening to our mother in those years after she left our father, after she started studying psychology and joined a women's group and subscribed to a bold, exciting new magazine called *Ms.* that had just started up. She was waking up for the first time in her life, realizing that her own feelings mattered, that women didn't have to put up with abuse and bad treatment from men, that women could be friends and allies rather than bitchy competitors, and that she was able to make it on her own, with three little kids, without a husband. When she'd been younger, and then married to Ralph, she had felt as if she were sleepwalking. Now she awoke into a sharper, clearer understanding of her past and her relationships with men, especially her own father and my father. Feminism was a dash of cold water, bracing and invigorating and clean.

My mother discussed all this with me: she always spoke to me as if I were a fellow adult, an understanding ear. Although she prudently, tactfully conducted her sex and dating life off-stage, and didn't tell us kids about it, there were few other things she didn't tell me. I read every issue of *Ms.* right along with her. I pored over her copy of *Our Bodies, Ourselves*, which made me squeamish and uncomfortable but which contained what struck me as blisteringly important information. I sang along with Helen Reddy, "I am strong, I am invincible. . . ." I inhaled biographies of Harriet Tubman, Susan B. Anthony, and Louisa May Alcott; the latter was called, appropriately, *Invincible Louisa*. I thought of myself as invincible. I also thought of myself as a feminist and proudly bandied the term about at school to my baffled classmates. Being female was powerful, I learned. Being a woman meant I was strong, I could do anything. It was all going to be okay. I look back on that heady time fondly, ruefully. Because of course it wasn't okay.

## CHAPTER 9

## The Tomato-Red Bus

In the early summer of 1971, I left my mother and little sisters in Tempe and flew to the Bay Area alone to spend the summer with my father in Oakland. I hadn't seen him in what felt like a very long time, all of third grade—he felt like a stranger suddenly.

My father had started a commune in his huge Victorian house on Regent Street. I was given my own room on the third floor under the eaves, a small room with a secret passageway behind the wall. There was a tiled koi pond in the backyard. There was a laundry chute in the butler's pantry off the kitchen and a dusty green velvet couch in the front parlor I liked to lie on.

My father had filled his house with young, righteous politicos, all of whom seemed to revere him. They did a lot of sitting around and talking through clouds of pot smoke. I was the only kid around the place that summer. I don't remember what I did all day, but I do remember feeling out of place and homesick and intimidated by my father, who was as distant and gruff with me as ever. I felt awkward around him, like a big lummox. I wasn't sure why I was there. Maybe he just wanted to upset my mother by enforcing his custodial rights.

One night, at a dinner with some friends of my father's, as I watched an enormous bearded man frying an odd dish he called peachburgers, which were literally hamburger meat mixed with chopped canned peaches, I blurted out to the entire assemblage of guests, "My daddy hit my mommy, and she cried."

There was something like a collective gasp from all the grown-ups. No one said anything for many ticks of the clock. They all stared at me as if I'd thrown a live grenade across the room.

After the party, as we were driving home, just the two of us, my father told me tersely, with controlled rage, never, ever, to say anything like that again. I had embarrassed him and upset his friends.

I was deeply, horribly mortified. What had I been thinking? I had wrecked the party. I had pissed my father off and hurt his feelings. I was such an asshole.

"I don't know why I said that, Daddy," I confessed wretchedly.

"You shouldn't have," he said. "Never do it again."

I lay awake long into the night, racked with shame and regret.

Soon after that, I took off with my father and his girlfriend, a kind, solid woman named Karen, in a tomato-red VW bus to drive around the Southwest, just the three of us. I remember straddling the Four Corners grid, my hands and feet in four different states. We went to Bryce Canyon, Canyon de Chelly, the cliff dwellings in New Mexico.

I couldn't stop annoying my father. I didn't mean to annoy him; it just happened. I pestered him to play cards with me and bragged when I won; I could feel viscerally how tense this made him. One night, very late, long past my bedtime, he left the campfire where he'd been talking with a group of people we'd met and found me whimpering and crying outside the bus, standing in the darkness.

"Why aren't you asleep?" he asked.

"You forgot to feed me," I said. "No one put me to bed."

"You're almost nine years old," he said. "Old enough to speak up. Don't let this happen again!"

I recoiled. I hadn't spoken up because I was not a kid who whined or asked for things, and I was shy with him sometimes. He gave me a yogurt, which I ate in silence, and then he packed me off to my little bed in the back of the bus. I lay there with a knot in my stomach, still hungry.

One day, Karen walked me into the desert alone and told me that I had to stop being such a pain in the ass. "Your father can't take it anymore," she said. "He's really at the end of his rope."

"Sorry," I said. "I'll try, I swear."

Following this little talk, which felt like a Mafia hit, things deteriorated. And so, after a summer of looking like a wild animal—with messy hair, dirt-streaked face, and ratty clothes—I found myself suddenly, abruptly scrubbed clean with freshly washed and braided hair, wearing travel-worthy clothes, being driven to the Albuquerque airport.

My father looked at me in the rearview mirror as he drove. "If the cops stop us, they'll think we kidnapped you," he joked.

He had called my mother and told her I was flying back to Arizona that night. Luckily, she was home, in the middle of her weekly poker game with her psychologist pals, or she wouldn't have known. She left my sleeping sisters in the care of a friend and drove to Sky Harbor airport.

When the stewardess who'd been put in charge of me walked me off the plane, there was my mother waiting at the gate. I had never been happier to see her.

## CHAPTER 10

## Food and Words

—— I got home from that disastrous summer with my father to find that my mother had painted my room a clear, rich, bright red while I was gone. She had wanted to surprise me; I had repeatedly asked for a red room in the months before I left. I was overwhelmed with joy; my room was now perfect. I had a mattress on the floor instead of a bed, just the way I liked it——all my furniture was flat and low so I could spread my many ongoing projects around my butter-yellow, fuzzy carpet. My bureau was the one tall thing in the room.

I had a low table to write on while I sat on the floor, cross-legged, hunched over my stapled-together books, grasping my pen awkwardly in my right hand. I had terrible penmanship; I was always impatient and slapdash at everything I did, so the aesthetic quality of my writing itself was completely irrelevant to me, far outside the realm of anything I cared about. I wrote as fast as the words could come out: a series of stories about girls my age and their adventures at school (not the most imaginative plots in the world); illustrated animal stories for my younger sisters with such inventive titles as "Sammy the Snake" and "The Bears on Vacation."

I drew endless pictures of huge families with sets of six or eight siblings in a descending line from oldest to youngest, with their vaguely Victorian names and ages carefully marked below each one: "Olivia, age 15; Abigail, age 13; Seth, age 11; Malcolm, age 10; Maria, age 8; Genevieve, age 6; Thomas, age 3; James, age 1." They all had solemn, big-eyed faces, neatly combed or braided hair, and my idea of nineteenth-century country clothes—pinafores, overalls, knickers, aprons.

I had a collection of names in a bowl, slips of paper folded up. Sometimes, when I was too lazy to draw or write, I would lie on the floor picking names out idly, letting them dictate people to me: "Victoria" was a beautiful, snobbish girl with a pouting expression who stamped her little foot; "Olaf" was an honest, industrious midwestern farm boy whose parents were old and poor; "Priscilla" was a cold, cruel, secretly sad rich girl whose mother was dead; "David" was a handsome, intelligent, studious boy with a full head of curly dark hair. I loved phrases like "a full head of curly dark hair." I rolled it around in my mouth silently, then put the slip of paper aside and picked out another one.

I hated my own name. It was all wrong. I was going to be a novelist, I knew very early on, and novelists were named Jane, Charlotte, and Louisa. When I learned cursive, I practiced signing the autograph I might put in all my books when I grew up: Laurina Kate Johansen. Laurette Johansen. Those substitutes never looked anything but faux Victorian and trampy, and Laura and Laurel weren't me at all, they were other girls I didn't know.

Over the course of two or more years, I invented and created an imaginary country called Zenobia; my imaginary friend, Charlie, was the emissary from the queen of Zenobia, and it was from him that I learned about the country. I wrote down the customs, holidays, and religious practices; I drew maps of the towns, set out to write a Zenobian grammar book with conjugated verbs and vocabulary words. I developed an ongoing drama about the royal family's internecine conflicts and rivalries.

I discovered a rhyming dictionary at the back of my mother's old *Webster's*, and wrote poems with it, the longest and most ambitious of which began:

> *One day, a wagon of hay*
> *Went down a gray*
> *Road made of clay.*
> *It came to a door.*
> *Who could ask for more?*
> *People by the score,*
> *They could ask for more. . . .*

In bed at night, I sat propped against my pillows and leafed through the dictionary, opening pages at random and avidly reading various new words and their definitions until my mother finished telling my little sisters their bedtime story and came to read me mine. Then we picked up where we'd left off the night before in whatever book we were currently enthralled by. We cried together when Bambi's mother was killed; we raced through *Swallows and Amazons* and all the rest of the books in the series by Arthur Ransome, cheering for Captain Nancy and her first mate, Susan. *The Princess and the Goblin* was our gateway drug to George MacDonald, then came *A Little Princess* and *The Secret Garden*. Sometimes, between books, my mother invented stories for me about a little goatherd named Roland who lived in a mountain hut with his father and had many adventures. She loved making up the Roland stories as much as I loved hearing them.

And I read books to myself, starting a new one as soon as I finished the one before it, checking out whole stacks once a week from the school library. I read as voraciously as I ate. The two activities went together perfectly. Like all kids, I read the back of the cereal box while I ate the cereal; everyone did, it was nonoptional. This compulsion, however, extended for me into other areas not everyone seemed to need to explore. The absolute greatest pleasure I knew when I was little was to eat along with characters in books I was reading, or to write about characters who ate what I wished I could be eating.

A keenly piercing brain hunger gripped me whenever a character in a book ate anything—an urgent craving for the pemmican in *Swallows and Amazons* (which I imagined as a chewy kind of Spam); the Turkish Delight in *The Lion, the Witch, and the Wardrobe* (I pictured pillowy glittering candy that tasted like perfumed nuts, and I wasn't far off); the dripping sweet flesh of the enormous traveling fruit in *James and the Giant Peach*; or some miniature version of the gigantic, caloric, wonderful *Little House on the Prairie* breakfasts, which seemed to consist of equal parts carbohydrates, cured meat, pickles, and preserves. Part of the excitement of all this food was the stuff that preceded or accompanied it—pirate sailing games, a sleigh ride in snow with a glamorous, dangerous witch, a perilous journey in an oversized fruit, the hard work and terrible weather of nineteenth-century midwestern farm life. With travel, danger, and adventure, it seemed, came food.

Once during an overnight at a friend's house, I snuck off and read *Charlie and the Chocolate Factory*. As a budding hermit, I used these overnights as an excuse to read whatever books my friends had that I didn't, sidling away from my hostess to read her books as fast as I could before she noticed I was missing.

I finished *Charlie* in my friend's bedroom beanbag chair and ventured back into the light, blinking with the force of the imagined taste of chocolate. On my way to the glass sliding doors that led to their backyard, where my friend and her sisters were playing, I ran into their mother. "Hello!" she said cheerfully. "What's up?"

"I just finished *Charlie and the Chocolate Factory*," I confided. "And I am craving chocolate now like crazy." I wasn't asking for chocolate; that would have been rude. I was simply answering her question, and I expected her to say longingly, "I know exactly what you mean," looking off into the middle distance as she viscerally remembered the book's lascivious, melting descriptions.

"Well, sorry," she said instead, her cheer undaunted, "I don't have any!" And off she went, before I could explain. This might have been the first time I realized that not everyone's brain was wired the same way mine was.

## CHAPTER 11

# Curios

For our first Thanksgiving in Arizona, my mother heard about a group of people who were having a potluck celebration near the Superstition Mountains just outside Tempe. Ruth Ann and Frieda, our former Berkeley neighbors, were visiting, so we all drove there together.

There was a huge tepee set up in the desert, a real one; we all sat inside it in a big circle around the fire in the middle. People played wooden flutes and drums, and there was a long table full of the food everyone had brought. Suddenly, we were all pseudohippies again; it was a comforting thing for us Berkeley-bred, culture-shocked kids. I remember feeling right at home there with the crowd of long-haired grown-ups in tie-dyed skirts, beards, and granny glasses. The other kids seemed familiar, too, more like us, somehow, than the other kids we knew in Arizona.

The food was the usual hippie stuff—vegetarian, heavy on the legumes, grains, nuts, and root vegetables. But there was no turkey. My family had never celebrated Thanksgiving with traditional dinners. As my mother put it, "It was the sixties and we were rebelling against turkey. Sorry you missed out on all that tryptophan!"

So we spent a perfectly nice day hanging out with some of the Arizona counterculture, and then later that night, we went home to Wildermuth, back to our Arizona desert life with the black widow spiders in the carport, the broom handle in our sliding glass door groove to keep intruders out, our swamp cooler, our cornfield.

The following Thanksgiving, we drove all the way up to "the snow"—this was a rarity for us, a luxurious and strange new thing. My mother's friends, two couples, Rich and Vangie and Steve and Debbie, organized a trip to Hannagan Meadow Lodge, nine thousand feet up in the Apache-Sitgreaves National Forest in the far eastern part of Arizona.

We all stayed together in a cabin with a front porch stacked with firewood and a big living room with a stone fireplace. We kids didn't have any coats warmer than light jackets, since we had never needed them before, but I remember my mother cobbling together some sweaters and knitted hats and mittens for us all. We spent all day outside, making snowballs and snow angels, running and shrieking around the vast forest meadows, and then we came back into the cabin and warmed up by the big fireplace, the tips of our ears and noses tingling, and our pants legs steaming as the snow evaporated.

On Thanksgiving Day, we all sat at a long table in the lodge dining room. "White meat or dark," the smiling wait-ress asked, going all the way down the table and back up again and writing it on her pad. "Dark," I said decisively when it was my turn, having no idea what it meant. The grown-ups drank wine, the fire blazed. I was sitting at the other end of the table from my mother and sisters, so I was quiet, listening to the grown-ups talking, eagerly awaiting my dinner. I was starving, as I always was, in those days, but the cold air had made my appetite even keener and more urgent. The plates started com-ing out, and they were loaded, laden, piled high with turkey, stuffing, mashed potatoes, and vegetables. I was mesmerized.

The people on either side of me got their food; the people across from me got theirs. Everyone started helping themselves to cranberry sauce and gravy. I figured they'd all asked for light meat, and the dark meat probably took longer because it had to cook more, so I waited. And waited, and waited, until finally I realized that everyone else was eating, I'd been forgotten, and I had to speak up for myself because my mother was all the way at the other end of the table.

I raised my hand high and looked at the waitress, of course, since every schoolchild knew that was how you got a grown-up's attention. She came over to me and leaned over. "Yes, hon?"

"I think . . . you forgot my food," I said, mortified. I'd been hoping she'd just see my empty place mat and bring me my plate without making me explain myself. I hated calling attention to myself, hated being pitied or worried about.

But of course all the grown-ups around me immediately put their forks down and made noises of sympathy and concern.

"Laurie, let me give you some turkey!"

"Here, Laurie, I've got enough for both of us."

"It's okay," I said through a knot of fierce pride that stuck in my throat. Absurdly, I was on the verge of tears, but it wasn't self-pity or hunger that was causing it, it was my mortification at being looked at.

"I'll be right back," said the waitress. "Hon, I am so sorry!"

I got my food, and it tasted as good as it looked. Turkey was gamier and richer than chicken. Cranberry sauce looked sweet, like strawberry jam, but tasted tart and hearty, both at once. The two things together tasted so good, I couldn't eat my dinner fast enough. And then that huge meal was followed by dessert: we all got pieces of both pumpkin and apple pie with whipped cream. I had never tasted pumpkin pie before. It was so creamy smooth, like pudding, but it tasted like cinnamon and wasn't overly sweet, and it melted on my tongue with the toothsome, flaky crust. Full as I was, bursting with food, I felt I could never eat enough pumpkin pie as long as I lived.

Mortification was becoming an increasingly common experience for me, the sudden, self-conscious, horrified realization that I didn't understand adults, no matter how hard I studied them, and that I had just done something totally oblivious and childish. I was a kid, and there was a barrier between me and the grown-ups, their world and mine. Often, it had to do with sex.

In the spring of 1972, we went camping with my mother's grad school friends in Mexico. Our car joined the caravan from Tempe down south across the border to Puerto Peñasco, or Rocky Point, on the Sea of Cortez. Back in the early seventies, Rocky Point was a tiny town with a wide clean sandy beach. It was the third or fourth time we'd gone camping down there, and we always stopped for lunch about halfway, in a town called Ajo, Arizona, whose A&W, in my family's collective opinion, had the best hot dogs in the world. They put grilled onions on them, along with relish and ketchup and mustard, which was how we ate them out west and how I always ate them until I moved to New York and caved to peer pressure and ate them with mustard and onions only, like the natives.

Camping trips meant special food, stuff we never got at any other time: orange and grape Tang, instant powdered lemonade, breakfast bars, and astronaut space-food sticks—the peanut butter ones were my favorite; they tasted like a combination of Elmer's glue and those chewy peanut-butter candies called Mary Janes. My mother also packed baloney and Cracker Barrel cheese, hot dogs and buns, marshmallows, and—wonder of wonders—potato chips. Of course, there were also whole-wheat bread, granola, peanut butter, strawberry jam, apples, bananas, carrot and celery sticks, those old staples, but even they tasted better on the beach, in the shade of the tent, with a fine grit of sand between our teeth.

We ate breakfast on the beach in the hot sunlight by the sparkling ocean before a day of running down to the waves to plunge in and jump over each one as it rolled into shore. Sometimes we had late-afternoon lunches in the inner court-yard of an old colonial hotel in the town of Puerto Peñasco. We ate shrimp with garlic over yellow rice, grilled fish, chicken enchiladas in green sauce. The grown-ups drank bottles of beer with limes; we got Shirley Temples. There was Mexican music playing, and an ocean breeze blew in through the tall open windows.

At night, we sat around big driftwood bonfires, eating charred hot dogs and marshmallows on sticks, singing songs around the campfire and stargazing. My sisters and mother and I slept in our big green and orange canvas cabin tent with our sleeping bags all in a row with the window flaps rolled and tied up to let the ocean air in through the screen mesh windows.

The beach was quiet and dark except sounds of the waves and the intermittent headlights and putt-putt-putts of beach buggies going by. I was always anxious about being crushed under those big rubber wheels in my sleep, and I did my best to whip my little sisters into a frenzy of fear so that I wouldn't be alone in it. In the mornings, miraculously still alive, we emerged from the tent's zippered door, already in our bathing suits, into sunlight and wind, hungry for space-food sticks.

One day, my mother's friend Claire, who was young and pretty, announced that she and her boyfriend, Keith, were going to take a walk down the beach. Everyone but me appar-ently grasped the significance of this.

"Can I come?" I asked instantly. It sounded like the most fun thing in the world. I'd been playing on the beach all day and was getting a little bored. Claire and Keith were so cool. It would be an adventure to take a walk with them.

They looked at each other. "We're going to take off our clothes," Claire said.

"Let them go," I'm sure my mother must have told me if she'd overheard this.

"Please?" I said. "I don't care if you take off your clothes. That's okay."

They didn't say no, so the three of us walked for a glorious mile or so along the hot, breezy beach. I couldn't believe my luck. I felt it was my duty to entertain them in return for letting me come, so I kept up a stream of information about myself—books I liked to read, gossip about people at my school. I offered the best shells I found to Claire. I ran ahead of them and back again to show them how fast I could go. I interrogated them: Where did they grow up? What were they like when they were little?

They were so nice. They listened to me and answered my questions and praised my sprinting. Eventually, we stopped walking and picked a spot on the sand as our base of operations for the afternoon. When they got naked and went out swimming together, I stayed on the beach for a while and guarded their clothes from nonexistent thieves and looked away, down the beach, to give them privacy. I dug in the sand with a big abalone shell and watched seagulls land and take off in the waves. I peeked—just once—and saw their heads close together, far out in the water, bobbing up and down.

On the walk back to camp, I was quiet and shy, having finally realized, too late, that they had really wanted to be by themselves. I couldn't figure out how to apologize to them for foisting myself into their private afternoon without making it more awkward than it already was, so I didn't say anything, but inwardly I was seething with embarrassment and regret.

When it was time to drive back to Tempe, our mother let the caravan drive on without us, and we spent the day in town. We walked around the streets, peering into open doorways (our mother was as shamelessly nosy as we were), spellbound by the seemingly romantic way they lived there, with hammocks and crucifixes and TVs in their front rooms, and by the exotic, delicious cooking smells emanating from their kitchens.

Afterward, we got to have lunch at the hotel, just us. And finally, our mother told us that we could choose one thing, anything we wanted, from the curio shop. We were all instantly in an agony of indecision, sure that if we chose the wrong thing, we would regret it forever. I had never heard the word "curio" before, but suddenly it struck me as the most glamorous, fantastic word in the world, and I couldn't stop using it as I walked around the little shop, inspecting all the curios. I fell in love with a round little turquoise ring, but then I saw a mermaid made of shells glued together, painted beautiful colors. I could only have one; I wanted both desperately. I chose the ring and yearned for the mermaid all the way to the A&W in Ajo, Arizona, where I drowned my sorrows in a root beer.

## CHAPTER 12

## Rattlesnake

In June of that year, two months before I turned ten, my sisters and I all went to Oakland to spend the summer with our father on Regent Street. Also in the house, along with the usual commune members, were our father's current girlfriend and her two sons, Elijah, who was my age, and Jesse, who was between Susan's and Emily's ages.

The five of us kids formed a wild, ragtag little crew, unsupervised for the most part and left to our own devices all day while the grown-ups did whatever they did. Elijah and Susan and I discovered that we could travel all over the neighborhood on rooftops, leaping from one pitched roof to the next, swinging on branches, until we were across the block. We played hide and go seek in an empty schoolyard. We hung out with the other kids on the street, including a girl who could swallow little glass bottles and burp them back up.

Once or twice, my father erupted at Emily the way he used to blow up at our mother. Apparently, Emily, of the three of us, was the only one who triggered his blind-rage mechanism. I remember him dragging her by the arm to his bedroom as punishment for her refusal to obey him. He threw her onto his bed and then around the room, scarily, violently. He didn't hit her, but he didn't have to—we were all properly terrified.

One day, Elijah decided we were going to rob the house next door. The people who lived there were gone all day, and he knew they left the back door unlocked. He and I would sneak in and take whatever loot we could find, and Susan would stand guard. The code word was "rattlesnake." We went through their back door the next afternoon and up the stairs to their bedroom. My heart was, of course, staccato, hotly beating. We took two twenty-dollar bills and some costume jewelry from a bureau top.

"Rattlesnake!" Susan yelled at the top of her lungs.

We tumbled out the back door and sauntered down the driveway as if we'd just been taking the air.

There stood my father. He had just come home from work. We managed to act normal, then we hid the costume jewelry under the side-entrance stairs of his house and crouched together in the tiny hidey-hole for a whole afternoon, eating dog biscuits we'd found—a fitting snack for hardened criminals.

The next day, Elijah and Susan and I went to the local Safeway via rooftops. We approached the lady behind the customer service desk with the two stolen twenty-dollar bills and asked her to break them for us. She peered at the three out-of-breath, wild-eyed, rat-haired hippie kids over her half-moon bifocals on a chain around her neck and asked where we'd gotten the money. We told her with insistent fake honesty that it had been our Christmas present. When she rightly surmised that something was amiss, since it was now July, and demanded our parents' phone number, we ran out.

We decided to put the money on my father's bureau top.

"Where did this money come from?" he asked us all when he found it.

We all pretended we had no idea, and my father, who was always mild mannered when he wasn't beating someone up, let it go.

When we got back to Tempe, I couldn't shake the feeling that something was wrong. I felt it in the pit of my stomach. During the months that followed, my inchoate fear took the concrete form of a terror of punishment for breaking into the house next door. Whenever the phone rang at night after I was in bed, I lay awake, staring into the dim light of the room with wide eyes, sure it was the cops calling to arrest me.

I finally confessed the crime to my mother and asked if she thought I'd go to jail for it. She assured me the cops weren't going to find me, but my fear didn't go away.

In fact, it intensified. One night, my mother was awakened by a tapping on her bedroom window. Terrified, she looked out to see my friend Beverly Begay standing under the swamp cooler with all her siblings. They asked if they could come in and stay with us because their own mother had gotten drunk and kicked them out and told them never to come back. They looked even more terrified than my mother was.

Although she badly wanted to invite them in for the night, my mother realized they might never leave if she did. So she talked them through the steps of breaking into their house without their mother knowing and slipping into their beds. Since they had no telephone to call the police, she told them all to stand up straight and tall and assert themselves to their mother in a loud voice if they had to. Then she told them to come back to her window if it didn't work out. It did. Beverly was at school, as always, the next day.

Soon after that, a strange man came to the door and threatened my mother, pointing a gun at her. He was the father of a shy, scared, troubled little girl who'd come over to play at our house only once, one of Susan's classmates. He was sure my mother was hiding her. Somehow she convinced him that his daughter wasn't in our house and got him to back down and go away.

Despite these incidents, though, things seemed to be okay on the surface. When Halloween came, I made my costume out of a cardboard box: I drew a screen on it with squiggly static lines, made antennae out of coat hangers, and wore it on my head with little eye holes, dressed all in black so I looked (I hoped) like a TV on a stand. As usual, the enormous bags of candy we lugged home were confiscated by our mother and doled out to us so slowly they would last till Christmas, and would have lasted even longer if she hadn't ransacked the stash at night while she was studying.

Then one November night, after we kids were all in bed, my father called and told my mother he was in Tempe and would be stopping by soon to take us with him for the weekend.

"The girls are already asleep," she told him. "You can't show up out of the blue like this. They all have things to do tomorrow."

"I'm coming over," he said. "Get them ready, I'm taking them."

My mother woke us up and drove us to our friends Mike and Jayne's house, where we all spent the night. We went home the next morning and resumed our lives. Before lunch, our father arrived. The front door was open, but the screen door was still locked. He yanked it open and leaped at my mother and beat her more savagely than he had ever beaten her before, yanking her hair out and punching her breasts. Susan and Emily hit his legs and tried to defend her while I hovered in the doorway to the kitchen, paralyzed with shock and fear.

"Dial zero, Laurie," my mother said to me, gasping a little. "Tell them to send the cops."

I reached up to unhook the receiver from the wall phone, dialed one long, slow zero, and said I know not what to the operator when she answered. I must have given her the correct information, because minutes later, a cop car arrived in a blaze of sirens. The cops, our saviors now instead of the pigs, came into the house, pulled my father off my mother, and led him away in handcuffs. We all stood in the driveway together and watched him get shoved into the back of the squad car, watched it drive away.

Then we all went back inside. My mother sat at the table, crying, pulling out hunks of her own hair while the three of us comforted her, patting and hugging her, telling her we loved her. The next day, her breasts were completely black and blue. Over the next week or two, the bruises faded. Her hair grew back.

My mother had declined to press charges, so my father was probably released soon after the cops took him away. We received no further child-support checks from him. He disappeared from our lives.

For months afterward, I kept my father's expired driver's license under my pillow; he had given it to me the summer before. The photo showed an old hippie with a long salt-and-pepper ponytail and shaggy beard, his eyes wild, probably from drugs. He bore little resemblance to the father I'd blindly adored as a small kid.

## CHAPTER 13

*Jim*

——— We had a lot of cats growing up, but I only ever cared about one of them, a handsome, good-natured little tabby called Toby who slept on the pillow by my head and whom I loved to cuddle and play with. He disappeared shortly after my father did. A neighbor found him in his air conditioner, dead. We guessed that he'd gotten stuck and died of thirst. How the neighbor didn't hear him mewing before he died, I could not imagine. It was a blow.

Without my father's child-support checks, we were suddenly very poor. Before, we'd been on the edge, but able to get by, but now my mother's worries about money made her serious and quiet and abstracted. The house felt dark and sad.

Then the head of the psych department at ASU threatened to cut or at least decrease my mother's stipend. At one psych department party at someone's house with a swimming pool, she sat with the department head and his administrator at a table while we all played in the swimming pool, laughing and paddling around together, three little girls.

"Cute kids," said the department head.

My mother was silent for a brief instant. Then she said, looking him in the eye, "They're the ones who will suffer if you cut my funding, you know."

Her funding wasn't cut. But we still struggled. One day, an envelope containing two hundred dollars in cash arrived in the mail, addressed to my mother. We didn't know whom it was from. It was a big help, of course, but the anonymity of the gift felt ominous somehow. Everything felt ominous.

Our neighborhood was turning seedy. Wildermuth had changed. My friends Debbie and Beverly and Shelly Renee had all moved away, and now there were strange kids on the street, kids we didn't know, older kids. Adolescence was suddenly in full swing on our street: the boys had faint mustaches and muscles; the girls had breasts, wore makeup. Hormones raged, teen psychodramas and sexual games; no one paid any attention to us skinny little girls. Our neighborhood felt even rougher and wilder. Our family was suddenly isolated there.

Early in the spring, a tall blond young man approached my mother after a classical music concert in Phoenix and told her, as an opening line, that he wanted to take care of her. He seemed earnest and kind and trustworthy. He was also handsome, sexy, and cultured. His name was Jim Christensen. He was the first man my mother had been with in any serious way since she'd left my father, so we got to meet him. He came over to pick her up for dates and tried to engage me, a ten-year-old girl, by tossing a ball back and forth and asking about school, as if he'd read a textbook on making conversation with your date's kids. I thought he was overly eager and boring, but he was nice to us. He was nice to our mother.

I remember one night when my mother was getting dressed up to go dancing with Jim; she put on a slinky hot-orange halter dress and strappy hot-yellow high-heeled sandals and a chunky bead necklace. She looked so beautiful, so tan and strong and sexy, that I swooned and threw myself at her, kissing her neck over and over.

It was so clear to me, I could even have articulated it at the time: I was madly in love with my mother, and I was losing her to a man. Before Jim came along, on Friday nights, I got to stay up after my sisters went to bed to watch *Sonny & Cher* with my mother, in her bed, just the two of us, laughing and chatting during commercials and sometimes, for a special treat, watching *The Tonight Show*—I was my mother's standing Friday night date, and it was easily the highlight of my week. Now those Friday night dates were Jim's, and I watched our TV shows with the babysitter.

Late in the spring of 1973, Jim moved from his apartment into our house on Wildermuth. I was not wild about this, even though we immediately felt safer with him around, and he adored all of us. And he was a catch: he was an architect, he dressed elegantly, loved jazz and classical music, smoked a pipe with Borkum Riff tobacco, and drove a Peugeot. He had a neatly trimmed beard. He drank a lot of wine, but he never got violent, no matter how much he drank.

And he liked to cook. The first time he made steaks for us, I came dashing into the kitchen demanding to know what that amazing smell was. It turned out to be garlic, sautéing with celery and onions while the steaks broiled. I stood by the stove, inhaling the smell as if it were a revelation.

And then we left Wildermuth. After my mother finished her course work and internship, she was offered a job as the school district psychologist in Glendale, on the other side of Phoenix from us. Jim, whom we now called Dad, had some money from the sale of a house he owned in Tucson, so they started looking for a house to buy together to be closer to her job. They found one on West San Miguel Avenue in Phoenix, and at the end of December, we drove away behind a packed-full moving truck. I felt nothing but relief: we were moving somewhere so much better, and life was going forward, and anyway, change was always an adventure.

### ANADAMA BREAD

*My mother often made this molasses and cornmeal bread. The story behind its name, as she told it, was that a husband whose wife, Anna, had just left him made a batch of bread in a fit of fury, and as he kneaded, he muttered, "Anna, damn 'er. Anna, damn 'er."*

*I used to wolf down almost half a loaf of this dark, sweet, soft bread straight out of the oven. I would jaggedly cut into the steaming-hot loaf and slather each piece in margarine and honey and chew it with ecstatic eye flutters and sighs, the kiddie version of a swoon, standing by the cutting board until I could eat no more. Then I drank a big glass of milk, pouring it down my throat.*

Grease a large mixing bowl with 2 tablespoons vegetable oil and set aside. Dissolve 2 packages dry yeast in ½ cup lukewarm water and set aside. In another large bowl, combine 2 cups milk, 1 cup yellow cornmeal, ⅔ cup molasses, 3 tablespoons melted butter, and 1½ teaspoons salt. Add 4 cups of flour and the yeast mixture and stir to form a dough. Add 3–4 more cups of flour a bit at a time, stopping when the dough becomes stiff enough to knead. Turn dough onto a lightly floured surface and knead until it's smooth and elastic, about 10 minutes.

Place the dough into the greased bowl, turning to coat, then cover with a clean dish towel and let it rise until doubled in bulk—about 1½ hours. Gently punch the dough down, then let it rest for 10 minutes. Shape the dough into 3 loaves, then place them into three greased 9-by-5-inch loaf pans. Let them rise until just about doubled, then bake at 350 degrees until browned and cooked through, 35 to 45 minutes. Invert loaves to cool onto a wire rack. Eat piece after piece, slathered in butter and honey, standing at the counter.

## FARMERS FRITTERS

*On many Friday nights, our mother whipped up a batch of thin,
crisp, tangy-sweet cottage cheese pancakes. She used to put her huge
rectangular electric skillet in the middle of the table, and my sisters and
I sat around it while she made fritters in batches, sliding them around
onto everyone's plates. While we ate stacks of them with homemade
applesauce and Aunt Jemima syrup, we told a story, going around the
table, with the sliding glass door open to the patio and a warm breeze
making the candles flicker. Someone started the story, and then we took
turns continuing it until it was finished.*

*The original recipe was written in our aunt Aillinn's handwriting on an
index card, with parenthetical additions by our mother:*

> 1 cup Blossom Time cottage cheese
> 1 egg (2 are better)
> ¼ teaspoon salt
> ⅛ (is that really an 8?!?!) cup milk (or a very little cream)
> ¼ teaspoon grated lemon peel
> 2 tablespoons melted butter
> ¼ cup flour (+ a little wheat germ)

Place first six ingredients in bowl and beat well with rotary beater. Stir
in flour. Drop by tablespoons on greased griddle. Serve with butter
and hot syrup. Serves 4.

PART THREE

*San Miguel*

## CHAPTER 14

## Household Politics

——— Although I didn't realize it yet, the era of blue plate specials was over, and so were those golden (to me, anyway) years of being just the four of us girls, all together against the world. Now, my mother had a grueling, stressful seventy-five-hour-per-week job, and she still had to write her dissertation. She was gone from early morning until late evening, and when she came home, she was tired and preoccupied and busy.

Also, her relationship with Jim was never, not even at the beginning, the fun, romantic partnership she'd had with my father. She was with Jim for security and companionship; it was obvious to me even then that this was no grand passion for her, although it was for him. Where my father had been dynamic and intelligent and charismatic, Jim was passive and weak willed and devoted——in other words, boring.

To make matters worse, he was laid off from his job shortly after we moved; the recession hit architectural firms along with everyone else. After he was fired, instead of tootling off in his Peugeot every morning, wearing a tie, trailing pipe smoke, he became a constant, needy, fretting presence around the house. He was too eagerly interested in our lives, asking us kids questions that seemed designed to "get to know us." He laughed too hard at our impromptu, over-the-top, silly variety shows, picked up on our private jokes a little too quickly, and repeated them a little too much. He was obviously trying hard to fit into the family. He flat-out adored my mother, and it was not hard to see that he loved having stepkids. He'd asked us to call him "Dad" right off the bat, as soon as he moved in with us. But I was embarrassed for him; I tried to humor him, to give him what he seemed to need from me, to be kind to him. But I didn't respect him. He struck me as pathetic, no matter how hard I tried not to think of him that way. It wasn't fair. He was everything my father hadn't been—gentle, fully present, doting. But being around Jim made me miss my father.

I also missed my mother now. I felt shortchanged, unfairly and childishly. I couldn't understand why she had let Jim into our house and lives and family. What was the point of him? He took so much energy. I had never been demanding or needy with her. I was always her supporter, cheerleader, shoulder, ear, ally, and champion. I kept my own needs and feelings far away from our equation. I was lucky, I knew, whereas my own mother had had a poetically tragic childhood she'd had to overcome. I knew her story by heart; it was my favorite childhood fairy tale.

Now my stepfather was my competition for her attention, and in my opinion, he was totally unworthy. He had upset the balance of our foursome. This was my mother's fault. I blamed her squarely. And I suddenly felt taken for granted.

Our new house was sprawling and fancy, or at least it seemed so to us after Wildermuth. It was a one-story ranch with four bedrooms, a living room, a dining room, an eat-in kitchen, and a huge tile-floored glassed-in porch leading out to a big fenced backyard. Everyone got her own room except my mother, who naturally shared with Jim. Their room was at the other end of the house, past the kitchen and laundry room, so my sisters and I had our own sort of wing. As the oldest, I got the bedroom with its own bathroom.

Our new neighborhood was solidly middle-class and suburban feeling, block after block of ranch houses much like ours with big front yards full of palm trees and saguaros and smooth, clean sidewalks on wide, quiet streets. San Miguel was just off West Bethany Home Road, which boasted a McDonald's, a Circle K, a 7-Eleven, and the fabulously cheesy new Chris-Town Mall. These were all within walking distance, as was our new school, Simpson Elementary, which went all the way through eighth grade: I could stay in the same school as my sisters through junior high. We could all walk to and from school together, if we wanted to.

Although it was nice to live in a neighborhood where there was no apparent threat of gunfire, and to have a man about the place for security reasons, in other ways our home life was harder now. My mother had, early on, made sure we three got used to doing chores. We'd learned long ago to set the table, wash the dishes, hang up wet laundry, clean the bathrooms, and vacuum the floors. We had always cleaned our own rooms, changed our own sheets, and taken responsibility for our own clothes. Our mother believed it was good for us to have jobs around the house, but primarily, she needed all the help she could get, and we were the only game in town.

To make sure dinner got onto the table every night now, even though she wasn't there most of the time, our mother instituted doughnut meetings every Saturday afternoon. Over a big box of doughnuts, we read and discussed the week's haul from the family suggestion box, and then we planned the coming week's roster of duties. The suggestion box (a cardboard shoe box with a hole in the lid) was generally filled with plaintive, heartfelt requests from the ever-beleaguered Emily, whom Susan and I teased constantly, not only because she was the youngest and smallest but because she had a tragic nature that required negative attention to fulfill itself. In other words, she asked for it. "No teasing," she wrote on strip after strip of paper. "No goosing."

Now that our mother was home so little, we got to add a

new skill to our mother's-helper repertoire: cooking. We were all assigned one weeknight to cook dinner and another to do kitchen cleanup: Susan, Emily, me, and Jim, who was now always home. On Fridays, my mother cooked; she got home earlier that night because it was the end of the week.

Susan and I didn't mind it so much, as we were older and more able to face the demands of cooking a whole meal. But Emily had to stand on a stool and be assisted by Jim. She was only six and hated cooking right away. To this day, she dislikes it, and she traces this abhorrence all the way back to a night when she spilled a hot pot of something on herself while she was taking it off the stove. She was too young to be cooking, clearly. But we all took a turn: that was how it worked.

On my nights, I made the pot roast from the *Joy of Cooking* as often as I could. I never got tired of either making or eating it; I have no idea how my family felt about it, and I didn't ask. In my opinion, it was always delicious and flavorful and never dry, and it always satisfied my infernal ravenous gluttony. And it was the first recipe I'd ever followed. The first time I made it, it came out well, and I saw no reason to risk failure with a strange new recipe when this one worked just fine.

I made certain minor modifications to the recipe, though, over time. First, I thought my changes made the pot roast taste better (I hated cloves and omitted them, for example), and also it has never been in my nature to follow directions to the letter—at school, in the kitchen, or anywhere. At some point, all my favorite teachers invariably gave me what I began to think of as The Talk: "You're not living up to your potential," said my junior-high social studies and English teacher, Mrs. Rodgers; "You seem to enjoy socializing more than you enjoy your schoolwork," said my third-grade teacher, Mrs. Clothier, "and don't blame your friends for distracting you"; and my favorite, "You're sloppy and careless. If you slowed down, you'd do so much better," said by many people, including my mother, who one morning had me called home from school over the loud-speaker for not wiping the counter after breakfast, which she had asked me to do repeatedly. She never had to ask me again after that.

But aside from that isolated incident, nothing anyone said or did cured, or even lessened, my slapdash tendencies. I could not be bothered to care about anything that wasn't something I cared about. When I was told to do something, I balked and chafed and became churlish. I wasn't rebellious or recalcitrant by nature; in theory, I wanted to do well, to help and please the adults I loved. But I had been born on a very narrow, certain trajectory, and nothing—not social studies, not Irma Rombauer, not my mother, and not that vague, ever-present institution I thought of as "the rules"—could deter my forward momentum, which was entirely self-generated and directed according to my own passions, internal dictates, and predilections. I was daydreamy, scattershot, and unfocused, unless I was doing something I deeply, urgently wanted to do: reading books of my own choosing or writing my own stuff or directing my sisters in a play I'd written or roller-skating or cooking according to my own palate's ideas of what might taste good. I failed to get the straight A's Mrs. Rodgers seemed to think I was capable of. I also failed to be the cheerful, helpful firstborn daughter my mother deserved. I had to be prodded, nagged, and threatened to do my chores, write thank-you letters, clean my room, go somewhere I didn't want to go, or talk on the phone (something I still try to avoid at all costs). This ingrained inability to do anything counter to my own desires has not improved with age; to the contrary.

## CHAPTER 15

## My First Date

⎯⎯ On my first day at Simpson Elementary, I wore the outfit my mother's stylish, groovy friend Jayne had taken me to buy on a special shopping trip, complete with lunch afterward: red bell-bottoms and a matching red and yellow top with puffy sleeves and a tight buttoned vest. It was the height of preteen fashion; I could feel that I made quite a splash when I entered the classroom, in spite of my braces and glasses. At recess, I was befriended by a pretty, bold, husky-voiced girl named Stacy. She invited me to sit with her in the lunchroom, and we were school friends from then on, meaning that we didn't do overnights or hang out after school, but we were allied during school hours. She was a loner, it turned out; I was her only friend, and we weren't at all close. I never learned much about her home life, but she occasionally mentioned rock concerts she'd been to, older guys, and friends in high school. Clearly, sixth grade was not where she preferred to be spending her days.

I liked my new homeroom teacher instantly. She called herself Ms., not Mrs., which was cutting-edge; it meant she was a feminist, which meant that she was smart and cool. Ms. Van Loo was young and pretty, with big blue eyes and fuzzy blond hair she wore in a loose bun and a smooth, olive-skinned complexion. She wore loose harem pants and Birkenstocks, and she liked to give creative assignments; that spring, she launched the whole class on a mad spate of story and poetry writing. In addition to our creative-writing notebooks, she had us give oral reports analyzing the lyrics of our favorite pop and rock songs and encouraged us to keep personal journals. I had been writing in my diary for years; I announced this to her somewhat smugly and was rewarded with a big smile.

"I'd love to read it!" she said.

"That's not really the point of a diary," I wanted to tell her, but I was too polite.

Then, to my pleased surprise, the cutest boy in the class, Paul Seifert, asked me on a date. He looked like a teen idol, tall, with a cleft chin, feathered dirty-blond hair, and piercing blue eyes. He wore sweatshirts, jeans, and Adidas. (I yearned for Adidas passionately; all the jocks and cool kids at Simpson wore them.) He invited me to ride bikes with him to the public library, where we would check out books and have a picnic. We were eleven; what else could we do? Paul was so impeccably polite, so old-fashioned and correct. He asked me on a date to the *library*.

He showed up at my house at noon on Saturday with a picnic lunch he, or more likely his mother, had made for us. We biked over to the big, modern library and browsed through the stacks together, and then we sat in the grass outside and ate cheese sandwiches and apples and brownies and drank, to my joy, cans of Pepsi. Then we biked back to Paul's house, where I met his family and hung out for a while. There was no way we would actually make out or anything, although I would have. At the end of our date, he biked me home and gave me a sweet peck on the cheek at my front door. That was as far as we ever went.

It seemed to be generally known in the class that Paul and I were "going out" for most of the rest of sixth grade. And everyone knew, too, when he dumped me for Stacy at the end of the school year. It took me a while to realize that he'd done so. Once I figured it out, I wasn't heartbroken; I was mildly perplexed. Since when did Stacy like Paul? Why did he like her better than me? Why had he liked me in the first place? It was all a mystery.

Paul and Stacy both moved away after that year, and I never saw either of them again.

## CHAPTER 16

## Crime and Surveillance

—— Despite the guilt I still felt at breaking into that house in Oakland, my criminal behavior resumed with a vengeance in seventh grade. My sister Susan and I liked to dress identically in short-sleeved black leotards and cutoffs and sandals and high ponytails (I was a head taller than she was and wore a bra, but we laughingly decided to tell anyone who asked that we were identical twins) and prowl around the Walgreens in the Chris-Town Mall, innocently pocketing strawberry lip gloss and chocolate. We never got caught.

One day before Christmas, I went to the mall alone. I bought a few things at Walgreens that were small and cheap and asked them to put them all into a big shopping bag for me. Then I walked around with the bag, putting it down and pretending to paw through it, as if I were looking for something, taking everything out and piling it right near or on top of whatever it was I wanted to steal. Under cover of being a confused kid, I finally put everything back into the bag, along with the object of my desire. This worked so well, I got away with whole Whitman's Samplers, which were dictionary-sized boxes of chocolates. I stole all my Christmas presents for my mother and sisters that year: necklaces, candy, knickknacks, bracelets, candles, and scarves.

Technically I didn't need to shoplift, except for the thrill it gave me, which was considerable. I was making money that year at my first job: after school on weekdays, I delivered the *Phoenix Gazette*—an afternoon paper—the Arizona *Republic* was the morning one—to various ranch houses in our neighborhood. On Sundays, though, there was no *Gazette*, so I delivered the early-morning *Republic* instead. I showed up at the station before dawn on my sturdy three-speed blue Schwinn with its three baskets, front and sides. I had the biggest route on my station and was the youngest carrier and the only girl, so I wasn't popular with the older boys. It didn't matter that I'd worked hard to expand my route, going door to door in my free time and drumming up new customers. I was the skinny, bespectacled girl in braces and braids who had the biggest stack of papers to fold, and so they acted as if I didn't exist.

The Sunday paper had to be assembled section by section and rubber banded. Our station was an empty lot. In the light of the streetlamps, in the chilly desert darkness, we yawned and loaded up our bikes and the canvas carrier bags we slung across our chests. The boys talked and joked among themselves. I worked as fast as I could to get out of there, then pushed my laden bike into the street, mounted it, and was off. I loved those silent, empty, sweet-smelling, predawn mornings, alone with my bike, my thoughts. I told myself stories under my breath as I rode along, sang songs, daydreamed about the people whose newspapers I threw onto their dewy lawns.

When I finished my route and all my baskets were empty, I rode through the bright morning sunlight and the churchgoing traffic over to the McDonald's on West Bethany Home Road, which was already open, and got myself a chocolate shake. I drank it on my bike as I rode home.

Years later, my mother told me that on a few Sundays, at the beginning of the school year, when I first started my route, she got up at 4:30 along with me, silently, so I wouldn't know, to make sure I was safe. She got on her own bike right after I left the house and followed me to the station. Then she waited, hidden from my sight, while I put the papers together and loaded up my bike, and followed at a distance while I wove my way through the wide, sleeping Phoenix streets. I never had any idea she was there.

## CHAPTER 17

## Church and State

——— Every Sunday morning, after my paper route, Susan and I rode our bikes to the Victory Baptist Church on North Twenty-third Avenue. My friend Jennifer Dominguez and her family attended services there every Sunday, and we had wicked crushes on Jennifer's older and younger brothers, Kevin and Todd. Kevin was in eighth grade, a year ahead of Jennifer and me. He was a dreamy combination of gentle and handsome, with a peachy, freckled face; doelike brown eyes; curly brown hair; and an athletic build. He was dating a girl named Hope, a tall, willowy blonde his own age, but I coveted him from afar. I thought he was perfect. Susan felt the same way about Todd, who could have been Kevin's younger clone.

When I got back from my paper route, we dolled ourselves up in skirts and blouses while listening to Casey Kasem's Top 40 countdown on KUPD. It was 1974, so that meant Olivia Newton-John, Chicago, War, Anne Murray, the O'Jays, Paul McCartney and Wings, Elton John, Cat Stevens, and Helen Reddy. My favorite song in those days was "Top of the World" by the Carpenters. (Sometimes, I called the KUPD deejay to request it and tried to keep him on the line by flirting with him.) "Everything I want the world to be," Susan and I sang in our chirpy girlish voices, "is now comin' true, especially for me. . . ."

In church, we sat primly during Brother Gil's sermon, bowing our heads like good Christians when it was time to pray, then singing earnestly from the hymnals, as we ogled the objects of our desire under our lashes, "Are you washed in the blood, in the soul-cleansing blood of the lamb?"

All my life, I had believed in glorious passion and swooning romance, but my fantasies had been pure and chaste. I'd imagined getting married to my true love and holding my husband's hand, but nothing beyond that. Now, for the first time, my feelings were carnal and direct. I gazed at Kevin's lips, fixated on his forearms. During the entire sermon, while Brother Gil intoned in his preacherly way about righteousness and sin, I daydreamed about making out with Kevin Dominguez.

When the service was over, the Dominguez family always went straight home, much to my disappointment. But it meant that Susan and I always made it back to our house in time for pancakes, our Sunday family breakfast. We all took turns making them, according to the roster of chores, from the *Joy of Cooking* recipe, which involved beaten egg whites. They were crisp and thick and fluffy and addictive. I smothered them in margarine and Aunt Jemima's and generally ate so many I was nearly comatose for the rest of the day—my record was twenty-seven at one sitting.

Brother Gil, the church's pastor, took Susan's and my regular attendance at his church very seriously, and so it came to pass that he showed up at our house one day and sat in our living room and asked our mother if Susan and I could be "saved," which meant having to go up to the front of the church to get our heads dunked in water while everyone—including Kevin and Todd—watched.

To our secret but vast relief, she said an adamant no: we were atheists in our house, and that was that. Brother Gil went away, and when we saw him the following Sunday, he was as cordial and unctuous as ever, but he never asked us to be saved again.

One of the duties on my paper route was doing collection, which meant knocking on every door and asking for that week's subscription money. I had a two-ring board with a sheet of tickets for each house; I wrote each address and name at the top and tore off tickets to give as receipts. I could always tell how many weeks' worth of subscription money my customers owed by how many tickets were still attached to their sheet. Sometimes people weren't home, and sometimes they couldn't pay that week, so I had customers who were generally behind, which was normal.

But there was one house I was afraid to go to, and so they racked up a staggering debt of $9.45, several weeks' worth of *Gazette*s. They were a household of several elderly women, mild as nuns, quiet and mousy, all of them gaunt, pale, gray haired. I don't know why I was afraid of them—they weren't really scary at all—but I had to talk myself into going up their walk and ringing the bell: I was short that week with my nut, so I needed them to pay up.

Two of them came to the door together, spectral wraiths dressed in cobwebs and ash. Their white, thin faces floated above me like the reflections of crescent moons in a lily pond. "Nine dollars and forty-five cents," they gasped. "So much at once . . . where have you been?" The door closed; I waited. The door opened, and one bony hand, trembling, counted out the money from a jar marked Grocery Kitty. The jar contained exactly $9.45. I took it all and gave them their tickets and rode away, wretchedly hoping they wouldn't have to live on cat food, or starve, until their next Social Security checks arrived.

When I handed my route over to a younger girl in the neighborhood at the end of seventh grade, I had saved $125, enough to buy the red ten-speed I had been coveting and saving up for. Whenever I rode my cool new bike by the old ladies' house, I averted my eyes, afraid they were at the front window, peeking out from behind their drapes, watching me enjoy the spoils of my plundering of their precious food jar.

The other house I was afraid to collect from was the LeBlancs', around the corner from our house. Diane LeBlanc was a year ahead of me at Simpson, and we were friends, sort of; my mother hired her to "babysit" us when she and Jim went out, because I didn't want to take responsibility for my sisters. Diane LeBlanc was fat, and she wet the bed, and when she came over to babysit, she wanted to talk out loud about our sex fantasies in my dark bedroom, on opposite ends of my bed, and then she wanted us to give each other massages. I had no problem with the sex-fantasy part; I had plenty of those, and I wasn't shy about sharing them (they were far more romantic than sexual, actually; they involved me being a haughty princess adored from afar by a shy woodcutter's son or humble peasant boy who proved his mettle and won my hand in marriage). But massages? With Diane? That was just oogie and gross.

One day at school, Kevin Dominguez came and sat in the grass next to me at recess and asked me if Diane was really my babysitter. I cringed and admitted that she was, kind of. Then he asked me for my locker combination; in our school, this was tantamount to asking me to go steady. I froze up, and my insides clenched. I blurted, "No way. Anyway, my friend likes you," and got up and walked away, fast, feeling like a weirdo and an idiot. Later, Jennifer told me that she had set Kevin straight: I liked him, not my friend.

This heralded the first of many such encounters of my spectacularly awkward adolescence, as far as boys I liked were concerned. I froze in their presence, could not speak to them or look them in the eye, pretended I wasn't interested, treated them with brusque condescension.

Meanwhile, Diane's brother Bill, who was sixteen and who looked like the older boy version of Diane, fat and doughy, exposed his penis to poor Susan in some backyard scenario, theirs or ours, I was a bit hazy on the details. Susan was even more creeped out by this, of course, than I had been by Diane's advances. The LeBlancs were really weird, we decided, and that was all there was to it. But still, they had a strange power over me. One day when I was over at Diane's, Diane's much-older sister interrogated me about my parents' marital status; I lied and told her they were married. Having to lie in order to appease the LeBlancs' nosy, small-minded, petty-bourgeois Christian curiosity and judgment made me loathe them all. But it also made me furious at my mother for not being married to Jim. I started pestering her about it, asking when they'd get married.

Diane's father, Mr. LeBlanc, was a fat, red-faced tyrant. Whenever I came by to collect the money he owed me for his newspaper delivery, he almost spat it at me. I suppose having to give a penny to a godless, heathen hippie girl with sinful parents filled him with seething resentment. And so, just as with the old-lady house, I stayed away too long from the LeBlancs' until, finally, when I realized I would be short that week unless they paid, I slunk up their drive and rang the bell with a hang-dog, unhappy dread. Mr. LeBlanc yanked the door open and saw me standing there.

"Well?" he said.

I told him how much he owed me.

"You're a liar," he said. "Let me see that book."

I showed him the tickets, uncollected.

"You must not have given me the tickets last time I paid!" he said. "You're cheating me!" He was apoplectic, a word I had just learned. I was interested to see it in action, and by interested, I mean outraged.

"I always give tickets when people pay," I said, a little apoplectic now myself. "I'm telling the truth."

"You are a liar," he shouted, and slammed the door in my face.

I went home shaking with anger. With my mother's help, I wrote Mr. LeBlanc a strongly worded letter that informed him that I was suspending delivery of his paper until he paid me, and furthermore, it was "very rude to slam the door in a young girl's face when she's just trying to do her job and collect money that is honestly owed to her."

Mr. LeBlanc telephoned. He didn't want his paper suspended. He would pay the money. He never apologized. I continued to deliver his paper, and he never balked again at paying me.

## CHAPTER 18

## Love and Marriage

Junior high was, for Susan and me, a time of trying out conventions, of feeling "normal," and fitting in for the first time. And not just us: we wanted it for our family, too. We put constant pressure on Jim and my mother to get married. They finally did, but not because of us. Our mother wanted us to have a father, and Jim wanted to adopt us. So they had a small wedding ceremony in our backyard with a few friends, a justice of the peace, and a cake. My mother wore a beautiful pale blue lace-trimmed maxidress that showed her cleavage, and flowers in her long hair.

Jim legally adopted us shortly afterward. I had mixed feelings about this. I was very sad to lose any proof of my father's relationship to me, but he had disappeared. My mother had even hired a detective to track him down in order to get his permission for Jim to assume paternity of us, but he couldn't turn up any trace of him. If my father ever magically changed his mind and decided he wanted to find us again, how, I worried, would he know where to look, if our last name had been changed?

On the other hand, we already called Jim "Dad," and he deeply wanted to be our father in a way that our real father never had. He cooked for us; was there after school; drove us places; laughed at our jokes; and, in every other way, had earned the right to make it legal. It was time to finalize it. After the adoption, my birth certificate was changed: Jim Christensen was listed as my birth father, and my legal name was now Laurie Kate Christensen. All legal evidence of Ralph Johansen's paternity was erased forever.

One very early morning, near dawn, I woke up and heard strange, sad music on the record player and went out into the living room to see Jim, sitting alone in a chair in the semi-dark, drinking wine and sobbing and listening to the Schubert C Major Quintet. He had always liked to drink wine and beer. But since he'd been laid off from his job, he had been drinking a lot more, and a lot more regularly.

He didn't see me; I went back to bed and lay awake with a knot in my stomach, the way I had almost every night at Wildermuth. I knew something was wrong lately. My mother seemed bored and impatient with Jim all the time; and Jim, for his part, seemed more anxious even than he'd been before. Although he never failed in his kindness to us, his patient attention and careful devotion to our homework, our chattering, our questions, there was a strain, a noticeable effort to present a good-humored geniality when before it had been unforced. After the wedding, it was clear, in a subterranean but unmistakable way, this new marriage was in trouble of some kind.

Jim's drinking was, it developed, a topic of concern among my parents' friends. All the grown-ups drank wine and beer; they all smoked pot. But Jim was the only one in their group who became drunk, who stumbled, who slurred his words, lost motor control, and sometimes even fell down.

But aside from their marital problems, Jim and my mother still had fun; they loved to dance together and, she told me years later, they always had a good sex life. They had a king-size water bed in their room, whose air smelled of stale incense and pot smoke. Their sheets always smelled of sex to me, even when they were clean. I had a passionate interest in, and simultaneous revulsion for, the idea of sex. When they weren't home, I was drawn to their room with a sick feeling in the pit of my stomach. I found *The Joy of Sex* (and read it from cover to cover) in their nightstand drawer, along with their pot-smoking paraphernalia, which I hated and which filled me with fear.

Before they went out together to go dancing or to a party, they disappeared into their room for a long time and came out on a waft of incense, dressed elegantly, smelling of pot smoke and giggling. I hated the smell, hated the way it made them act, hated that it was illegal, that my parents weren't straitlaced and proper like all my friends' parents. And Jim sometimes made sexual jokes to my mother in front of us; it made me gag. Jim had started to actively repulse me. He had pink lips in a close-cropped blond goatee. He had silky pale hair and watery blue eyes and a tall, lanky, slinky body. His voice was high and breathy. He always kissed us on the lips, he insisted on it—I cringed at having to let his pink, wet lips anywhere near mine. The idea of him and my mother having sex gave me palpitations of nausea.

Still, I had crushes on boys and thought about them with increasing physical urgency. I had finally gotten contact lenses, my braces had come off, my hair grew long and thick. I was still stick thin and totally without curves, but I had some semblance of a teenage body suddenly, along with the usual hormones.

I reacted by becoming aggressive. There was an older neighborhood boy who had an obvious crush on me—I don't even remember his name. He was tall, already an adolescent, with a nascent mustache and a low voice. One day, bored, I blindfolded him with a bandanna and led him around the neighborhood, narrating to him in a low, bossy voice the things I would do to him later. I took him into bushes, behind houses, along the sidewalk. He stumbled. I led him. He was totally in my thrall. I hardly touched him; I just promised future delights.

When I was much littler, I had been sexually aggressive with boys: in third grade, I chased a boy I liked at every recess, and when I caught him, I kissed him. In second grade, I'd played house in my garage with a neighbor boy; he lay on top of me and we kissed. Even earlier, I'd convinced a smaller boy to show me his penis, which was uncircumcised with a tip that I thought looked like a strawberry. I had never been shy about bossing a certain type of boy around.

Now, I could feel this neighborhood boy getting charged up, excited, waiting to hear what I would say next. His excitement was the whole point. But he was too passive to sustain my interest for long. Soon I was done with him, bored and sated with power. I ripped the bandanna off his face and ran home. The next night, as I was washing dishes in the kitchen, whose window looked out at the street, I saw him standing on the sidewalk under the big palm tree in our front yard, looking in at me. He threw something into the bushes beneath the window and ran away. I went outside and found a folded-up piece of paper on which he had written a love poem. Dispassionately, I read it, found it trite and lacking in beauty, and threw it away. I never spoke to that boy again.

One day after school, I went over to my friend Jennifer Dominguez's house to hang out. My mother was late picking me up. Jennifer had to go to the church with her parents for some function or another, so I stayed behind with Kevin, just the two of us, playing cards together on their front patio while I waited for my mother.

That night, for the first time ever, I found that I could talk to him, could look him in the eye. Over gin rummy, I flirted brashly, made bold eye contact, felt triumph when he looked away, grinning and blushing. His evident attraction to me turned me on.

When I got home, I found blood in my underwear for the first time in my life. I didn't tell my mother about it. She had bought me a box of pads already; I had it in my bathroom cabinet. Telling my mother was so fraught with untenable implications, I could not bring myself to do it, even though I knew I should—what girl doesn't go running to her mother at the first sign of womanhood?

I didn't want this. I wanted to be a boy. I didn't want these breasts, either; not that I had much, but what little I did have freaked me out. Before the onset of adolescence, I'd been safe in my skinny, strong, broad-shouldered body. Now, here was the irrefutable proof that I was not like my father; I was like my mother.

Also, since Jim had come on the scene, I had become aware of the ways in which my mother had always appropriated me, how I'd made sure to have no needs of my own so I'd always be available to her. I was so firmly entrenched in the habit of not asking for anything from my mother, I tried to hide all signs of weakness from her. Grimly, I launched myself into womanhood alone.

## CHAPTER 19

## My First Muse

Every now and then, Jim or my mother would pull a hairy two-pound zeppelin from their alarmingly productive backyard garden. My mother would chop it up and fold it into a casserole and serve it to us horrified kids for supper. Lettuce, tomatoes, cucumbers, and green beans also issued forth from the neat rows by the fence. Those were delicious, but the mealy, seedy, weirdly sticky, and spongily dense zucchini was a new object of loathing. Along with tofu—that chalk-white substance that tasted vaguely of some sort of low-vitality bodily humor and had an appropriately slimy, coagulated texture—it was suddenly everywhere, all the rage. I hated it on first gag.

We were also given new things to snack on: "soy nuts," toasted, salted soybeans that were crunchy and not too bad, as well as dried banana chips, which were sweet and crunchy and not too bad, either. Freeze-dried apples came along, as soft and chewy as ears, and so did yogurt-covered raisins, carob instead of chocolate, and fruit leather roll-ups. Supposedly, these things were better for us than potato chips and candy, but I suspect they probably weren't, that they just had the aura of health food that was so trendy all of a sudden.

Food was splitting off into two distinct categories in those days, and parents and kids stood on opposite sides of a widening divide. Kids craved Big Macs and hot apple pies, baloney sandwiches on Wonder bread with mayonnaise and Kraft cheese slices, Pop-Tarts, and Mountain Dew; whereas our parents championed wholesome grains with vegetables and a baked fillet of fish, homemade carrot cake, and milk. Grown-ups liked tofu, or pretended to; I couldn't imagine why anyone would ever choose to eat that stuff (to my mother's credit, she hated tofu; Jim was the one who bought it).

My longing for what I couldn't have turned out to be a source of inspiration. Maybe because we weren't allowed to eat junk food or drink pop, maybe because I craved forbidden sugar cereals and potato chips and root beer but couldn't have them on a daily basis, writing about food gave me a sense of heady power that was in some ways even better than eating the forbidden items in real life. I couldn't always have what the characters I read about ate, but I could feed my own characters all the things I wasn't allowed to have.

In eighth grade, I wrote a short novel that might be pegged these days as a YA thriller. The thirteen-year-old heroine, Claudia, and her little brother go into the remote Arizona desert on the heels of their evil band teacher, Mr. Aragones, a kidnapper and possible murderer. After the scary parts are over (Claudia finds a severed arm in a cupboard she's hiding in, "a dead human arm"), after everything has resolved itself, they end up in a diner, where Claudia orders almost everything on the menu. I remember hungrily listing with the bottomless appetite of pubescence every conceivable thing I myself would have ordered in such a situation—french fries, baked beans, chicken, hamburgers, meat loaf, blueberry pie, ice cream, etc. I wasn't trying to be funny; I wrote it in a state of vicariously swooning, single-minded earnestness.

My muse for my first novel, which I called *Life Can't Be a Penguin*, was my eighth-grade crush, a short, stocky boy named Kenny who wore glasses and had bushy brown hair and brown eyes. He sat behind me in Mrs. Rodgers's social studies class; I passed him chapters of this novel as I wrote it and felt a thrill when I heard him chuckling as he read the funny parts. He had a crush on a girl named Penny who was far prettier, nicer, and smarter than I was: she got straight A's and had a lovely, oval face and long, straight, silky blond hair. Penny was sweet and good and perfect, and I was not, but she didn't crack Kenny up the way I did, so I assured myself that secretly he liked me better. I was sure I would grow up and marry him. He smelled like warm toast and was so comfortable to be around; I could see us as grown-ups in our easy chairs together in front of the TV, eating dinner and chuckling, then going to bed afterward in our twin side-by-side beds like Rob and Laura Petrie. I had no sexual interest in Kenny at all; I just wanted to marry him, which seemed like a completely different thing. What I liked best about him was that he had a crush on someone else. He was unattainable, a challenge.

Kenny and Penny and I were all in the gifted program together, along with bespectacled, bubbly Patty; serious, deep-voiced Judy; a smart-alecky redheaded boy named Chris; and my best school friend, Curtis. The gifted program was a new thing at Simpson, and the teachers hadn't ironed out the kinks yet, which is to say, they had no idea what to do with us, but they had to do something. Finally, owlish, gruff, old-school Mrs. Rodgers stepped in and proposed a project. And so the seven of us were sent to the cafeteria once a week to brain-storm on a patriotic theme: we were in the early months of 1976, and the country was catching bicentennial fever. In the end, the gifted program kids spent the afternoons doing what-ever we felt like, doodling and talking and hanging out, and then scrambled at the end of the year to make a cheesy banner to hang in the cafeteria during the big end-of-school assembly. What this had to do with having high IQs, I do not know: a monkey could have drawn that thing.

That whole year, Curtis and I were inseparable. He was in love with me, I knew because he told me repeatedly, but I couldn't return his love, even though he looked like a Slavic prince, broad shouldered, slender, with black, long-lashed eyes and thick glossy black hair and creamy skin, and he was smart and funny. He was too goofy for me to take seriously, too playful and smitten with me—I liked Kenny's solidity, his husbandly, inscrutable aloofness, his complete lack of interest in me. I liked having to woo him; I liked that he was slightly boring, because it meant I could spice him up. Curtis understood everything I said, got all my jokes, and always seemed to sit next to me during the school day in class, at lunch, even at recess. I never got sick of him, though; we had a lot of fun together. We were collaborating on a science-fiction novel about an exiled princess in a future dystopia. He drew cartoon strips about futuristic androids and interplanetary adventures; I drew one based on the misadventures of a hapless, screwed-up but well-intentioned character named Quigbert with a triangular head and a nerdy suit with short pants. We spent many recesses at our homeroom desks, drawing floor plans of our modern dream houses together. How could I have any romantic interest in someone who was so clearly my soul mate?

My other best friend, Susie, went to a different school. She was the daughter of one of my mother's psychologist colleagues, and since we were the same age and both played the violin, our parents had set us up. I went over to Susie's house first, and then she came to mine, and then we were best friends. Every time we had an overnight, we played violin duets, especially the Bach Double Violin Concerto. All the hours and years I'd spent sawing away at Kreutzer, Hřímalý, and Wohlfahrt were finally paying off. Susie and I shared the first stand of the second-violin section in Symphonette, the Phoenix youth orchestra, and were roommates together at the Northern Arizona University summer music camp.

I remember the moment I learned that Susie was Jewish, very early in our friendship. I was ridiculously excited—I'd

never met any Jews before (although of course I must have).
No one in any of my schools, to my knowledge, had ever been
Jewish. Susie's family invited me over for Shabbat dinners and
Hanukkah, to her bat mitzvah, and to a seder. I went to Hebrew
school with her a few times, and we jokingly told people that
my name was Laurie Christenstein. Their house was fancier
than ours; it had powder-blue shag carpets and a den with a
big TV and nice, matching furniture and dishes and drapes. I
had a mad crush on Susie's older brother, Mike, so going to her
house was a triple or even quadruple treat. I fell deeply in love
with everything that had to do with Judaism, most of all the
food—bagels with lox! matzo-horseradish-haroset Hillel sandwiches! brisket!

At Susie's bat mitzvah, when she read and sang in Hebrew
up on the bima, I got teary-eyed with pride for her. Then we
all went back to her house for the party, and we kids hung out
in the garage rec room and played pachinko, flirted, listened to
music, ate big plates of buffet but did not drink Manischewitz,
if only because the grown-ups made sure we had no access to
booze.

On several occasions, Susie came camping with my family
up on Mingus Mountain in northern Arizona. To get there, we
had to drive two hours north, through the Verde Valley and up
a winding road, through a ghost town called Jerome, a vertical town of rickety wooden Victorian houses perched on stilts
on the steep slope of Cleopatra Hill. My parents had spent a
summer there years ago, before I was born, with some of my
mother's Juilliard friends, making a spoof film called *Two Brides
for Three Brothers*, and my mother had always had a romance
with the place. As we drove through town, she pointed out the
building where they'd shot a scene from the movie. Then we
left Jerome behind and climbed even higher on the road toward
Prescott until we reached Mingus Mountain's campground.

Susie's parents had heard from other friends that Jim had

drunk too much one night, as he generally did, and had fallen and hit his head. Now they were worried that he had a concussion, a drinking problem, or both, and they made it very clear that their daughter's life could not be entrusted to his driving. It was deeply embarrassing to me, but nonetheless, whenever Susie came camping with us, we had to wait till my mother got out of work and drive up with her, arriving to find Jim and my sisters at the set-up campsite.

We loved it in northern Arizona, but we didn't necessarily want to live there. However, in the late winter of that year, at a doughnut meeting, my mother and Jim announced that they were selling the San Miguel house and that we were leaving Phoenix and moving up to Jerome.

All my life until then, every time we moved, I had been happy about going somewhere new. But now I didn't feel that way at all. I didn't want to leave Susie. I didn't want to leave my violin teacher, Symphonette, this nice, safe neighborhood where I knew everyone, the Chris-Town Mall, or our backyard, where Susan and I sometimes slept in a tent and woke up to the smell of the dew on the grass, a spookily beautiful, pink desert dawn. I didn't want to leave Curtis, either. In Phoenix, I was a normal kid in a normal family in a normal neighborhood with normal friends; at thirteen, this was the most important thing in the world to me. Moving to a ghost town, even though a few hundred people did actually live there, was weird. We didn't know anyone there. I'd have to start all over again from scratch, after I'd established myself here in Phoenix so well. I'd be the new girl again, an outsider.

But all my arguing did no good. My mother was determined to get out of that awful hot suburban hell and move somewhere more interesting and beautiful; she had just survived more than two grueling years. She had turned in her dissertation and passed her orals and gotten her Ph.D., and she was ready for a new adventure, ready to start a private practice and live in a Victorian house and make a new life in a place she had such nostalgic associations with.

Our San Miguel house was put on the market and sold shortly thereafter. During my last months of eighth grade, we drove up to Jerome for several weekends and stayed in an old hotel above the Spirit Room bar on Main Street and looked at houses for sale. My parents quickly bought the Central Hotel, a big wooden apartment house right on 89A, the main highway that wound up through the town. It was in good shape and had wraparound porches with balustrades and a little store on the first floor.

At my graduation from junior high school, as one of three valedictorians, I was assigned a speech on "The Home," which I made boldly feminist by announcing that "the home" was a place of equality now, where men changed diapers and baked bread, where women came home from work and opened a beer; this elicited shocked laughter from much of the audience, who clearly had no idea what I was talking about. Afterward, I said good-bye to Curtis. I told him I was sorry I wouldn't get to go to Alhambra High with him.

"But we'll see each other this summer, right?" he said. "This isn't the last time I'll see you."

As it turned out, it was. I never saw him again, and during most of my hard, lonely freshman year of high school, I missed him so much that I began to suspect that I might have returned his feelings all along; I just hadn't realized it at the time.

---

## CAMPING PEAS

*Camping meant, of course, hot dogs on sticks stuck into the flames of the campfire until they were spitting and charred; it meant marshmallows' black outer husks melting in your mouth and the rest of the white part, now soft and raw looking and naked, thrust back over* the fire. In order to get some vegetables down our gullets, my mother opened a can of peas and we passed it around with a spoon, not even heating them, slurping the olive-green, mushy, sweet peas along with the syrupy water they were packed in.

---

### POT ROAST

*The recipe, with my own preteen modifications to Irma Rombauer's, goes like this:*

Preheat the oven to 325 degrees, unless you're using the stove-top method. Rub a 3–4 pound chuck (or other) roast with garlic. Dredge in flour. In a Dutch oven or cast-iron pot, heat 2 tablespoons of vegetable oil "over lively heat." Brown the meat on all sides, but don't let it scorch. When the meat is half browned, add 1 chopped carrot and 1 rib of diced celery and an onion stuck with cloves, says Irma, but I always skipped the celery and cloves, which I detested. Then add 3–4 carrots peeled and cut into chunks as well as a large quartered onion without cloves and 3–4 peeled quartered potatoes.

When the meat is browned, spoon off the excess fat, says Irma, but I always left it in. Boil a cup of dry red wine (in those days, Gallo), a cup of beef or chicken or vegetable stock, and a bay leaf, and add to the meat. Cover and bake 3 to 4 hours or simmer on top of the stove. Turn the meat several times and, if necessary, add additional hot stock and season to taste. When the meat is tender, spoon off excess fat (or not), remove bay leaf, and serve with the pot liquor as it is, or slightly thickened with sour cream.

# PART FOUR

# Verde Valley
and Spring Valley

## CHAPTER 20

## Fame and Misfortune

In the summer of 1976, we moved into the Central Hotel in Jerome. The town had been reinvigorated in recent years by a scruffy bunch of baby boomers—artists, entrepreneurs, and hippies—who bought up the old Victorian houses and opened cafés and pottery shops and hung out drinking beer at the Spirit Room. It was just becoming a tourist destination: Winnebagos and campers jammed the narrow, steep streets in the summertime. But in the winters, it was snowy, eerie, deserted.

My family lived on the top two floors of the hotel, which had views out over the whole Verde Valley, and rented out the apartments on the two floors below us. My sisters and I got the penthouse, a self-contained apartment with its own bathroom, all to ourselves: Susan got the former kitchen, which still had a sink and linoleum floor, and which had no view because it was at the back, street end of the house. Emily got the middle room, a dark room with no privacy. And I claimed, by dirty pool, the private front-facing room with the enormous picture window and amazing view, meaning that I bribed my gullible, malleable little sisters with huge Hershey's chocolate bars and five dollars apiece to let me have it.

The Verde Valley was in those days a flatland of dull-green cactus and cottonwood trees, bisected into a rough quadrant by the Verde River and highway 89A. There were a few dusty little towns down there—Clarkdale, Cottonwood, Camp Verde, Cornville—and the trailer-park cluster called Centerville. Cottonwood was the biggest; it boasted a strip of highway that had one alluring, well-attended fast-food place after another: Kentucky Fried Chicken, Pizza Hut, McDonald's, Wendy's, Dairy Queen, Burger King, Taco Bell. These were the big attractions for teenagers and no doubt everyone in general; there was nothing else in the way of hangouts or cultural life for many miles in any direction.

That fall, I started as a freshman at Mingus Union High School, down in the valley, in Cottonwood. I finally dropped the name Laurie forever on my fourteenth birthday and adopted my middle name and forced my family to accept this. I registered for high school as Katie Christensen; the diminutive seemed less angular, more friendly and cute than Kate. This was all well and good, but unfortunately, I had a horrible new haircut—much too short. My mother had chopped it too enthusiastically, then tried to even it up and there I was, looking like Prince Valiant.

Mingus was a newly built one-story building, bright shiny classrooms around a central hub whose front half was an enormous, expensive open auditorium with a big, professional-quality stage and a state-of-the-art sound system; all visiting orchestras and musicians performed there. The front doors and lobby of the school opened right onto the auditorium, and kids hung out there between classes. Just behind the auditorium was the glassed-in school library. A wide hallway ran around it, sprouting classrooms and the cafeteria and the door to the huge gym, in back.

On my first day, I took the school bus and sat alone and walked into school and around the circular hallway during my free period alone, sat by myself at lunch in the cafeteria eating my sandwich, brought from home, made with my mother's homemade bread. I watched everyone, stared at everyone, wondering who would be my friend, brightening at any spark of eccentricity or quirkiness (there were few) in someone, inviting anyone at all to make eye contact with me, say hello, anything. No one did: I was invisible.

For the first months at Mingus, I went from the school bus to class to my locker to class all day long, saying nothing unless I was called on by a teacher. I was stunned to find myself so completely alone at school. I'd never had any problem making friends before. All the kids at Mingus seemed different from any others I'd ever gone to school with. They were a foreign species with an unfamiliar language and culture and strange social habits. They talked among themselves about things I didn't understand, places I'd never heard of, TV shows I didn't watch, football, cheerleading, drinking, clothes, boys, gossip about people I didn't know. No one even looked at me.

I gradually found three other loners and fellow invisibles: Jane, a prematurely middle-aged-looking senior with Coke-bottle, beige-framed glasses and a rocking, lurching gait—one leg shorter than the other and turned in at the ankle; Ovalea, who was beautiful, hilarious, and sharp, but permanently hunched over and knotted in her wheelchair, slated to die young of muscular dystrophy; and Celia, a chubby, fresh-faced toughie who was an obvious butch lesbian at a time when no one ever showed even the remotest outward signs of being gay. I befriended all of them aggressively. I cornered them like the wounded gazelles of the pack and bit their necks till they succumbed. Then I had three friends. Jane and I ate lunch together. She blinked at me from behind her thick glasses as she told me everything about herself in a shy rush as if no one had ever asked her about herself before. I rode the back of Ovalea's electric wheelchair between classes, the two of us cracking up so hard I almost fell off, and she almost fell out. Celia took me with her kind, shy parents for a week on their sailboat in the Sea of Cortez; she had a crush on me, obviously but quietly and no doubt painfully.

My sisters fared far worse than I did. We all three went to different schools—Emily was in Cottonwood at the elementary school, Susan was at the junior high in Clarkdale—and they were both struggling, as I was, to make friends, to fit in, to find some common ground with anyone at all. Emily, who was loud and not at all timid, was teased for being weird, which was at least a form of attention; Susan, who was painfully shy and meek, disappeared altogether.

Then, near the end of that miserable first semester, as the town got emptier and darker and colder and spookier and lonelier, our mother announced that she was leaving Jim. Although there were signs, none of us had had any inkling that this was coming. Emily took the news with equanimity, but Susan and I were furious with our mother. We had just moved to a lonely new town, uprooted our perfectly happy lives in Phoenix, and now our parents were splitting up? It was too much for us to take.

But our mother was adamant: Jim was going to move downstairs to the dark, dingy little one-bedroom apartment on the second floor, and we kids would all stay in our penthouse suite and go downstairs for dinner with him every other night. So on Jim's nights, we trooped down to his depressing apartment to eat the usual steak with sautéed garlic, celery, and onions while Jim drank and sighed sadly. By the end of dinner, he was always drunk.

Our mother was no better. She was quiet and brooding and deeply unhappy. We were broke, and both my mother and Jim were struggling to make money: he had opened a private architectural office in Sedona and was just starting to get clients, and she was collecting a small amount of unemployment and trying to open a private psychotherapy practice down in Cottonwood, but hadn't gotten it off the ground yet. On top of that, the whole town turned against her; former friends even crossed the street to avoid her. Evidently, Jim had been hanging out at the Spirit Room, drunkenly crying to the bar at large about how heartbroken he was, how he would have done anything for Liz, how much he loved his family. And thus the tide of public opinion had turned decidedly toward him.

"This is what happens when you leave your husband," my mother told me. "People take sides."

We all spent a grim winter together, trying to make sense of what had happened to us, to our family.

In the spring, I met Valerie, who was a freshman, like me. She was flamboyant and smart and weirdly seductive and crazy. She looked and acted like a hot twenty-five-year-old television star. She was writing a *Star Trek* teleplay on spec that she hoped to sell to the show's producers, and she belonged to the Mingus drama club. I spent a few nights at her house, a fancy modern split-level in the red rocks of Sedona. Each time, we stayed up till past midnight, and she whispered to me under the covers about some new rare or unheard-of disease that she was suffering from, a rare brain infection or a blood cancer no one had ever seen before; she claimed that she was written up in all the medical journals.

"Tryouts for the spring musical are next week," she said to me one day at school. "You should come!"

After school, on the day of the tryouts, I followed Valerie down to the auditorium stage and met the drama teacher, a neatly bearded, Shakespearean-looking guy everyone called by his first name, Von. Von's assistant director, a bitchy redheaded senior named Carol, handed each of us a script of *Cheaper by the Dozen*, a musical based on a book I'd read many times and loved. Von asked several of us to read for the part of Anne Gilbreth, the ingenue, the lead, the part Valerie knew she was going to get because she was fated to be a star. I couldn't act, but I could read aloud. Then Von had us gather around the piano and, one by one, sing a solo.

Somehow I got the part. Valerie swallowed her jealousy and became my greatest supporter. She continued to pretend to be happy for me when I got cast as Gloriana in *The Mouse That Roared* the following fall (she even loaned me the beautiful satin green dress, formfitting with puffy sleeves, that she had been planning to wear herself for that part) and then as Julie Jordan in *Carousel* the following spring.

Suddenly, after months of being invisible and knowing no one, I was the star of the drama department. In that little cluster of towns in the middle of nowhere, this was a big deal. My name was regularly splashed on posters all over the school, all over what passed for Cottonwood's downtown shopping district. My name and picture appeared in the local paper advertising the high school play, the big event of every season. Overnight, everyone seemed to know who I was. It was one of the strangest years of my life.

## CHAPTER 21

## The Talley House

——— That summer, a year after we had moved to Jerome, Jim and my mother got divorced. Jim moved back upstairs and stayed in the Central Hotel, while Emily and I moved with our mother up the mountain to the Talley House, the ramshackle but beautiful former mansion of the local Copper King himself. Susan had left home, at barely thirteen, to study ballet in Flagstaff, where she lived with another family whose daughter studied ballet at the same school. She came home sometimes on weekends, increasingly pale and alarmingly thin (she later confessed that she'd lived on chocolate Ex-Lax during those years), but she never lived at home again. Our years as a complete family were over.

The Talley House sat high up at the top of the cobblestoned, steep little Magnolia Street above the Catholic church, set into the mountainside, so the road wound up and around the back of the house at rooftop level. My mother paid two dollars a month in rent to the Jerome Historical Society in exchange for restoring it. She spent countless hours stripping and refinishing the original woodwork in the kitchen, living room, and stairwell; she had time to do this, alas, because her fledgling psychology private practice had hardly any clients—no one in the Verde Valley quite knew what to make of a psychologist. Maybe it didn't help that the parking lot by my mother's office was visible to anyone driving by: who would want their pickup truck to be recognized by the neighbors? Consequently, the Talley House gleamed with refinished old wood. Still, the roof leaked, the house was freezing cold in the wintertime, there were broken windows in the sleeping porch, and the plaster was cracking. I didn't care; I had always dreamed of living in a house like this. There were window seats in the bay windows, hidden porches, a sunroom upstairs, Victorian curlicues. The front windows looked out over the whole Verde Valley to the red rocks of Sedona and the San Francisco Peaks and Mogollon Rim beyond.

Winters were lonely and cold, but in the summers in Jerome, honeysuckle grew around our porch railings, massive, amazing thunderstorms crossed the Verde Valley every afternoon, and there was always a potluck to go to. The mid-seventies was the golden age of many things, among them the casserole, the naked-adult party, and the uninhibited smoking of marijuana. Those three things went together far too often for my liking. I dreaded the nude-sketching potlucks at John's sculpture commune down in the valley in Cornville, as much as I dreaded the naked bacchanalian potlucks at Gary's hand-made sauna down in the Jerome gulch. My unself-conscious Berkeley-born little sisters shucked their togs along with the adults and other kids and joined the crowd while I, a fiercely modest fifteen-year-old, stayed fully clothed, reading my book in a corner, averting my eyes from the horrifying display of boobs and nut sacks and butts and (oh my God) penises, dangling softly while dudes squatted over their sketch pads, eyeing a naked woman draped over a couch or chair. Of course my family teased me for being such a puritan, which made it all worse.

Every weekday morning, I got up at 5:30 to curl my bobbed hair under, which was the prevailing style at Mingus (either that, or curled out so it flipped up), with a curling iron in front of the propane heater in the kitchen, the only other heat source in the house besides the woodstove in the living room. Then I made myself two buttered pieces of whole-wheat toast, which I washed down with a protein shake consisting of a cup of whole milk, a tablespoon of chalky but sweet Super Pro powder (very trendy at the time), a raw egg, a dash of vanilla extract, and a banana.

My mother and Emily were still sleeping when I left the house and walked a mile and a half down highway 89A through the town and along the ridgeback to the old Jerome high school to catch the school bus. During the winter months, I saw no one else the whole way down, and no cars passed me; Jerome really felt like a ghost town, dark and cold, deserted and wind-swept. I was one of only four teenagers who caught the bus there; the other three, Desiree, Julie, and Dani, were blond, bubbly, popular cheerleaders and athletes. I had little to say to them, or they to me. I did all my homework on the long bus ride to school as we wound through the little towns, picking up the respectable children of Clarkdale citizens, then the Indians, Mexicans, and poor white kids from the trailer parks of Centerville, then the "rich kids" who lived in the new developments outside Cottonwood.

In the Mingus cafeteria, we had the option of getting the hot lunch or buying junk food; naturally, almost everyone went for the junk. I had pocket money because of a Saturday job at a pottery store, so my lunches generally consisted of Ding Dongs, Doritos, and, as a nod to health, a carton of milk. I never brought food from home anymore. When I got back from school, I went to the kitchen and pulled out the Cracker Barrel sharp cheddar, an oblong orange block I sliced thickly. With a handful of Triscuits, I went upstairs to read whatever novel I was currently engrossed in, spending the whole cold afternoon under the covers, luxuriantly munching my afternoon snack until it was time to go downstairs to help with dinner or to walk with Emily down to Jim's if it was one of his nights.

I often stayed late at school for rehearsals, and Jim or my mother picked me up and drove me home afterward. I had almost no talent for acting, but I loved the excitement and camaraderie, the rush of adrenaline, the gathering I felt viscerally of my own forces as I walked onstage in order to command the audience's attention. I liked the other kids in the drama club. They were the interesting, fun, offbeat people I'd been looking for during my first semester. I had a lot of friends now; I finally felt as if I belonged here.

That year, for a playwriting class, I wrote a one-act "avant-garde" play, inspired by Ring Lardner and Woody Allen, essentially a dramatic monologue by a New York guy in a New York apartment talking about his New York life; clearly, I was in love with the idea of New York. Watching my fellow actors perform my play, I was seized with a panic-stricken urge to edit it on the spot. I had to hide my eyes at one point, as if that would help. It was so overwritten, so self-consciously clever, so manifestly not funny. Instead of the urbane, witty satire I'd intended, I had a long-winded fiasco. It was a useful lesson.

Jim's drinking, which had been bad before, was now dangerous for himself and for others. One day, as he was driving my best friend, Dale, home from a rehearsal of *Carousel*, with me in the passenger seat and her in back, he worked his way rapidly through a six-pack of Coors, driving up the hairpin switchbacks to Sedona, where she lived. He drove fast and drank fast and hardly talked to us as he threw the empty cans at my feet. Dale and I sat silently in shared mortal terror.

After Dale got out of the car, safely arrived at home by some miracle, and said a shaky good night to me and went inside, I said stonily to Jim, "You're drunk. You shouldn't drink and drive like that."

Instead of apologizing, he spent the entire way back to

Jerome droning obsessively and repetitively about how hurt he still was by my mother, his lack of money, his health problems, and his car troubles. His unhappiness was so complete, it was as if he were wrapped in it for warmth along with the alcohol. There was nothing I could say to help him then, or ever.

## CHAPTER 22

## *Alec Wood*

——— In the spring of my sophomore year, I discovered alcohol myself. I was in Mexico with the Mingus Spanish club on our yearly trip to Mazatlán, a trip intended to allow us to try out our supposed language skills in a natural setting but which in reality allowed us to do whatever we wanted in a country without a minimum drinking age. Alec, our chaperone, was the father of one of Susan's classmates and also some sort of pillar of the community. Alec was thirty-six, handsome in a lean, wolfish, nervous way. He was recently divorced, although I didn't know it at the time. I had met him on last year's Spanish club trip, when he had also been the chaperone. We were pals then, but he'd been married, and I had been very much a kid still.

And so, on our second evening in Mazatlán, when Alec asked me to come to his room for a drink, I went without a second thought.

He mixed two drinks, told me they were Tom Collinses, and handed me one. I took a sip and loved it instantly and took a bigger gulp and felt my chest get warm. While we drank out on his little balcony, we gossiped, as we usually did, analyzing all the other students on the trip together—who had a crush on whom, who was making out with whom, and were they doing it or just fooling around.

The theme of sex well and truly established, Alec mixed us another round.

"So tell me, Katie, have you done a lot of things with boys before?" he asked me.

Drunk and naive, I answered honestly: "Not a thing."

This was true basically. I'd gone on several first dates with various boys, cute ones I had crushes on, all of which involved some minor league French-kissing, but that didn't count. After each date, I hadn't been able to talk to the boy anymore or look him in the eye. I was rendered paralyzingly shy at even the whiff of potential romance with someone I liked. So nothing had ever proceeded beyond that.

It was time to go to dinner. We all climbed into the van, about twelve of us altogether, ten students along with Alec and our Spanish teacher, Mr. Fallon. I sat in the back of the van by the window and looked dreamily out at the nighttime Mexican resort city sliding by. I loved being drunk. At dinner, we sat at a long table and ate enchiladas and tacos. I made obscure, urbane jokes I thought were witty but that no one got, and I flirted brazenly with Hector, a senior I'd never really noticed before but who suddenly seemed irresistibly cute.

After dinner, we all went to a big, glitzy disco near the beach. It was the era of the Bee Gees and Donna Summer; all the girls wore sundresses and wedge sandals. On the dance floor, Alec took my hand and put his arms around me and nestled me against him and kissed my neck. Startled out of my intoxicated dreaminess, I looked him in the eye but didn't say anything. At the end of the song, I went back to the group of girls I'd been hanging out with. I didn't dance with him again.

Later, I watched him dance with Jody. She was only one year older than I was, but to me she looked fully grown-up. She was a sexy, plump blond girl with a wide, rapacious mouth, a smutty laugh, and a gap between her front teeth. She danced with her arms around Alec's neck, laughing up at him, her body pliant and curvy against his.

For the rest of the trip, Alec always seemed to be right nearby. We hung out by the hotel pool together, sat together at meals. The sudden sexual feeling between us was strange and confusing to me. I had thought we were friends; everything had tilted and shifted. The alcohol had made my brain cloudy. For days afterward, I had a hangover.

Just across the border, on the way home, when we stopped to eat at the same A&W in Ajo that I'd loved as a kid, Alec asked me if he could drive me home when we got back to the high school. I agreed: I had some things to say to him. About an hour later, in the van, one of the other girls offered me a ride. Embarrassed to admit that Alec was driving me, not wanting to cause gossip, I kept my mouth shut. After a tense second, Alec said blandly, "I'm driving her home." I sensed a few people exchanging glances. Still, I didn't say a word or look at anyone. I knew they'd talk, but there was nothing going on: there was nothing I could say in my own defense.

When the bus parked in the high school lot in Cottonwood, I went with Alec to his little green TR7 (a midlife-crisis car, I realize now). Without a word, we got in. We were silent on highway 89A, through the Verde Valley to the switchbacks up to Jerome. The sexual tension had come with us from Mexico like a souvenir.

In Jerome, just before we got to the old high school, I said dramatically, like a soap opera character, "Can you please pull over? I have to say something to you."

Alec pulled the car onto the shoulder and turned off the engine.

I said in a heated voice, "You know, Alec, nothing can happen between us. It's inappropriate. I'm too young."

No doubt I had learned the word "inappropriate" from my mother, who had no doubt picked it up in her feminist consciousness-raising group in grad school. Wherever she'd found it, it was useful to me now.

"I wish you were five years older," he said, as if it were my fault that I wasn't.

Then he drove me home. We said good-bye.

All through the spring of my sophomore year, as I rehearsed the part of Julie Jordan in *Carousel*, wrote lengthy essays for my gifted-program independent study on the American short story with the school vice principal, and educated my regular English teacher (to his very obvious irritation) on the subjunctive mood and proper usage of "lie" and "lay," I sent away for brochures from expensive, arty, faraway boarding schools, Putney and Interlochen. I was dying to get out of the Verde Valley. I felt as if I'd never get anywhere in life unless I could get a "real" education. I pored over these brochures and application forms with desperate concentration, but I could see no way to go to any of them. We were broke and had no connections.

When my grandmother finagled me a summer job waiting tables at the Threefold guesthouse in her Rudolf Steiner community in Rockland County, New York, I took it. Here, at least, was a chance to be near New York City for a summer, which was the place I most wanted to be, the place I intended to live someday. My mother scraped together the money for a plane ticket, and I was all set.

Early that summer, before I left, Jody asked me out for lunch. She drove up to Jerome in her yellow Toyota Corolla and picked me up at the Talley House and drove me over to a restaurant in the Schoolhouse, a new arts-and-crafts cluster of shops in the old elementary school building. The café she had chosen was chichi and touristy, the kind of place middle-aged women went for lunch. We weren't friends; I barely knew her. She seemed decades older than me; I was a goofy kid without a driver's license who daydreamed all day and wore cutoffs, and she was dressed like a grown woman with an imitation Chanel scarf, sophisticated perfume, and a pearl necklace. It seemed surreal to be sitting there picking at our salads and sipping our iced teas. Why had she invited me?

"I want to talk about Alec Wood," said Jody finally.

"Okay," I said, suddenly understanding. "What about him?"

"Well, I figured we should," she said. "Since we're both involved with him."

I realized that she had slept with him in Mexico, that night after the disco, and again after that. I wasn't sure what to say.

"Right?" she said, watching me closely. "I thought maybe we should talk it over."

So she was in love with him.

"Oh," I said, trying to figure out how to tell her the truth. I had developed a fantasy crush on Alec inspired entirely by my flattery at his frank and ongoing interest in me, but nothing had ever happened with him, or would ever happen, even though we had gone running alone together a few times that spring.

In my fantasies, though, I was Alec, molesting some idealized version of myself. It was too freaky to actually imagine my fifteen-year-old self having sex with a grown man, so I did what I'd always been so good at doing: I took an upsetting situation and transposed my identity to the person who had the power, like a version of Stockholm syndrome in my own head.

Anyway, I happened to know that he was sleeping with Lisa Hatch, a teacher at Mingus. She was twenty-five, of perfectly legal age. He'd brought Lisa running with me the last two times we'd gone, and it had been obvious to me that they were a couple.

"No, he's sleeping with Lisa. Miss Hatch," I said.

Jody's expression was complex; I was still too immature to have had any experience in parsing out the nuances of female competitiveness over men. But her face told me a few things at once: she was relieved that I wasn't sleeping with Alec, that I wasn't her rival; she was grateful to know the truth about Lisa;

but most of all, she was devastated to know for sure that Alec was in fact with someone else. She might also have felt foolish for asking me to lunch, now that she saw how naive and insignificant I was in this story.

Of course, she said none of these things aloud, maybe because I didn't invite her to, and I didn't tell her my own feelings about Alec or cozily initiate an exchange of lovelorn confidences. She seemed miles ahead of me—she had actually had the guts to sleep with him, while all I'd done was fantasize about him and hold him self-protectively at bay. I felt gauche and reserved; we made small talk for the rest of the lunch. When we were finished eating, Jody paid the bill and drove me home.

## CHAPTER 23

*Tomcat*

—— Two weeks after my awkward lunch with Jody, I left the Verde Valley to spend the summer in Spring Valley, New York, among my grandmother's fellow Rudolf Steiner disciples. The Threefold Community included a Waldorf school (where my grandmother was the librarian) as well as an anthroposophical center, a eurythmy school, an enormous mystery drama auditorium, a Weleda store where they sold anthroposophical medical and beauty products, a small but productive biodynamic farm, and the Fellowship, an old-age community up the hill from the community proper. It was a suburban-rural enclave nestled into a valley and a hillside between two thoroughfares, thirty miles from New York City. There was a pond; there were woods. When I arrived, I was shocked at how lush and green and humid it was there. I loved the East Coast instantly; being in the trees felt cozy and enfolding and safe after the stark, dizzyingly open desert, which had always made me feel exposed and minuscule. I never wanted to go back out west again.

That summer, I lived in a room above the old summer kitchen, which was behind the main house of the Threefold Farm guesthouse. I waited tables every day for the main meal at midday and for the simpler evening supper. The long tables in the dining room were filled with spiritual types, followers of Rudolf Steiner, eurythmists and philosophers and seekers of truth, who accepted their plates of food as if the notion of eating were simply a necessary function to sustain their investigations into Ahriman and Lucifer, the astral and etheric bodies, and the threefold nature of man. There were grandiose, batty old ladies with hectic rouge on their cheeks and alarmingly loud clear voices; willowy, ardent men in sandals with Adam's apples bobbing in their slender necks; robust Germanic women in corduroy jumpers, with loose gray buns and faint mustaches; twinkly-eyed white-haired old gents in corduroy trousers who smelled of lavender soap and tobacco; and wispy young women who swanned around in flowing sundresses looking like exalted poetesses.

I was fascinated and repelled by these people, and wrote letters to my mother filled with laughing, satirical descriptions of them. She had of course grown up among similar types, had been forcibly inculcated since birth in all this hogwash, and had fled the instant she got the chance. For years, my grandmother had been dying to bring a granddaughter into the fold; I was a sort of pawn between the two of them, but I had my own agenda, having nothing to do with theirs.

When I wasn't waiting on and observing the local fauna, I fell in with the community teenagers, all of whom went to Green Meadow, the Waldorf school just up Hungry Hollow Road off Route 45. With these kids, I smoked Marlboros, ate meatball heroes up at the Barn (the local deli) and drank beer at the Silo (the local bar), went to Shakespeare in the Park in "the city," swam in the local pond, and got drunk at parties. I made out with a boy named Christopher one drunken night and instantly fell in love with him, but he left the next day and wouldn't be coming back again until school started at the end of the summer, so I figured I'd never see him again. I made fast friends with a red-haired, hilarious girl who was a year younger than I was and who waited tables with me. The older kids, the seniors and recent graduates, all rightly thought I was provincial and full of myself, but they accepted me enough to encourage me to apply to their school.

To my surprise, Green Meadow accepted me. They gave me a scholarship, and then my mother offered to pay the amount it didn't cover, about seven hundred dollars for the year; where she got the money, in addition to paying for Susan's ballet school and boarding, I have no idea. After asking around, I found free room and board with Mary Sterne, one of the high school English teachers, in exchange for doing housework, cooking, and after-school babysitting.

I had presented this plan to my mother as a fait accompli; I had to get out of Dodge, I needed an education, and Green Meadow was infinitely better than Mingus. She had no choice; she let me go. That fall, I flew back to New York and moved in with the Sternes. My mother and Emily stayed in the Talley House, where they would live alone, just the two of them, for the next two years, playing dominoes by the woodstove and reading novels together over their supper.

Green Meadow was another culture shock for me, completely different from Mingus. For the first time in my life, I was in a school where all the kids played instruments, sang choral music, and spoke foreign languages; there was no Spanish class, so I took French my junior year, Italian my senior year. With a few other kids from the Green Meadow Special Chorus, I sang with the local Bach Society, an adult semiprofessional chorus, for two years. We studied each subject intensively in blocks and wrote and illustrated our own textbooks. My entire class had only thirteen kids in it. There were fewer than sixty kids altogether in the high school. Many of the kids had known one another since kindergarten; they weren't overtly cliquish, but deep and ineradicable lines had been drawn in the sand long before I got there, lines I couldn't always read. For the first time, I had to work for room and board instead of slouching off to my room after school with my cheese and crackers to read until dinnertime. Now, I had to make dinner; help the young-est daughter with her homework; clean the house on week-ends; and answer to the demands of Mary, my hardworking, stressed-out teacher, who was a stranger and now also my boss.

My math teacher, whose ominously apropos nickname was Tomcat, Tommy for short, lived next door with his wife and three small sons. He was famous for molesting all the teen-age girls. He had even gotten one of them pregnant, I heard from several other girls—a girl two years older than I was; she had a secret abortion—and he went right on being a respected community member and teaching math at Green Meadow and molesting every other girl he could get his mitts on. Naturally it didn't take long for him to suss me out as vulnerable prey: a fatherless girl, far from home. He started coming over and taking me on "walks" after dinner, ostensibly to give me guid-ance and sympathy because I seemed to be "having a difficult time" but in fact to lead me into the deserted fields and rub his hard-on against me while trapping me in his arms as I struggled to break free. He was short and bald with large, hot, pale blue eyes in a round egglike head, a smooth face, and a big hard belly. He smelled of mint, the most sinister child-molester smell possible. I loathed and feared him, but I couldn't tell him to go fuck himself: I had lost my nerve. I was frightened of him. I had been able to tell Alec that I couldn't sleep with him; with Tommy, I felt like paralyzed prey, and, because of my silence, I was therefore complicit somehow, or so he made me feel. I had fallen right into his trap. His rationale for abusing so many girls was that they didn't tell him not to, and therefore they wanted him to. It never seemed to occur to him that laws protecting minors from predators like him were in place because we were too young and vulnerable to protect ourselves. He didn't actu-ally rape me, but some of my friends weren't so lucky.

My grandmother, Ruth Pusch, lived in a tiny apartment near the school and took a sympathetic but distant interest in my adolescent goings-on, most of which (my smoking and drinking, of course, as well as Tommy's ongoing molestation of me) she had no clue about. I was close to her in a formal, chipper sort of way—she was highly intelligent and literary, a writer, translator, and prodigious reader, energetic and stoic until she died of the flu at ninety-three with all her faculties intact, bright-eyed, culturally awake, politically aware. She was also impenetrably independent, determinedly stoic—she never admitted any negative feelings, never copped to aches or pains. One didn't in my family; one carried on cheerfully. I've often wondered what lay underneath Ruth's armor, what loneliness, insecurity, or unfulfilled desires haunted her; I've often imagined she was a lot more like me than either of us allowed ourselves to know.

That fall, I turned into someone I didn't recognize, someone shy and weird and furtive. To comfort myself during that first semester, I gorged on bread and granola and quickly gained about ten pounds. I spent recesses and lunch breaks picking my face and writing in my journal in an empty classroom, adolescent maunderings about loneliness and alienation. I listened to Carole King's *Tapestry* and Fleetwood Mac's *Rumours* over and over and over.

In late December, I flew back to Arizona for Christmas break, feeling determined not to let my mother know that I was unhappy and depressed at Green Meadow. I had to prove that I had made the right decision to leave Jerome, not only out of pride but also because she had been so heartbroken to see me go. I wanted to show her that it was all worth it, the sacrifices we'd both made. I told my family that Green Meadow was an academic and social idyll where I spent the days hanging out with my interesting, cool, smart, close-knit classmates, rehearsing Bach's St. John Passion and Mozart's Requiem Mass, giving oral reports on Wordsworth and Thoreau, playing the Brandenburg concerti in chamber orchestra, writing and illustrating my own main lesson books, and playing right wing on the girls' lacrosse team—all of which, of course, was true, so I wasn't lying, but it made me feel lonelier not to be able to confide in my mother and sisters how hard things were for me there.

One day toward the end of that winter break in Jerome, I took a walk through town for some fresh air and exercise. I strode down the mountain, swinging my arms, my face frozen and olive green and broken out in pimples, wearing too-tight jeans and a puffy down coat, my formerly straight, thick hair now cut in a shag and frizzy with an unfortunate perm. I rounded the corner past Main Street onto the series of switchbacks that led down to the gulch. As I approached the end of the first switchback, I glanced up at the house I was walking toward. There, framed in an upstairs window, was Alec Wood. The house he was standing in belonged to Lisa Hatch.

When I waved at him, he just stared at me as if he didn't know who I was.

"Hi," I yelled. "It's Katie Christensen."

He opened the window a little and flinched in the sudden freezing air.

"Hey, Katie," he said. I heard disappointment and indifference in his voice and saw myself through his eyes, the way I looked now compared to how I'd looked when we were in Mazatlán less than a year before. We had a stilted, very brief conversation, and then I went on my way, feeling wretched.

Shortly afterward, I broke down and told my mother about Tommy. She was horrified and livid and immediately wrote a letter to the school to report him. She told my grandmother, who said she'd go and talk to the school about it; if she did, it had no effect, because nothing changed. Later that year, when my mother came to visit my grandmother and me in Spring Valley, she called Tommy and asked him to come over to my grandmother's. He arrived and sat down, and my mother told him he had to stop molesting me. She was apparently very firm about it and very insistent.

After my mother left, Tommy showed up at the Sternes' house and came into my bedroom and sat on my bed. I stood with my back against my bureau, my arms folded over my chest, and stared at the floor. He said, "I want to hear it from you. I don't believe you feel that way."

I mumbled something, terrified, unable to look at him or tell him to stop.

And he kept taking me for walks.

## CHAPTER 24

## My First Diet

For the rest of that year, I went deeper and deeper into solitude and loneliness and alienation, writing long journal entries, excelling at schoolwork and choral singing and chamber music and writing, reading novels as fast as I could fly through them, sustained by a lot of alcohol on Friday and Saturday nights at parties in the fields or someone's house or Hong Fat, our nickname for the empty old green garage on Threefold property where we all hung out. On Sunday mornings, I waitressed, always hungover, at the Threefold guesthouse for pocket money. And I ate and ate and ate.

I glutted myself on carbohydrates and fat: meatball subs on long, soft white rolls dripping with meat juice; entire big bags of Doritos; and calzones, those soft bricks of dough encasing melted, oozing white cheese. And those were just my after-school snacks. (As meager compensation, I took to drinking Tab, the ubiquitous diet soda of the era, but of course it didn't help.) Soon, not surprisingly, I was not fitting into my jeans anymore. Being sixteen, I squeezed myself in anyway and hoped for the best and looked marshmallow-like.

I was a terrible cook when I moved in with the Sternes and a better one when I left two years later, thanks to my fear of Mary's disapprobation. She made it clear that she thought I was a lazy, dim-witted layabout who ate too much and did too little to help her. At night, since she usually had to go to faculty meetings and various activities after school and didn't get home until fairly late, I cooked dinner for the family. She taught me to make soup from scratch, as well as chili, macaroni and cheese, and lasagna. I ate mounds of all of it and took seconds. And she also taught me how to reuse leftovers; the rest of a ham, for example, could be cubed and turned into risi bisi, a quick, easy Italian children's dish of ham, peas, and rice. The remnants of a meat loaf and mashed potatoes could be turned into a shepherd's pie with cut-up vegetables and instant gravy.

She taught me to make the best granola I've ever had, with oats, almonds, walnuts, sunflower and sesame seeds, honey, and oil from the local co-op, baked at a very low temperature for a long time until it was crunchy and deep with caramelized flavor. I covered it in whole milk and couldn't stop eating it. Mary groused at me frequently about hogging all the granola, but it was more than my self-control could handle; the kitchen was right outside my bedroom door, and the granola was right on the counter in a big jar. She also bought loaves of big, soft, wheaty bread that I paved thickly with cream cheese and slathered with strawberry jam or toasted and ate with mayonnaise and sliced Muenster cheese or with a dense layer of peanut butter with honey drizzled on top. I didn't see how I was supposed to resist any of it.

I ate anything, including, after my waitressing shifts on Sundays, the coarse, damp zucchini bread that issued forth from the guesthouse kitchen as dessert. This stuff was wretchedly wholesome, granular with whole-wheat flour and sweaty with oil. Flecks of grated zucchini crisscrossed each piece like the thick cloth ribbons we used to make pot holders with at day camp. I didn't care; I ate it anyway. I missed my mother.

But I was mortified when Mary patted me on the butt one day as I was loading the dishwasher and told me that I was putting on weight. I decided then and there to go on a diet. I minimized my breakfast: one piece of toast in the morning with a little butter. For lunch, every single day, I had a large, unpeeled carrot dipped in salad dressing and a grapefruit, which I peeled and ate section by section as slowly as I could to make it last. At dinner, I had a small portion of whatever the main course was, plenty of salad or vegetables, and no seconds and no dessert. I was stringent about it; once I'd decided to do this, I never deviated from my new regime: no more granola, no more lavish cream cheese sandwiches or calzones after school, no more zucchini bread at the guesthouse on weekends.

I was surprised to find that this strategy worked; I hadn't expected it to. I hadn't ever realized before that there was a correlation between what I ate and how I felt or looked.

I ate my carrot and grapefruit lunches in the guesthouse dining room, where I had access to salad dressing. Most of the other kids in my class went up to the Barn for subs and Cokes or ate bagged lunches they brought from home, downstairs in the high school common room, draped on the couches and chairs, sitting on stools around the counter. My diet made me antisocial and shy; I was obsessive about it. It was a private ritual, ascetic. At lunch hour, I went along the wooded path across the brook, up the steps, and into the simple dining room, where I ate alone amid a smattering of eurythmy students and teachers.

The guesthouse dressing was a simple vinaigrette: olive oil and vinegar and dried herbs. I poured myself a plastic teacup, filled it a quarter full. Sitting at an unoccupied table, I opened my soft leather sack, which I called Kermit and which came with me everywhere, and took out my lunch and my journal and pen. I made that carrot last as long as I could. The rule was that I could coat it with as much dressing as would adhere to it, but I couldn't scoop the oily stuff out of the cup with a spoon or drink it, which was what I wanted to do. I craved the oil; the carrot was my means to getting it, and so I dipped it in and swirled it around and quickly scooped it to my mouth and licked off all the dressing I could and took one tiny bite of carrot. In this way, I managed to ingest enough olive oil every lunch hour to keep me from keeling over during afternoon classes.

Then I slowly peeled and carefully sectioned the grapefruit and bit off one end of each and teased the little striated fluid-filled sacs out one by one, then ate the collapsed outer skin. This went on for as long as I could make it last.

While I ate, I looked down at my journal and wrote. I wrote and wrote and wrote; I was so lonely and hungry, and writing was an outlet for the voice in my head that ran on and on and on like a stream in the dark. I wrote about how lonely I was and instantly felt less so.

## CHAPTER 25

## The Edible Complex

The summer after my junior year, I went back to Jerome. Shortly after I got home, my mother and sisters and I took a road trip to California to drop Susan off in San Francisco, where she was spending the summer as an intern with the San Francisco Ballet.

While we were there, we saw my father for the first time in almost six years. My mother had found him through Ruth Ann, our former neighbor on Acton Street, who casually mentioned that he was back in the Bay Area; she sang in a chorus with him. My mother looked him up in the phone book and called him, just like that; and just like that, he picked up and seemed happy to hear from us and said he would like to see us.

We arranged to meet him at a restaurant called the Edible Complex, which he chose. He was already there when we arrived, sitting at a table in the front patio. He saw me first, since I was the tallest, and said, sounding a bit baffled but proud, "You're beautiful!" He took in my sisters and added with the same proprietary surprise, "You're all beautiful!"

He still had a beard and a scraggly ponytail; he still looked like the photo on the old driver's license I'd kept under my pillow for so many months. And he was as affable, charming, and distant as ever. I could hardly bear the intensity of my feelings for him, and I could hardly talk to him or look him in the eye. Here he was, my father again, after all these years of my thinking about him, imagining that we were so much alike, feeling allied with him as a source of comfort and strength, believing somehow that one day, we would be father and daughter again. That had been a fantasy father, I realized with lurching disappointment.

Seeing my parents together again was disconcerting and sad, too. They had both changed so much since Berkeley days, back when we all went camping together, back when we were a family. Then, my parents had been easygoing, young and carefree and glamorous. Now, my father was grizzled and wayward. My mother had been through another painful marriage and hard divorce; she looked as beautiful as ever, but she was beaten down inside, I could feel it constantly. They were no longer friends—my father's violence and departure in the cop car almost six years before hung over the table like a cloud of smoke. And I had called the cops on him; I had been the one who had caused him to go away.

When my mother asked my father point-blank where he'd been all these years, he said something vague about driving a truck in Greece and Turkey. I suppose we told him about ourselves. Throughout the meal, my heart thudded slowly and I shook with nerves and I could hardly pay attention to what was said. I felt like weeping. When we all said good-bye, my father parted from us as if we were old, long-lost acquaintances of his that he had been glad to see again in a fond, removed sort of way but wouldn't much miss now that we were saying good-bye again. My mother and sisters and I drove off, feeling sad, troubled, and unsatisfied. The next day, we took Susan to the ballet school and left her at her new dormitory. That summer, she saw our father several times while she was in San Francisco. He gave her tennis lessons, took her to lunch. He was his usual charming, affable self with her, but she never felt quite at ease with him. He made her feel shy. She could never fully trust him.

When my mother and Emily and I got back to Jerome, I found a job working as a chambermaid at the Poco Diablo Resort in Sedona. I hitched a ride to and from work every weekday with Jim, who drove to his office in Tlaquepaque, an upscale adobe plaza of restaurants and shops and professional offices. All day, I scrubbed toilets, made beds, vacuumed, collected tips from dressers and coffee tables, and fended off the occasional weirdo. After two months of very hard work, I ended up saving the vast sum of seven hundred dollars, which covered the part of my tuition at Green Meadow that my mother had somehow paid the year before. I handed over the cash all at one go to her, and then we toasted my joy at leaving that awful job behind with a bottle of champagne.

My mother turned forty-one that summer; I turned seventeen, Susan fifteen, and Emily was twelve now, going into seventh grade. My mother and Emily had lived peaceably together the past year, but my mother was still having a hard time of it. Many people in the town, seemingly so bohemian and openminded but really as narrow and conventional as anywhere else, still judged her for leaving Jim and continued to shun and avoid her. She'd had a heartbreaking affair with a man she'd fallen in love with who had left her, and was alone again, still trying to get her private practice going, working hard on the Talley House, smoking a lot of pot and listening to records all day as she stripped and refinished wood, and painfully missing her two older daughters.

I didn't know it at the time, but my mother was beginning a slide into a protracted breakdown that would last on and off for the next decade. She had seemed so stalwart and brave and invincible to me throughout my childhood, but now that my sisters and I were teenagers, leaving home, leaving her, she was no longer propped up by the scaffolding motherhood had afforded her. Her painful childhood and past caught up with her; the present was hard, too. She became increasingly absent, more and more caught up in her own internal storms.

Emily was ripening into a precociously sultry beauty and had become a prodigy on the piano. She was an eccentric loner. Always warmhearted and quick to champion the underdog, she befriended poor lonesome Father John at the Catholic church down the street. He was a sweet, humble old man, but when he died, an enormous collection of women's left shoes turned up in his basement.

Susan was succeeding as a ballet dancer, but she was painfully anorexic and living far from home, as lonely and out of place in her new life as I was in mine.

Jim, for his part, was also lost and forlorn and sad. He still loved us, but he wasn't our real father, and no amount of trying on anyone's part could make him so.

For months after seeing my father, I felt devastated, heartbroken, in a way I could neither articulate nor acknowledge, even to myself.

## CHAPTER 26

*Senioritis*

—— During my senior year, Tommy stopped pestering me for the most part; his hugs now seemed less urgently aggressive, anyway. But he continued to pester one of my friends. She told me he wouldn't stop forcing her to give him hand jobs, although she'd asked him to leave her alone. She also told me that her father and another relative had molested her as well.

Who could we tell? They were all doing it. Almost everyone in that supposedly spiritually righteous community knew what was going on, but no one said or did anything to stop it; there was never the slightest sense that they thought they were doing anything wrong, having sex with the teenagers they taught, mentored, and hosted. Tommy was far from the only one. One of my other teachers had had a long affair with a former student that had started when he was her teacher; two other male teachers (married, with children) had sex with two sixteen-year-old girls at some drunken party.

It wasn't only the men. A female teacher was involved in a longtime liaison with a recent graduate that had started when he was in high school, and another female teacher had slept with a boy in the class above mine. Almost all these teachers were married; many of them had kids who were students in the school themselves.

I was flat-out shocked by this, but many of the students

seemed to be complicit in these affairs. It was almost fashion-able, like a trend. All the same, it felt as though the adults around me were falling apart and behaving like adolescents, as if there were no sense of grown-up responsibility or account-ability or dignity. But there were notable exceptions to this lack of generational distinctions. Several high school teachers actually managed not to have sex with us. In fact, they behaved as if their job were to teach us.

One of those was May Eliot. She stood out as a bright light for me in that place. She seemed hardly older than I was—I thought she was probably in her early twenties, when she taught me English—but she was fierce and intimidating. It never occurred to me that she even had a sex life, she was so proper, so formal. One night, I dropped a late essay off at her house. When she answered the door, I saw that she had a guest for dinner, a man. I averted my eyes quickly: I sensed that she was very private, and her personal life was totally separate from her work life. It was a vast relief to have such clear boundaries set by one of my elders.

She was also an inspiring, brilliant teacher. For our senior play, May had our class put on *King Lear*. I played Regan, one of the evil older sisters, and by all accounts, we pulled it off, a bunch of seventeen-year-olds, because May was determined that we could and willed us to. In her class, we wrote creative essays, stories, and poems and shared them with one another, as we would in a writing workshop. Her criticism was fair and strong. Her praise was rare and hard-won and always gave me a rush of confidence.

May did not take any special interest in me—that wasn't the source of her influence on me or of my gratitude to her. She simply showed me in her clear, uncompromising, impersonal yet warm way that there were still a few adults who hadn't lost all sense of propriety.

Meanwhile, normal life went on among us kids. My closest friends that year were twin Jewish boys named Seth and Jason Silverberg who lived in a big, sprawling house in Upper Saddle River, New Jersey. I went there on Friday nights for Shabbat dinner, Passover seders. Their house was full of their mother's pottery, rugs and pillows and couches, books, a piano, a big table in the big dining room where we did our homework together on school nights.

Our class spent many nights in the Silverbergs' basement rec room, lying around on couches and listening to the White Album, the Eagles, Led Zeppelin, and Supertramp, drinking vodka mixed with anything we could find. There were the usual adolescent heartbreaks, worthy of a French farce: Sara, whose older sister Jessica was Seth's girlfriend although he had a crush on Amy, who had a crush on Jason; Jason had a crush on me; I had a crush on Christopher; Christopher had a crush on Gina; Gina was off at college because she had graduated the year before, but eventually they got together, and I was officially heartbroken.

My crush on Christopher was deep and painful and obsessive for my entire time at Green Meadow. Whenever he tried to talk to me, typically I couldn't answer or look him in the eye. Every so often, we made out; I suppose that is the term for the rolling around and groping and pawing that happened. I was virginal and petrified and much too in love with him to allow anything real to happen. I identified with and envied him more than I lusted after him—he had all the qualities I lacked and desperately wanted to develop: confidence, autonomy, a backbone, a strong sense of self. I was insecure, introverted, self-conscious, and shy. My crush on him propped me up, but until I could develop those things in myself, I would never be able to connect in a real way with someone I was in love with. I knew it at the time and it made me jumpy with frustration, with anxiety and impatience to grow up and leave adolescence behind.

At the very end of senior year, when it was safe to do so because we were all going our separate ways after graduation, I succumbed to Jason, who was easy to talk to, enamored of me, and not at all intimidating, but I could never return his feelings or take him seriously. It was the same old thing, all over again. We became sexually involved, but only to a point. I couldn't give myself fully to him. I wasn't ready to give myself fully to anyone, and I saw no point in rushing into full-on sex.

While most of my classmates were busily visiting various colleges with their parents, prepping for SATs at their parents' prodding before taking them multiple times, and spending hours researching their higher education decisions, I approached the whole thing with a lackadaisical confidence that was entirely at odds with my longtime desire to get the best education I could. No one prodded me or asked me what my plans were. I took the SATs once, because I had to, and the achievements once, because Jason offered me a ride with him. My class adviser, realizing that I was completely directionless, took me aside one day and asked where I was applying. I said I had no idea, but I preferred a small school out west, so I could be closer to my family; I didn't really know anything about colleges, but I thought that would be the best thing.

He told me he had a hunch I might like Reed, which was in Portland, Oregon, and handed me a catalog whose photos reminded me of those long-ago brochures from Putney and Interlochen—interesting-looking, unconventionally dressed kids in classrooms, hanging out in the grass, talking in groups, playing instruments, working in labs. "It's a very good school," he added. "Academically, one of the best."

Reed was the only college I applied to. Luckily, they accepted me, and gave me an immense amount of financial aid.

But as it turned out, the aid I got was for the wrong year. Evidently, my high school chairman was too busy sleeping with and then running off with a girl in the class below mine, abandoning his pregnant wife and small sons, to realize that the financial aid form he had given me was a year out of date. The college admissions department was as frankly perplexed by this mix-up as I was. Why they hadn't caught it right away, I have no idea, and now that the deadline was past, it didn't matter. I had to defer my admission and reapply in a year for financial aid.

So I went home to Jerome for the summer to figure out what the hell I was going to do.

---

### RUTH'S BREAKFAST

My grandmother ate breakfast in bed every single morning, as long as I knew her. The night before, she put oats to soak in milk in a small covered pot; laid out her wooden tray with teapot, bowl of turbinado sugar, eggcup, plate, knife, bowl, spoon, china cup, and cloth napkin.

When she awoke the next morning, sometimes before dawn, she went out to her kitchen in her nightgown and robe, put on the kettle, simmered her cereal until it was very creamy, soft-boiled one egg, toasted some whole-wheat bread, and added to her tray a creamer, a butter dish, a pot of crystallized honey.

She carried this laden tray into her bedroom and put it on her wide, flat, firm bed. She climbed aboard and leaned against her "husband," the corduroy, triangular pillow with arms that was so popular in that era, turned on NPR, poured out her first cup of tea, and opened her latest library book.

Leisurely, over the next hour or so, she ate her oatmeal and toast and egg and drank her strong black tea with cream and sugar, played a few hands of solitaire, read several chapters of whatever novel she was currently ensconced in, and eased into her day.

This always struck me as the most civilized, cozy breakfast on earth. I have tried to replicate it, but I have never approached the Zen perfection of hers.

# PART FIVE

# *France*

## CHAPTER 27

*The Allier*

⸺ When I got home after graduation, I learned that my mother had decided to leave Jerome at the end of the summer and move to upstate New York. She'd been offered a job at a mental health clinic in the town of Hudson. So, at the end of August, right after my eighteenth birthday, we loaded up a U-Haul and drove it east. My mother had rented an old brick farmhouse on the edge of a tiny town called Harlemville, which was, ironically, an anthroposophical community, with a Waldorf school and biodynamic farm. Emily enrolled in eighth grade at the Hawthorne Valley School. Susan had just turned down an internship at the Joffrey Ballet in New York, decided to quit ballet for good, and started her junior year at Green Meadow. She also got a scholarship and worked for a family for room and board, as I had done, and turned out to be as miserable there as I had been.

Meanwhile, my grandmother had managed to find me a job at yet another Waldorf school, this one in France. I was hired as the *fille au pair* for two immensely kind, impecunious, scattershot, warmhearted teachers named Vivian and Pierre della Negra, taking care of their four little boys before and after school, with weekends and school holidays off. The salary was room and board plus the equivalent of sixty dollars a month in francs, a tiny amount, but they couldn't afford to pay more. The school, which doubled as an anthroposophical seminary for young adults, was located in the dead geographical center of France, a muddy and otherwise nondescript farming region called the Allier. I would naturally much rather have been going somewhere exciting, like Paris or the South of France, but I accepted this job and felt lucky to get it. It seemed to be a good solution to my dilemma: I'd get out of the States for a year, learn French, and have some adventures, at least.

I bought a round-trip plane ticket with money I'd earned that summer, working as a dishwasher in a Sedona greasy spoon called Auntie Maud's. The cook was a mean little hard-ass who listened to the same Blood, Sweat, and Tears album over and over during all our shifts, all day, every day. He seemed to take sadistic pleasure in burning things so I'd have to scrub extra hard. "Ride a painted pony let the spinnin' wheel turn" happens to be the perfect rhythm for pot scrubbing, but that did not mitigate my hatred of the album. He was mad at me because his wife had wanted my job and they'd given it to me instead. He did everything he could to try to force me to quit, but I needed the money and jobs were hard to come by that summer, so I stuck it out.

At the beginning of September, with a crammed-full backpack and a brand-new pair of cowboyish Frye boots that gave me blisters, I flew to Europe. It was my first time across the Atlantic, and I was going alone. I was excited and nervous.

I landed in Brussels, since that was the cheapest destination in Western Europe, in the late afternoon and figured out how to change money and how to take the tram to the train station. I was very proud of myself and felt that this augured well, but then I found out that it was too late; there were no more trains to France that day. I sat on the platform by the tracks anyway, and smoked a Gauloise, feeling very romantic, looking up at the spires and mansard roofs of Brussels. At a kiosk in the station, I had a coffee and a baguette with tomato and cheese, then

I wandered around the streets by the station, over a bridge, slumping under the weight of my pack.

I didn't know yet about youth hostels and couldn't afford a hotel room; I thought I had no choice but to sleep in the station waiting room. I put my pack on the floor by a wall and leaned against it and settled in for the night. Just past midnight, a young guy in a station uniform stopped and spoke French to me. I shook my head, hoping he wasn't telling me I wasn't allowed to sit there all night. Then, in broken English, he invited me upstairs to stay with him and his girlfriend. "I work here," he said. *"J'ai une chambre, la haut.* I have a room."

I followed him upstairs to a long institutional hallway of doors. There was, of course, no girlfriend. Omar and I sat on the floor of his tiny dorm room all night. He spoke French, I spoke English. We smoked hash, ate a melon, played cards, and listened to a radio station that broadcast from Tangiers, where he was from. He was gentle and sweet and not much older than I was. Finally he unrolled a sleeping bag for me on the floor, and then he got into his own bed. Exhausted and stoned, I closed my eyes and was almost asleep, five minutes after he'd turned out the light. But then he snaked his hand down to find mine, stroked it, and asked me to come into his bed with him. I felt I couldn't refuse after his hospitality, so I woke myself up and slid in next to him. "Just don't go inside me," I said several times. *"Non, non,"* he assured me. I gave him a blow job, then slid back into my sleeping bag. As we fell asleep, he said with some anxiety, "We are still friend, yes, Katie?" I assured him that we were. Early the next morning, I woke up, wrote him a note to thank him, and crept out without waking him. On the train, I sat by the window, staring at the countryside going by, amazed. Here I was, in Europe.

I had some time to kill between trains in Paris, a few hours. I plunged into the city and walked and walked, agape. I wanted to stay, I even considered blowing off the della Negras, but I had nowhere to go in that city, nothing to do there, and hardly any money. And I'd arranged for Vivian della Negra to pick me up that night at the station in Moulins. I had to go.

It was dark and raining when my train pulled in. Vivian had come to get me in the family's rickety old Citroën. She was a tiny Englishwoman in her late thirties with a coppery, loose bun and dark red-brown eyes, dressed in baggy corduroy trousers, an oversized cardigan sweater, and knee-high rubber boots. She peered up at me from under a gigantic black umbrella.

"We're all very glad to see you," she told me in her dry, laconic accent. "The school year's already started and it's just been brutal. Well, you'll see."

We drove along tiny country lanes lined with trees, past wet, dark fields. We turned in at a huge wrought-iron gate and climbed a slight hill to the Château de La Mhotte; I caught a glimpse of it, a crumbling, grand old edifice with French doors and enormous, tall windows, mansard roofs, and a terrace. Vivian parked behind the château in a large bare inner courtyard. The Waldorf school itself, I would learn the next day, was up on a rise in Quonset huts, temporary and makeshift until more permanent structures could be built. The three huge, drafty, radiator-heated dormitory buildings around this courtyard housed the seminary students, a few teachers and their families, including the della Negras, and me.

I lugged my backpack into the della Negras' cozy, warm apartment at the end of one dormitory block and hastily met Pierre, Vivian's bearded, gaunt French husband, who was on his way to bed. He was much older than his wife, I guessed; his hair was shot with gray and his back was stooped. The four boys were asleep; I'd meet them tomorrow, early, when I showed up for my first day of work. I said good night to Pierre, then Vivian led me out into the courtyard and through another door and up a wide, echoing staircase.

This part of the dormitory was entirely empty and dark and silent. All the other little rooms were unoccupied. She showed me mine: a small, bare room on the second floor with an iron bedstead, a sink in the corner, and a table and chair and dresser. An enormous casement window looked out over the courtyard. A big radiator ticked and steamed. The big bathroom was down the wide, dark hallway. There were three toilets in little closets lit by bare lightbulbs with string pulls; they were nothing but holes in the ground with places to put your feet and a pull chain overhead. I had never seen toilets like that. The showers had no curtains; they were just nozzles sticking out of the wall with a large common drain in the middle of the room. I felt as if I were in a Turkish prison.

I got into my new bed, which sagged a bit but was otherwise comfortable and warm. I was so tired I was almost hallucinating, but I lay awake a long time, my head buzzing, listening to the rain and hearing the empty old building creak all around me. It was pitch-dark, there in the rural middle of France. Omar and the past night in Brussels seemed a thousand light-years from here. I didn't dare think about my mother because I was suddenly, stabbingly homesick. I pushed it away: it would pass. I would not give in to it.

The next morning, a little bleary-eyed, I got up and put on my tan corduroy overalls and Frye boots and twined my hair into two French braids. I clumped downstairs and went over to the della Negras'. The household was in a full-out welter of chaos, it seemed to me, but Vivian sat calmly at the breakfast table, peeling a tangerine and smiling at her offspring. Four small, thin boys tore around shrieking, throwing their boots at one another's heads, making a mess of toast crumbs and spilled milk: the oldest, Mark, was ten; the youngest, Jeremy, had just turned three. They barely acknowledged me. Pierre flapped around them like a mother duck, laughing, shouting at them in French, marshaling them into their sweaters and rain boots, swiping at their faces with a wet rag while Vivian combed all four of their heads.

"I hate it when I find lice," she told me. "They don't have it now, but they all get it sooner or later when the school year gets under way. We all do. You will, too."

Then the horde of boys was suddenly gone, off to school like four ducklings quacking behind Pierre, and the house fell silent.

"Well," said Vivian. "How did you sleep, Katie? Why don't you have some breakfast before we do the washing up. I'll put the kettle on."

And so my life in France began.

## CHAPTER 28

# Les Courgettes

———— I spent my first three months in France, the entire autumn, struggling inarticulately to express the most simple phrases. The two semesters of French I'd had at Green Meadow had vanished, leaving only the more-familiar Spanish in my brain, so I knew nothing when I arrived beyond *merci* and *bonjour*. Mark, James, Alain-Michel, and Jeremy all spoke English, of course, since their mother was British. It would have been easy to speak nothing but English with them, but I tried to get them to speak French with me as often as I could. We played Monopoly in French. I read their French storybooks aloud to them at bedtime; they sleepily corrected my pronunciation and helpfully translated into English. I asked them to teach me the names of things—tree, bush, wall, road, field—when we went for walks in the woods. I helped them with their schoolwork in French as well as I could.

Every weeknight, in order to help me learn French, and to alleviate my isolation, I was invited to eat in the château dining room with the seminary students. They were about two dozen French people in their twenties, all of whom seemed incredibly good-looking and cool to me. We all sat at a long candlelit table together. I listened to them jibber-jabber away and tried to imitate the way they ate, which they seemed to do better, being French, than anyone I had ever observed at a table before.

They interacted with their food, looked at it, chewed thought-fully. They made clucking noises at a particularly good *potage*, buttered their bread with ostentatious ceremony.

The food at the château was not typically French. It was, in fact, not much different from the wholesome, simple food I'd eaten at home. Most of what we ate came from the bio-dynamic farm attached to the château. The evening meal was always a light one; the main meal was at midday, when I ate with the della Negras, who came home for lunch. And the cook at the château was, in fact, American. His name was Jeff. He was something of a ne'er-do-well who loved to discuss Schil-ler and Hegel with anyone who would engage with him, but who wasn't much good at supporting his family. He was mar-ried to Hélène, a tiny, beautiful, rather dim-witted French-woman with deep dimples and huge brown eyes and a helpless expression. They had four tiny milk-pale urchinlike kids with walleyes and snotty noses. They were a sweet, lost, struggling family who'd washed up at La Mhotte and who hung on here because Jeff was the school cook. They lived in the apartment above the kitchen, the spacious grand rooms on the second floor of the château.

One night, the entire supper consisted solely of boiled zuc-chini, boiled potatoes, and homemade bread and cheese. They called the zucchini *courgettes*, but they didn't fool me: I knew that stuff when I saw it. I remembered all too well the hor-rible stuff from our Phoenix backyard, the zucchini bread at the Threefold guesthouse. I sat down with disappointment and dread.

And then I tasted the zucchini. It was sublime, subtly multidimensional in flavor and velvety in texture, not like zuc-chini at all but some fairylike, delicate thing of palest green, very fresh, with an herblike essence.

That zucchini woke me up to the idea that food had possi-bilities and qualities that I had not suspected. After that supper,

I began to pay closer attention to what I ate; I began to see it not as a substance to assuage hunger or homesickness but as something to savor when it was good, like a well-written book or piece of music.

Throughout that autumn, as I tried to speak French with a thick tongue and total unfamiliarity with the language, I fought to stave off my homesickness. I kept up a cheerful bravado with everyone at La Mhotte and also in my long, frequent letters home, but I was horribly lonely there, and I missed my mother and my sisters terribly. My letters were full of amused stories about the kids' troublemaking, wry asides about how bad my French was, confident cheer; but sometimes, in the evenings, after I'd finished the dishes, I would lean out the casement window of the della Negras' kitchen and weep tears of loneliness.

At night, alone in my little room, I sat at my desk with my red French verb-conjugation book, my dictionary, and my phrase book. I made charts, wrote notes, memorized, studied, until I'd stuffed my cranium brimful, and then got into bed, hoping osmotic energy would sear it all into my brain and I'd wake up magically fluent. I read in bed, before I went to sleep; I'd found a box of English-language novels up in the attic in the della Negras' storage trunks, Vivian's books, a mishmash of writers—Irving Stone, Jane Austen, Agatha Christie, Ngaio Marsh, Ernest Hemingway, Nikos Kazantzakis—and that year, I read through all of them.

Every morning, I woke from a deep sleep, not quite sure where I was at first. My days were long and busy and full of blundering mistakes and cringe-worthy misunderstandings and hard domestic labor. Vivian had a cold-water washing machine with a faulty wringer and no dryer. My hands were constantly chapped from squeezing load after load of wet, cold laundry and hanging it up outside. She had a straw rug that I had to sweep underneath and then water, flinging drops from a pitcher, so it wouldn't dry out. Dust was everywhere. "France is crumbling," said Vivian cheerfully; I dusted the whole house every other day. Alain-Michel set the wastebasket in the living room on fire while Jeremy had a tantrum on the toilet, waiting for me to wipe him. I didn't know a thing about small boys, and I had no special affinity with little kids.

I put salt instead of baking powder in a birthday cake because the boxes they came in looked identical and I couldn't read French yet; I had to throw it out and start over, with expensive ingredients. Cooking was a whole new thing here. Under Vivian's tutelage, I learned to make dishes that I had never made before—soufflés and mousses, stews and soups. When I encountered crème fraîche for the first time, I could not believe it existed. I ate spoonfuls of it when no one was looking.

In mid-October, Vivian told me it was time to make the mincemeat for Christmas. "I'll show you how," she said. "It's an English tradition. My mother taught me." In the kitchen, she stood at my elbow while I roasted and chopped beef heart and liver and mixed them with minced apple and dried fruit and spices and nuts, then bound the whole thing together with beef suet and brandy.

I had decided to be a vegetarian before I came to France, simply as an experiment, to see what it was like not to eat meat. A lot of people were doing it, so I thought I'd try it, too. I wasn't moralistic or puritanical about it; I just wanted to do it for its own sake.

And so I found this mincemeat-making exercise disconcerting but thrilling. The resulting mixture looked like the aftermath of a psychopath's murderous spree—small, firm chunks of organ meat interspersed with luridly moist nuggets of fruit and fleshy nuts—but it smelled amazing. I packed the redolent, dense mess into a large glass vacuum-sealed jar and didn't see it again until just before Christmas, when I baked it into two pies.

Those Christmas pies, when they came out of the oven, looked magnificent. I stood over them, filling my nose with the steam that rose through the vents in the top crusts. After the heady brandy updraft came a fierce admixture of currants, apples, cloves, nutmeg, and cinnamon, with pungent meaty bass notes. I couldn't eat them, but I was comforted by their smell, which reminded me of cinnamon-raisin toast, that dessertlike staple of American childhood breakfasts. It was a dark, rich smell that simultaneously alleviated and intensified my homesickness.

Early in the spring, I was still a vegetarian, still trying to commit to something that wasn't at all compatible with my character and inclinations. Then one morning, I was confronted with a whole rabbit, sinewy and red. Vivian took me through the steps of turning this poor creature into a *lapin à la cocotte* for dinner: when it was done, I sat at the table with the della Negras, eating salad and buttered egg noodles with grated cheese and watching them devour the stew I'd made. After I'd cleared everything away, I stood in the kitchen over the pot of leftover stew, of which there was hardly any, and forked a small chunk of rabbit into my mouth. I couldn't help myself. Then I ate another bite, and as I finished the stew, I knew I was done with vegetarianism forever.

## CHAPTER 29

# Les Orties

Being around kids who didn't always finish their food made it very easy to overeat. Nursery food is both comforting and fattening, and French nursery food was totally irresistible: buttery scrambled eggs with brioche; *tartines* made of baguette and Nutella, that cracklike chocolate-hazelnut goo; four platefuls at a time of uneaten potatoes au gratin—I was the family dishwasher; instead of scraping it all into *la poubelle*, it seemed so much more responsible to eat it.

After five or six months of this, I was husky again. So, early in the spring, just as I was rediscovering meat, I put myself on yet another stringent, ascetic, no-nonsense diet. Since I was adamantly strict with myself and never once deviated from it, I lost all the weight I'd gained since I got to France, but it was no fun. I ate fruit, salad, meat, and vegetable soup, drank a lot of tea, and took myself on three walks a day. I awoke before dawn every morning, even weekends, and struck out into the countryside for a brisk half-hour walk. I repeated the exact same circular route just after lunch, when I had a short break, and in the evening, when the kids were in bed and the dishes were done and I was free to leave the della Negras' and do as I liked until it was time to eat with the *seminairists*.

I walked fast, swinging my arms, marching along. Cars passed me in the mornings, parents driving their kids to school. Often, they waved and honked at me. When I saw them later at the morning assembly in the château, kids often pointed at me and shouted *"la marcheuse!"* and laughed.

Evidently I walked like a German soldier on patrol.

My French was improving slowly. I was beginning to be able to make jokes at dinner with the *seminairists*; I could understand at least the gist of almost everything they said. I started dreaming in French. The more French I spoke, and the more often I spoke it, I felt myself developing a sort of French personality: more wry and snappy, less naive and earnest than my American one.

That was a great relief to me; when I spoke French, I could feel my imprisoning cage of self-involvement lifting away and setting me free. Apparently, the French part of my brain was capable of a detachment and maturity the American part of me could only stumble toward.

I was starting to like life at La Mhotte, or at least to feel like I had become part of the place. I was fond of the little boys I took care of; and I liked Vivian, whose nonchalant warmth was a great relief after Mary Sterne's constant harried resentment of me.

And the longer I lived there, the more I learned about food. In addition to the vegetables I took from the big kitchen garden shared by everyone who lived at the château, there were things around the place that just grew naturally, things I could go out and get and bring back for us to eat. I picked up basketfuls of glossy chestnuts in the forest beyond La Mhotte that we roasted in the fireplace around Christmastime. Peeling them hurt our fingers, but the meat was so sweet and rich, it was worth it. In the spring, I gathered the peppery, bright-green watercress that grew in a large, stream-fed stone pool, and put it into salads with lamb's ear lettuce.

Foraging in this way was something of a revelation to me. The only other time I'd ever done it was in 1969, right before we moved to Arizona, when my mother and sisters and I spent the summer with my grandparents in a rented farmhouse in Maine. It was near a beach whose name I don't remember; we called it Blue Boat Beach because of an upside-down dinghy that was always there. That summer, we picked wild blueberries that grew in a meadow for anyone to eat. They were warm and sweet and bursting with juice. My sisters and I gorged on them as fast as we could pick them.

One of the students at the *seminaire* was a six-foot-tall blond Swedish girl named Elisabeth. She was fearless and funny, and we instantly became friends. One night, on a whim, we'd set out on foot across the fields together, following the sound of live rock music. It sounded pretty close, but it took us two hours of bushwhacking past sleepy barns, barking dogs, and dark woods before we came to a faraway little country village where a street festival was in full swing. We drank wine and danced, and then, because it was very late and everyone back at La Mhotte was surely asleep, we had to ask two gendarmes for a ride home. They were nice enough about it, but they came back to La Mhotte the next day and demanded to see our papers. The della Negras were nervous: I had no visa or permit, so I wasn't supposed to be working there. I told the gendarmes I was visiting. They said sternly, with fussy French bureaucratic fervor, that I could stay exactly three months from the stamp on my passport, maximum, and then I would have to cross the border. They drove off, leaving us all very consternated. I could tell the della Negras blamed Elisabeth for this misadventure. She was twenty-two, so much older than I was, and should have known better. I tried to defend her, but there was nothing I could say.

In February, the night before *le Carnaval*, which was celebrated as a medieval church festival at La Mhotte, Elisabeth and I painted our faces and dressed in wild colors, then headed to a party at the farmhouse down the road. We showed up to find the seminarians sipping tisane, herbal tea, talking softly by beeswax candlelight with the biodynamic farmer and his wife. We came in, raucous, with wine, and sang medieval drinking songs: "*Si vous avez du vin claret,*" and "*Quand je bois du vin claret,*" songs we had learned at morning assemblies with the school in the château but evidently not in this context appropriate. Again, Elisabeth was blamed for what was perceived as our joint misbehavior. "She always does everything too much," I heard someone mumble. "It is not carnival yet."

Then, one weekend in March, Elisabeth invited me to hitchhike with her to visit a count in a medieval village in the northwest of France. Back then, it was still considered safe for young girls to hitchhike around Europe, so we got a ride with a teacher to the highway near Moulins, and then stuck our thumbs out, headed northwest. Within minutes, a trucker pulled over, and we were off on our adventure.

The count lived in a rambling medieval house built on the road that wound through the village, the upper floor acting as a bridge, spanning it, curved on its underside so cars passed underneath an arch and between the outer stone walls of the first story and traffic literally drove through the house.

The count himself was a fat, sardonic, lonely man with a pendulous, wet lower lip who looked like a Roald Dahl character. He was married to a tiny, much younger Japanese woman who, as soon as we arrived, took Elisabeth and me to gather stinging nettles, *les orties*, for a soup.

Wearing white cloth gloves, we pulled the weeds from the side of the cobblestone road and put them into a big straw basket, being careful not to brush them against our forearms. When it was full, we carried it into the big kitchen where we washed all the sand and grit off and chopped them into small pieces. Then we sautéed a diced onion in lots of butter in a soup pot, added the nettles, chopped potatoes, and enough water to cover it all, and boiled it until the potatoes were soft. After that, we added some cream, salt, and black pepper and ran it through a Mouli. It was velvety and savory and surprisingly good. We ate it that night with a plain lettuce salad and a loaf of chewy *boule* and a board of good cheese to go with it, and wine, of course. I felt that it was wonderful to be in a French household that served wine as a matter of course with food. At the château, we almost never had it.

After supper, while Elisabeth helped with the dishes, the count took me up to his study, a book-lined room in the bridge part of the house whose two windows on either side looked right down at the road so that headlights and taillights of pass-ing cars showed in them. He poured me a cognac, which I sipped while he had a cigar. We discussed literature; I pre-tended to be much better read, much more erudite, than I was. His English was far better than my French, but I tried to speak French with him. I didn't dislike him, but I was wary of him. Even so, I was thrilled to be drinking cognac with a count in his library. It felt like a scene in a novel.

After I had befriended and perhaps charmed the count by discussing novels and poetry with him, he confessed to me that he was in desperate need of real companionship and hoped I would come to live here with him and his wife. I balked and demurred, but I was secretly, weirdly flattered. Ever since my own father had disappeared, I'd been open to a replacement. Talking to the count felt a little like trying to win my father's approval. I felt like a boy with him, like a "hail fellow, well met," an expression I liked because it sounded exactly like what it meant.

Meanwhile, Elisabeth had befriended the count's wife, who confessed to her that the count treated her cruelly and beat her. Hitchhiking home the following day, as we stood by the highway with our backpacks on and thumbs out, Elisabeth told me she was disappointed in me for flirting with the count.

"I didn't flirt with him," I said, feeling misunderstood and miffed.

"You did," she said. "You should be careful."

When the count kept telephoning me at La Mhotte long after I stopped taking his calls, Elisabeth's disappointment in me became clear. I knew I should have taken what she said as a warning. Instead, I defiantly chose to ignore it. I'd done nothing wrong. I'd been misunderstood. I hadn't been flirting; I had behaved with the count as if I were a guy, like him.

In the decades since, this particular misunderstanding has plagued me again and again and again. I am still defiant about it. I have never been able to take Elisabeth's caution properly to heart.

Shortly after this trip, Elisabeth's mother got very sick, and Elisabeth went back to Sweden to nurse her. She wrote later to tell me that her mother had died and that she wouldn't come back to La Mhotte at all. I'd lost my only true friend there. I could never bring myself to write back to her; she wrote again a few times, and I tried to answer her letters, but something stopped me.

By then, I was well and truly in the habit of letting people go.

## CHAPTER 30

## *Ménage à Trois*

——— My high school friend Jason had written to me earlier in the fall, inviting me to Israel for Christmas and New Year's. He was living there that year, studying intensive Hebrew at an ulpan and working on a kibbutz. His whole family was gathering in Jerusalem to take a trip into the Sinai desert in jeeps with Bedouin guides. "Come with us," he wrote. "Christopher will be here, too."

I felt a lurch of simultaneous dread and excitement. I had to leave France for the holidays anyway; the gendarmes would check to make sure I had. Because my salary was so small and I'd worked so hard for them all autumn long, I summoned the nerve to ask the della Negras for a plane ticket to Israel, the equivalent of about a hundred dollars, as a sort of Christmas bonus. They had no extra money that I knew of, but they graciously paid for me to go all the same.

I met Jason and Christopher in Jerusalem, where we hung around together for a few days. We flew in a prop plane down to Eilat, a town on the Red Sea near Aqaba, where we met up with Jason's family. There were a dozen or so other Americans and a handful of Bedouin guides. We all piled into open jeeps and drove into the desert.

On the first night in the Sinai, we camped in tents near an open corrugated-tin shed that housed a number of camels;

I shared a tent with Jason's younger sister. I awoke at dawn to the sound of the muezzin on the radio, the Muslim morning prayers broadcast from Mecca, and the snorting of camels nearby. When I poked my head out of my tent flap, I saw our guides lying prostrate on mats in the sand, praying.

Our breakfast was Turkish coffee, very strong and sweet, made in tiny brass pots over an open flame, and halvah, sesame-honey candy. We drove all day into the Sinai, through a warm wind, lurching over rocks. It was the winter of 1980–81: the Sinai Peninsula was slated to be given back to Egypt soon according to the Egypt–Israel peace treaty signed by Sadat and Begin and brokered by Jimmy Carter. This was the last year that it would be in Israeli hands. But whomever the place belonged to, this was a holy land for everyone, travelers and guides alike.

This desert was so different from the verdant, bursting-with-life rocky one I'd grown up in—the Sinai was nothing but undulating dunes from horizon to horizon. Out in the sand, there was just the wind and the shifting shapes of the dunes. We all stood shoulder to shoulder in the open jeeps, holding on to the roll bars, staring at shades of gold and straw and beige, watching each mountain as it hove into view far away and grew until it towered before us. There was nowhere to hide here in the frank bright sunlight and wide-open baking landscape.

At mealtimes, we got the Middle Eastern version of camping food. The Bedouins baked flat disks of dough on hot rocks in an open fire; these fresh pitas were unlike any bread I had ever eaten before, fresh and chewy and full of flavor—a hint of ash, a metallic tang of rock. And it was on this trip that my lifelong passion for potato chips began. We were supplied with enough to last an army two years, and I loved them with Turkish coffee and halvah for breakfast. But I didn't realize I was putting on weight until one day, as we all took turns sliding down a giant sand dune on our asses, Jason's father made a remark about how having a nice big butt made it more fun to slide. He meant me. I tried to laugh it off, but I was mortified.

Near Sharm El-Sheikh, we rode hired camels to the Red Sea. It was a cheesy tourist thing to do, but I found it completely thrilling. A Bedouin helped me mount and settle on a platformlike saddle, and then we were off, lurching like a ship on high seas along a sandy road, the ocean in sight ahead. We rode single file, Jason ahead of me, Christopher behind.

I was right back in that same paralyzed, wordless, shy welter of love for Christopher that I'd been in for two years at Green Meadow. It was unbearable, one of those feelings that's too intense to stand for long—euphoria, pain, yearning, and dread all at once. I could barely talk to him, and when I did, it was with mock bravado and an arrogant hardness I didn't remotely feel.

In fact, I was completely self-absorbed the whole time. Here I was in the biblical wilderness, surrounded by natural beauty and ancient history and present-day complexity, and all I could think about was myself. I told my dreams at tedious length to Jason's mother. I interpreted everything Christopher said and did as a sign, all of it having to do with me. I looked straight out at the wonders we drove through and saw everything only dimly, through the thick scrim of my adolescent egocentrism. I was all too aware of this, and would have done anything to be able to lift myself out of it, but I couldn't. My private phrase for my ailment was "self-blindness."

After the Sinai trip, Christopher, Jason, and I took a bus up north to a kibbutz called Hazorea, where Jason was living. Most of his fellow volunteers seemed to be beautiful Scandinavian girls. The three of us slept like puppies piled together in Jason's room. On my last night there, we got drunk with a group of kibbutzniks, then all went off to sleep. The three of us all got into the one bed together; Christopher and Jason, on either side of me, gently pawed me for a while. All I wanted to do was push Jason away and glom myself onto Christopher and fuse with him and never let go as long as I lived, but instead, Christopher slithered down to his sleeping bag on the floor, I disengaged from Jason, and the three of us fell asleep separately.

I took the bus to Tel Aviv the next morning and flew back to France.

During the della Negras' Easter vacation, I got two weeks off again. I stuffed a purloined sleeping bag and a few books and clothes into my backpack and took a train from the middle of France to Venice to meet Jason. Our first two nights, we stayed in a hotel; he treated me, since I couldn't afford it and he could, but I didn't feel right about it. It was strange in Venice. Sharing a bed was awkward for us both; somehow, we managed to negotiate the fact that I was not interested in him sexually without ending our friendship. We walked all day long through the city. Our room had French doors that opened onto a balcony, looking out over the water, where we sat together at a little table eating bread and cheese and drinking Chianti and watching the gondolas go by.

Then we left Venice by train and met Christopher in Rome, on the Spanish Steps, on the exact day and time we'd agreed on several months earlier. The three of us bought some food at a market and took a long bus ride to a campground on the Tiber, where we paid for a campsite, set up Jason's tent, and made camp. We stayed there for a week, living together in one tent, in our by now typical *Jules et Jim* arrangement in which Jason pined for me, I pined for Christopher, Christopher remained merry and aloof, and no one had any sex. Christopher was as broke as I was; we lived on bread, cheese, olives, tomatoes, Chianti, salami, and fruit. Every day, we took the bus into Rome together, explored the city, and took the bus back out to the campground in the evening. At night, we ate our simple food, read by flashlight, and fell asleep early side by side by side in the tent.

It was Passover; Jason, who always kept kosher, was also not eating any bread. When I accidentally plunged the bread knife into the cheese, possibly contaminating it with hametz, he snarled at me. One night, he went off to a seder at the house of friends of his parents', and I had a night alone with Christopher. I managed to make awkward, stilted conversation with him over our picnic supper at the campground, then we read our books with flashlights in the tent and turned in early and lay far apart chastely. Jason came back later and took the spot in the middle.

We moved on from Rome to Florence, where we stayed for a couple of nights in a cheap *penzione* near the Duomo, sharing a big, beautiful old room with more than enough beds for the three of us. One day, we all three went our separate ways for the day. I headed straight for a monastery, San Marco, whose cells all had paintings by Fra Angelico. I spent the day staring at them; their startling vibrancy and pitiless objectivity snapped me out of my self-absorption. I returned to my room to find Jason and Christopher already there. I tried to express my excitement about the paintings. I flung myself onto my bed. On that trip, I wore the same thing almost every day: a blue and purple Indian print wraparound skirt, a T-shirt, French sandals I'd found on sale in Moulins. I braided my hair, always, in two French braids. I was tan and strong.

I kicked off my sandals. "You guys, it's so *amazing* here," I said.

They were quiet. Wondering whether they were laughing at me, I lifted my head to find them both staring at me. In that moment, I had an inkling that I looked . . . beautiful, maybe.

"Let me lie with you a minute, Katie," said Christopher. He came over and got into my bed and lay next to me and put his arms around me. My euphoria vanished. I went rigid. This was the thing I most wanted in the world. I stiffened until Christopher gave up and went back to his own bed.

The next day, since Christopher's and my money was running out, the three of us moved to a campground in the hills above the city. Every day, we zipped up our tent and hiked down to the city to see the churches, museums, monasteries, and walk through the crooked, walled streets. I bought as many postcard and poster-sized reproductions of works by Michelangelo, Leonardo, and Rafael as I could afford and fit in my backpack. I wanted to take them back to France, to hang them up in my room, and gaze at them for solace and perspective: I would be an adult someday. I wasn't stuck in adolescence. There were larger things in the world than my own damn self.

After dinner, we got drunk on red wine on the Ponte Vecchio, hanging out with all the freaks and vagabonds and backpackers. Late one night, we came back to the campground to find that my sleeping bag had been stolen. That meant, we all knew without discussing it, that I would sleep in Jason's bag with him, since Christopher didn't offer his. I didn't want to sleep with Jason, didn't want to do anything to encourage him romantically. But I also didn't want to sleep with Christopher, who made me so nervous I got nauseated around him.

And worse, it wasn't my sleeping bag. I'd borrowed it without permission, taken it in fact, from my friend Maryse, one of the seminary students at La Mhotte. It had belonged to her dead brother; she was sentimentally attached to it. And it was a lovely sleeping bag—pale blue and soft, filled with down— it was like zipping yourself into a duvet. I didn't know how I would confess to her.

In fact, I never did; I couldn't bear to. I let her think the sleeping bag had vanished from the storage shed.

During the day, our little threesome subsisted on the usual salami and cheese and tomatoes, but at night, we ate at a Florence university cafeteria; for less than two bucks, they gave us a full dinner: spaghetti with meat sauce, bread, salad, a small bottle of Chianti, and dessert. It felt good, sitting with the university students. I wished I were one of them. More than anything, I craved the intellectual rigors, social variety, and freedom that I imagined college afforded. Having to take care of four small boys and clean a family's house and cook for them day after day was tedious and frustrating, and living in the middle of nowhere, even a French nowhere, was lonely and depressing. I couldn't wait to get to college, to emerge from my stifling cocoon of self-involvement and fly off into ideas and literature, love affairs and friendships. I felt as though my life could not begin until I got there.

Unfortunately, I had let the window of opportunity pass for applying for financial aid again for the following autumn, so I began, in my dreamy, abstracted, scattershot way, to awaken to the fact that I was going to have to defer my admission to Reed yet another year.

When I was finally in full cognizance of this fact, I wrote to the admissions office and asked if I could take another year off. They wrote back telling me I was welcome to come to Reed any time I was ready. Then I arranged with my mother to live at home the following year with her and Emily in upstate New York. I would find a job, work for the full year, and save money for tuition.

CHAPTER 31

## Paris in the Springtime

⸺ One weekend in June, toward the end of my year at La Mhotte, I hitched up to Paris with my friend Monica. She was the only other au pair girl at the school, a placid but intrepid girl from Leeds, also eighteen, who earned several times more than I did from the family she worked for, taking care of one small baby instead of four energetic, demanding boys.

Our occasional trips together that year had been weekend adventures, larks. In the fall, we'd hitchhiked to Switzerland to stay with my punk friend Knut in Dornach, my mother's birthplace, where we admired the Goetheanum and stayed up all night listening to bands with names like Stiff Little Fingers and Kraftwerk and walked around town with Knut in his tight black leather pants and Doc Martens.

On the way there and back, truckers stopped for us, genial, bored Frenchmen who wanted to bask in the company of two girls for an afternoon in exchange for driving them a few hundred kilometers. We understood the deal. When a truck pulled over and stopped for us just up the road, we ran to it so the driver wouldn't have to wait long, hopped up into the cab, and introduced ourselves with profuse thanks to the driver. We were a good team—two fresh-faced, pretty, friendly, seemingly innocent teenagers. We were young and fairly naive but instinctively good at gauging people. We obligingly flirted and chatted with our truck drivers, shared our picnic lunches with them, and always arrived safely exactly where we wanted to go.

Earlier that spring, we'd taken a long weekend and hitch-hiked down to Provence. In the lilac and sunflower fields near Aix, we stayed with an older couple on their spread of land that included an orchard, a garden, a vineyard, and a goat pen. Acquaintances of Monica's parents somehow, they fed us rounds of their excellent homemade goat cheese of three different ages, young, middle-aged, and old, that they took from wire baskets hanging from trees in their orchard. I had never eaten *chèvre* before; at first it tasted strange, and then, all at once, it was unbelievably good, gamy and creamy.

We ate meals at a long wooden table in a shady arbor of grapevines: lunches of chewy, crusty bread and *chèvre*; salads made with the lettuce they grew; and for supper, a soup or stew and once a leg of lamb with *flageolets en pissenlits*, beans with dandelion greens. Our hosts were great cooks and had good wine, not that I knew anything about wine, but their local red *vin de table* tasted fantastic to me. Their stone house was cool and dark and sprawling. I never wanted to leave. I wanted them to adopt me.

In June, in Paris, Monica and I stayed in a tiny studio apartment that a guy we hardly knew had generously loaned us while he stayed with his girlfriend. We couldn't afford to eat any meals in restaurants; we lived on those excellent staples of the young backpacker, baguettes and cheese and tomatoes and cheap red wine. All day, we walked through the city crisscrossing the Seine.

One day, we saw a man jump off the newly built Centre Pompidou. I noticed him standing up on the roof. Before I could wonder about this, he fell and hit the courtyard with a hard, wet crunch. We watched, dazed, as an ambulance came screaming into the courtyard to pick up his corpse. We barely spoke to each other for hours after.

On our last night in Paris, as we were walking back to our apartment after a glass of wine at an outdoor café, we headed down a deserted side street near the Place Pigalle. Two men appeared at our elbows, as if they had materialized from the darkness. Each of them took one of us by the arm firmly and tried to pull us into an alley. I protested in indignant French; one of them answered in quiet, monosyllabic Arabic, which scared me even more for some reason—we had no common language. Nonetheless, their intentions were very clear. It occurred to me with a fizz of adrenaline that they planned to rape us, here and now.

Monica went passive and quiet, but something exploded in my head, some surge of pure, red-hot rage that enabled me to simultaneously kick and throw my attacker sprawling into the gutter and then to slam Monica's against a parked car. Before they could recover and come after us again, I grabbed Monica's hand and pulled her, sprinting, back to our apartment building, where we unlocked the door with shaking hands and then collapsed together in hysterical tears.

The next day, having run out of money for a train home, I had to hitchhike alone back to La Mhotte; Monica was going on by train to stay with friends in Dijon. It was my first solo hitchhiking expedition. I was too scared to sleep that night, imagining various scenarios, the attempted rape naturally fueling my already paranoid imagination. I had no other way to get back, though, and I was expected on Monday morning early, to make breakfast for the boys. Just after dawn, I took the Métro to the end of the line, got out, found the highway south, took a deep breath, and put out my thumb.

After a few minutes, a Renault full of boys about my age pulled over. I got in with some trepidation, but they were a nice bunch of rambunctious French *mecs* who treated me like a kid sister, lecturing me about hitching alone, teasing me about my bravado when I protested that it was no big deal, and complimenting me on my French. Because I had not one sou, they bought me lunch in a roadside place, a ham-and-cheese baguette I ate ravenously and much too fast. They left me off about an hour from home and drove away honking and waving. I was sad to see them go.

My next ride was a lone middle-aged man in an old Citroën deux chevaux. I was even more worried this time, but there was only one of him, and he was gray-haired and slight. I was cautiously, warily confident that I could fend him off. I'd beaten two strong would-be rapists last night, after all. So I got in.

My new chauffeur turned out to be even more protective and solicitous than the boys. He was a sociology professor at the Sorbonne, a deeply kind and fatherly man who gave me a very frank, touchingly agitated lecture about traveling alone.

"Not everyone is like me!" he said. "There are bad people in this world."

"I know," I said. "Believe me. I can't thank you enough."

He went more than twenty-five kilometers out of his way to drive me to the front gates of La Mhotte so I wouldn't have to take my chances with another ride. He waited until I had walked halfway up the long driveway, I suppose in order to make sure no one attacked me before I was safely inside, and then he drove off down the little country road lined with poplars, back toward the highway and wherever he'd been headed.

## CHAPTER 32

# L'Amour

———— Shortly afterward, school let out at La Mhotte and the della Negras went off to the south for their summer *vacances*. My job was over, but my plane reservation back to the States wasn't until the very end of August, so I stayed on at La Mhotte and worked with a group of European Waldorf alumni to organize that year's annual international Waldorf students' conference, which was taking place at La Mhotte. I acted as a French-English translator whenever they needed one, and the rest of the time I cooked for the organizers in the now-empty (the *seminairists* were gone, and Jeff, the cook, had taken his family to the States to visit his parents) château kitchen.

Since we had a superabundance of vegetables from the kitchen garden and biodynamic farm along with plenty of grains, like brown rice and bulgur, and a general shortage of meat and fish, I made soups primarily, which I served with bread and cheese. My success with soup varied: once in a while, I lucked out and accidentally made a good one, but generally, since I hadn't yet mastered the fundamentals of making soup from scratch, with a base of well-sautéed aromatics and stock enriched with herbs and tomato paste and wine, they were watery and bland, like prison or boarding school soup. Consequently, I got my fair share of complaints, which I accepted cheerfully: I wasn't being paid, I was volunteering out of the goodness of my heart and because I had absolutely nowhere else to go right now, so they could either teach me to make better soup or shut up.

For breakfast, there was always Bircher muesli; every night before bed, I cut up all the ripest plums, peaches, and apricots in the larder and soaked it all in milk overnight with a heap of steel-cut oats. The next morning, the vat held a slightly fermented, sticky, thick mass that smelled like library paste on a rotting orchard floor. The German, Scandinavian, Dutch, and Swiss kids couldn't get enough of it. Along with all the French and Italian kids, I ate a piece of toast with butter and apricot jam. I dipped it in my bowl of sweet, milky coffee.

When the conference began and hundreds more kids poured into La Mhotte with backpacks, tents, and musical instruments, I continued to cook, but now I was joined by a whole staff who had actual experience in cooking for a big crowd; the pressure was off, and I could just do prep work—gather and chop vegetables—and then, my duties finished, go off and have fun. With a group of other kids, I drank a lot of wine by campfires at night, went swimming in a nearby lake, visited the nearby Bourbon-l'Archambault, the castle built by Louis Bourbon in 1300, and joined the work crews who were clearing the forest and hauling wood. When I was asked to be the singer for the band that played at the big party halfway through the conference, I memorized Pink Floyd's "The Great Gig in the Sky" from the sheet music, having never heard it before. On the night of the party, I sang into a mike turned so loud, the entire countryside heard me for miles around. There were some grumbles later about the decibel level, but most people were remarkably tolerant.

Toward the end of the conference, I fell abruptly in love with a darkly handsome French boy named François who kept pursuing me. He was a cellist who had just graduated from the Paris Waldorf School and was planning to study philosophy at the Sorbonne. We spent a couple of nights together in my tent; I was still a virgin and determined to stay that way, at least for now, but that didn't dampen our lust, at least not mine. When the conference ended, we took the train up to Paris and stayed in the empty apartment in Versailles where he lived with his mother, who was away on vacation. I had three days before my flight back to the States; they were the most preposterously, ludicrously romantic days I'd ever had in my life. It was like some cinematic vision of young love in Paris. We swooned around together, kissing madly in the Métro, going to see *The Marriage of Figaro* and watching the entire thing with our heads together, our arms around each other; we both loved Mozart. We strolled through the palace and gardens of Versailles, walked along the Seine, went to the Louvre. We lay around on the Victorian couches in François's high-ceilinged, airy, French-windowed, nineteenth-century apartment, listening to classical records and talking for hours. He serenaded me with his cello first thing in the morning. We had big bowls of coffee for breakfast and then nothing much else till late at night when we realized we were starving and fell like hyenas on our stores of bread and several kinds of cheese and huge, ripe tomatoes. Even then, we could hardly stop kissing and talking to eat.

On my last night in France, we didn't go to sleep at all. François played a new recording of Stravinsky's *Rite of Spring* on the record player over and over while he baked me a caramelized peach tart with a *pate sucrée*. We lay on big pillows on the rug in his bedroom with a bottle of wine. François fed me pieces of warm tart and we drank wine while we listened to *Rite of Spring* until the sun rose.

François took me on the Métro to the Gare du Nord, where we said good-bye. I boarded a train to Brussels, the same station where I'd met Omar, exactly a year earlier. That afternoon, I flew across the Atlantic, toward home.

## LAPIN À LA COCOTTE

Chop a rabbit into pieces. Fry 3 or 4 cut-up slices of very thick, fatty bacon in a skillet until they're crisp and all the fat has rendered. Remove the bacon with a slotted spoon and watch Vivian munch on it as you make the rest of the stew. In the bacon fat, sauté a large chopped onion and 2 cloves of garlic. Add the rabbit pieces and sauté till they begin to turn brown-gold. Sprinkle them with 3 tablespoons of flour and sauté them for about 5 more minutes, turning. Add a cup of beef broth, ½ cup of wine, minced parsley, dried thyme, salt and pepper, and a bay leaf. Simmer, covered, for an hour, adding more broth as necessary. Serve over buttered noodles with a crisp green salad alongside.

## FLAGEOLETS EN PISSENLITS

*I love the French word for dandelion greens, pissenlits, which means bed wetters, probably because of their diuretic properties. Monica's and my Provençal hosts made this beans-and-greens stew to serve with a rare, tender, garlic-studded roast leg of lamb.*

Soak a pound of dried flageolets or navy beans in water overnight and then drain them. In a Dutch oven, heat a tablespoon of vegetable oil or bacon fat (I might throw a handful of lardons in, too, if I had some on hand) and sauté a mirepoix (minced onion, carrot, and celery) with 2 crushed garlic cloves and thyme. Add the beans with enough water or stock to cover by 1 inch, plus a bay leaf. Cover and bring just to a boil, reduce the heat, and simmer for 2 hours, adding additional liquid if necessary to keep the beans covered. When the beans are soft, add 2 cups of chopped *pissenlits* or other bitter greens and continue to cook for another half hour, until the beans are creamy. Stir in 2 tablespoons of butter and season with salt and pepper to taste. Eat immediately.

---

### YORKSHIRE PUDDING

*Vivian taught me to make this perfect, quintessentially British accompaniment to roast beef. Made correctly, it emerges from the oven looking like a big popover, brown and puffy around the edges, golden and firm in the middle.*

Half an hour before the roast is done, take a large bowl and in it, combine 1 cup all-purpose flour, ½ teaspoon salt, 1 cup milk, and 2 beaten eggs. Mix until smooth. Remove the roast from the oven and spoon ½ cup of drippings into a 9-by-9-inch pan. Increase oven temperature to 425 degrees. Return the roast to the oven. Pour the pudding batter into the drippings and bake for 10 minutes. Take the roast out of the oven; continue baking the pudding for another 25 to 30 minutes. When it's cool enough, cut it into squares and serve it with the best, most perfectly rare and tender rib roast ever made in Christendom and Jewry.

# PART SIX

# Upstate, Oregon, Iowa

## CHAPTER 33

## The Bleak Midwinter

I arrived back in the States to find my mother in a very bad way professionally, financially, and emotionally. She was deeply lonely, even more so than she'd been in Jerome. Her job at the health clinic was stressful and hard; the hours were long, the pay was bad. She had left the brick house in Harlemville and was renting half of a divided white frame house over in Spencertown, on the main road through town. The other half of the house was empty. Behind her lived a burly bearded tattooed guy, above a garage. He tinkered with his motorcycle and pickup truck engines constantly and never smiled or said hello.

My grandmother visited us shortly after I got back. When she and I had a moment alone, she told me that it was good I was living at home this year so I could take care of my mother.

"She needs you to help her," she told me.

Instantly, I felt an internal, immature, rebellious quailing. I was in no shape then to take care of anyone. In fact, I had been secretly hoping, irrationally and naively, that my mother would take care of me, now that I was finally home again.

I found a job right away at the Hawthorne Valley Waldorf School, where Emily was in the ninth grade. I worked for $4.25 an hour, helping Nick, the architect and contractor, build the new high school next to the lower school building. Over the course of that year, I learned to sweat copper pipes together and install plumbing, install electrical wires and outlets, lay joists and flooring, frame out studs and hang and tape drywall, cut wood on a table saw, pour concrete, and install windows. It was hard work, which always felt good, but I had absolutely no aptitude for it. I made so many mistakes I started to feel deeply deficient. I also assisted in pottery classes, for which I had even less aptitude than construction. One day, I overlooked the melting of the little cone that signaled doneness and wrecked the entire ninth grade's raku projects. I wanted to run into the woods and hide in shame. Instead, I faced them all at the start of the next class and told them what I'd done. They forgave me, amazingly, even Emily.

I found the Hudson River Valley to be a lonely, bleak place, closed in and dark, even on hot sunny days. I ate steadily throughout that year, as if I were homesick, even though I was home. On weekend mornings, Emily and I cooked French toast, big square stacks of egg-and-milk-soaked whole-wheat bread with cinnamon and vanilla, slow cooked in lots of butter until they were crisp on the sides and custardy in the middle, served up and drenched in Aunt Jemima. In the afternoons, when I got home from work, she from school, we loved to make a snack of bean burritos fried in plenty of vegetable oil, enormous flour tortillas wrapped around mounds of grated cheddar and dollops of canned refried beans—big, crisp, savory bundles of fat and carbohydrates.

I baked constantly—gingerbread, brownies, biscuits, carrot cake, and muffins—and I ate everything I baked as fast as it came out of the oven. At the school, when it was finally lunchtime, I went to the cafeteria, ravenous, and loaded my plate with bread and butter; macaroni and cheese; baked beans; chicken with dumplings; thick, rich beef stew—anything filling I could get my mitts on. I went back for seconds. The cooks remarked, laughing, on my appetite, which had evidently become something of a joke among them; I didn't care. I was hungry. And of course I was also "fat" again, as I called it to myself, although in photos from back then I see that a more accurate word would have been my mother's term, "husky," which I certainly was.

It was a long, raw, cold winter. We heated our house by going every hour or two down to the basement and shoving enormous logs into the wood-burning furnace. When the fire went out, which it did whenever we didn't pay attention, the house almost instantly became freezing cold. We blasted through one cord of wood and stacked another one, me, my mother, and Emily, in a chain from the backyard through the basement door onto the woodpile by the furnace. It took most of a dark, windy afternoon.

One day, I walked home from work in a severe blizzard, five miles, because no cars could get up the hills. The whole way, I craved a grilled cheese sandwich on rye bread and a bowl of Campbell's tomato soup. As I tramped along in my work boots and down coat, I could barely see the road ahead or the dim headlights of any cars brave enough to try to drive in this maelstrom. When I finally got home, I burst into the house and found my mother and Emily, warm and safe, playing gin rummy over their supper. I didn't say a word to them; I was so angry at my mother for not even trying to pick me up, even though her little white tin can of a VW Rabbit would have slipped and slid on the steep hills between home and Harlemville. To comfort myself, I made myself a hot, oozing cheese sandwich fried in butter. Then I heated up a can of Campbell's tomato soup with a cup of whole milk, and ate it all defiantly, sitting at the table with my mother and sister. After that, I had a cup of hot cocoa and a brownie left over from the batch I'd made the day before, until I felt warmed and cared for enough to be friendly again.

By Christmas of that year, my mother was in a deep depression. She was unable to stop crying; she stayed in bed for three days straight. Susan came home, and on Christmas Eve, we three sisters went to the little cemetery in Spencertown and sang carols together. Christmas lights twinkled from the houses all around us. " 'In the bleak midwinter, frosty wind made moan,' " we sang dramatically, like heroines in an Alcott novel, and then we went home to put more wood in the furnace and try to cheer up our poor, ailing, wretchedly unhappy mother with Christmas cake and hot chocolate.

I'd been raised to be cheerful and make the best of things. I'd learned from my mother that the way to get through hardship was to pretend I had it all together, that nothing was wrong. This year, that all went out the window. My mother and I were in openly grim moods for almost the whole year. We were both depressed and lonely, and, for the first time in my life, we didn't get along at all. She resented me for living there and not being more helpful to her, and I chafed at her resentment; if I couldn't be in college, all I wanted when I came back from work was to be left alone to read E. M. Forster and Agatha Christie and write long letters in French to François. My red verb book was always with me, on my nightstand, at the breakfast table, in my backpack at work. My phrase book and dictionary were never far away, either. François and I sent each other almost daily letters on tissue-thin airmail paper. When I got home from work to find a letter from François on the table, I took it up to my room and opened it and savored it. His letters warmed me, gave me joy and hope.

I wrote pages and pages to him of thoughts and dreams and ideas and romantic assurances, and he wrote back in kind, sometimes laughing at my mistakes, encouraging me as I got better. Little by little, my written French caught up with my spoken French, until I could dash off a letter and say whatever I wanted without having to look anything up.

Then, in the late spring, François broke up with me, sadly, apologetically, with his usual delicate articulateness. He had fallen into the arms of his former girlfriend, he wrote to me. The possibility of our ever making a life together seemed remote. We hadn't seen each other in nine months. I was starting college in the fall. Although he loved me, it had become clear to him that we should both move on.

I wrote back in tears, agreeing, saying good-bye. By that time, I had saved a lot of money. I could have flown to France to see him, but I thought I needed the money for college, and François had become an abstract idea to me by then; he existed for me only as beautifully written thoughts and feelings on onionskin paper, not as a real man with a real body and soul. And I had plans for the summer. Emily and I had been offered a job together at a Waldorf camp on a lake in Ontario as the counselors for the older girls' cabin; we were heading there as soon as her school got out.

It was a good time for us both; after the hard year I'd just been through, it was a relief to be far away from it all with my little sister, floating around on a lake, singing songs and laughing so hard at our private homespun jokes, we almost fell into the leech-filled water. We took our six preteen girls on overnight canoe trips to a nearby island, where we all sat around the campfire eating corned beef hash from cans, toasting marshmallows, telling ghost stories.

That summer, I had sex for the first time. It was just before I turned twenty, in a hand-built sauna on the lake, with a Canadian guy who'd been a year ahead of me at Green Meadow. His mother was camp director. He relieved me of my virginity obligingly and expertly and without undue fanfare; Canada seemed as good a place as any for that particular rite of passage, and he was a fine man for the job.

When I got back to Spencertown, I found out that my mother had met and started seeing a very handsome professor named Ben La Farge who taught English at Bard College and wrote poetry and had a roguish way about him. He was smart, charming, and funny. They seemed genuinely in love, and I was happy for her. She had been alone, and lonely, for so long. Suddenly she was more cheerful, distracted from her worries.

Reed offered me a generous combo platter of financial aid; it turned out that I didn't need any of the money I'd saved that year, because my mother offered to cover the rest of my tuition. My money was mine to spend as I liked. I bought a viola, a backpack, some new clothes, and a plane ticket to Oregon.

At the end of August, I said good-bye to my family and flew off to the other side of the country to begin, finally, at long last, my adult life.

## CHAPTER 34

## Scroungers

As soon as I arrived in Portland, I moved into a tiny, shared dorm room, registered for classes, and started to study like I'd never studied before. I made a few friends right away. My professors were brilliant and intimidating, and I was too shy to open my mouth in class. The campus was green and misty with rain. I couldn't believe my luck at finally being at Reed. I placed into third-year French classes and started writing papers, giving oral reports, and having class discussions in French. I got into the Collegium Musicum, a small medieval and Renaissance chorus, and joined the school chamber orchestra, playing the viola now, which I had switched to for its deeper, richer tone. I started sleeping with a guy named Bill who was nice enough, not too interesting or exciting, but generous and experienced and frankly adoring. Sex was fun, I was discovering. I was glad I'd waited, but now I felt like making up for lost time.

My first semester at Reed, I ate all my meals in Commons, the school cafeteria. I watched in fascination as my fellow freshmen, most of whom were two years younger than I was, piled their plates at breakfast with sausage, French toast, pancakes, and fried eggs. All around me, homesick kids were pigging out. I had done enough of that for one lifetime in the past year alone. But after my summer in Canada, I was thin again, and this time, I was determined to stay that way. I ate fruit and toast for breakfast, soup and salad for lunch, and not much for dinner, always conscious of the strangely satisfying pleasures of asceticism, of self-control, of slenderness. But I thought about food, as always, lasciviously, lustfully. That year, my sense of food became bifurcated. I ate little, but I thought about it a lot. The idea of great food, my memories of the rabbit stews and chocolate mousses and Yorkshire puddings I'd made and eaten in France, sustained me as I ate the mediocre fare of Commons. My jeans fit loosely around my hips and stomach, and I moved easily around and felt light and clean, like an arrow. It seemed to me that I had found the best of both worlds.

There is a long and honorable tradition at Reed of scrounging: A motley group of students waited by the dish line at every meal and took uneaten food off other people's trays and ate it. More than a few of them had dreadlocks and bare feet and ratty clothes. They were, Bill told me, trust fund kids with enough money to eat in the best restaurants in Portland every night if they wanted, or even to buy a restaurant of their own. In my dorm, kids binge drank, played records all night, and made a mess in the kitchen. It was a grimy, institutional place of shared fluorescent-lit bathrooms and cramped quarters, and my roommate and I couldn't stand each other. I felt too old for this shit.

And so, after one semester, I moved off campus into a two-bedroom apartment with my friend Lisa, who was my age. We ate the same thing every day: breakfast was a cup of freshly brewed, strong French roast coffee with a well-toasted English muffin with butter and raspberry jam. I got a bowl of soup and half a sandwich for lunch in the Reed café; and then, back at home in the evenings after classes, we made stir-fries with garlic, ginger, scallions, broccoli, red pepper, and mushrooms, with chicken or ground beef, that we ate on top of baked potatoes. Every day, same food. The routine was soothing to my newfound model of monastic eating, and it made grocery shopping a snap.

The summer after my freshman year, I was hired by Jo, a senior at Reed, along with five fellow Reedies, to cook at a camp for emotionally disturbed children near Shawnee, Pennsylvania, in the Delaware Water Gap. For the eight-week program, the kids lived in cabins with their counselors, and we cooks lived together in our own cabin—Jo, Jen, Lucy, Patty, and I, on five little cots in two straight lines. Ben, the only man on the kitchen staff, was in a cabin with the grounds crew and maintenance guys.

We had a rotating roster of duties. Breakfast duty, for example, meant showing up before six in the morning and breaking eggs into a mixer from pallets that held several dozen each (we all got very good at the double one-handed egg crack); beating them with the electric paddles; adding milk, cinnamon, and vanilla; and soaking loaf after loaf of generic wheat bread in batches in the egg mixture and frying them on the huge griddles.

Lucy and I were frequently on breakfast duty together. She was my favorite person on the crew, little and fine boned but very strong, with wavy long blond hair and a wry, calm disposition. She wore white wifebeaters and baggy canvas shorts and Birkenstocks. We listened to Bob Marley nonstop.

Jo, our sterling, superresponsible, serious boss, armed us with ring binders she'd assembled, full of recipes proportioned for two hundred people. It was classic cafeteria food—red-bean chili, which we stirred with paddles in tall stainless-steel pots; spaghetti and meatballs; and various casseroles like baked ziti and mac and cheese, which we baked in industrial ovens in pans the size of small sleds.

Because the children all had varying degrees of "issues" and disorders (which these days would probably be medicated but weren't back then), their diets were severely restricted. The recipes were filling and healthy—heavy on vegetables and starches, light on meats and fats. The kids weren't allowed to have any sugar at all. Desserts were sweetened with sugar-free applesauce, industrial-sized cans of it; we made vast sheet pans of gingerbread and brownies and cobblers, which always came out of the oven looking and smelling delicious but tasting disappointing, at least to me.

One day, I came into the kitchen for my shift and was confronted by a walk-in fridge filled with boxes I was evidently expected to haul forth and deal with: forty whole, plucked, very dead chickens, all of which needed to be hacked apart into the usual components: breast, thigh, drumstick, wing. I had never butchered a chicken before. I took the first one from its tightly packed box and laid it on a cutting board. The chicken looked small and vulnerable and goose pimpled, as if it were chilly and wanted a blanket. It was about the size of a very young human baby.

I looked at Ben, who was on duty with me that day. "Have you done this before? You're the guy."

"No," he said. "And don't be so sexist."

Ben was sweet faced, intellectual, pale skinned, and mild mannered. All things considered, I was the more viable candidate.

"Here's a chart, I think," he said, handing me a piece of paper. Then he went off to make a vat of potato salad.

I looked askance at the chart, put it down, and hefted the cleaver Jo had handed me before she went back to the cabin for a nap.

The first attempt went badly; I've never been much good at following directions, even harmless and potentially helpful ones. I was glad the poor chicken was already dead. The second attempt was a little better. I now had a heap of hacked-up bird parts and was starting to feel a bit like a serial killer. I arranged the third one for dismantling. It looked as daunting as the others.

With inward resignation, I consulted the chart finally. According to the instructions, birds came apart neatly. It was a matter of knowing where the joints were and severing them, not cutting into bones but liberating each piece from its neighbor with a sharp, well-placed chop. The carcass itself likewise came apart with little resistance if you sort of tugged it open like a book and cut through the hinges of cartilage.

About ten chickens in, I basically had the hang of it. By my thirtieth, Ben could have blindfolded me and I would have taken that thing apart no problem, chop-chop. I stopped seeing the chickens as once-living beings, stopped worrying about desecrating their little corpses. They were food, damn it. They were going to be coated in spiced bread crumbs and baked. They were going to feed a bunch of kids who were hyperactive, depressed, out of control, manic, hypersexual, maladjusted, violent, and/or learning disordered. And this was my job.

At the start of my sophomore year, after I'd had my heart well and truly broken by a stoner physics major named Kip with long blond hair and a dudely, passive-aggressive sweetness I could neither resist nor penetrate, I razored off my own long hair into a spiky boy's cut full of cowlicks in an attempt to rid myself of my femininity entirely. I was skinny and muscular and angular, bristling with ambition, impatience. I had all but forgotten my past bouts of gluttony; I ate now so sparingly I sometimes got light-headed and had to remind myself to get some food. My brain felt electric and engaged, like an engine being tested and pushed and let out at full throttle. My obsession with food was sidelined, suppressed, displaced.

In the spring of that year, having finally recovered from Kip, I fell in love with a guy named Stephen, my skinny, angu-

lar, spiky-haired, literary twin. We quickly became inseparable. We had several classes together and slept together every
night in my narrow little bed; occasionally, we even had identical dreams. We loved Wordsworth; danced like pogo sticks
to the Clash and the Specials; tried to puzzle out Ezra Pound;
wrote villanelles and sonnets; ate cheap, easy suppers of Top
Ramen (twenty-five cents a packet) with eggs and scallions and
chicken thrown in; and laughed as hard together as I'd laughed
with Susan as a kid.

## CHAPTER 35

## Tuckernuck

That summer, and for many summers there-
after, I joined my family for three weeks on an island off
Nantucket called Tuckernuck. Ben, my mother's now-third
husband, had a family house there, a shingled cottage with
a breezeway; a library with window seats and shelves of old
books; a gas-powered generator in a shed that pumped water
up from the well; propane tanks to run the stove, fridge, water
heater, and washing machine; and a boathouse down on the
East Pond containing a barnacled dory, a small sailboat, and
a couple of canoes. The island had no paved roads, electricity,
or stores, nothing but twenty or so old shingled cottages scat-
tered through grassy moors and scrubby woods. I slept in the
small bedroom off the kitchen, a whitewashed chamber just big
enough for a lumpy single bed and small wooden bureau. I read
and wrote over coffee in the mornings, then walked after lunch
with my sisters to the white beaches on the other side of the
island for an afternoon of swimming and sunbathing.

In the evenings, we all played cutthroat, killer games of
croquet, with our cocktails on the mown lawn that overlooked
the water, like proper WASPs. When dinner was ready, someone rang the gong and everyone came to sit around the wooden
table with its straw place mats and porcelain water pitchers.
Above the fireplace was a wooden carving of an enormous fish.
The dining room windows had ancient, wavy glass; through

their small, mullioned panes, the sky and water and moors looked watery and distorted in their greens and blues. As it got dark, we lit the kerosene lamps. After dinner, we went into the library and played charades or dictionary, or Ben read aloud to us. The nights were very dark and very quiet. I lay in bed watching the moon through the clouds and listening to the wind.

Sometimes, when the tides were right, we carried rods and lures to the beach and went surf fishing for striped bass and bluefish, casting out into the waves, standing waist-deep in the water. When I reeled in a fish, I clonked it on the head to kill it, then slit its belly open with a sharp knife and reached in and pulled out its entrails and threw them to the seagulls. Later, on the breezeway of the house, I attached each fish I'd caught by the tail to a big, rough clipboard and scaled it with a knife, feeling as macho as Hemingway.

My mother used to stuff the oily, strong-tasting bluefish we caught with whole garlic cloves, lemon slices, and sprigs of fresh rosemary and thyme that she pulled from the kitchen garden. She doused it in olive oil and surrounded it with potatoes and baked it. She had found the recipe in a cookbook somewhere; it was the best bluefish I've ever eaten—rich and tender and so garlicky and herby, its gamey-fishy flavor was overwhelmed and conquered.

At low tide, we took quahog rakes and a bucket in the dory around the point to pull huge, knobby quahogs from just under the sand on the shallow sea floor. I soaked them in salt water all afternoon so they'd spit out the sand in their gullets, then steamed them in a big pot until they opened. Then I chopped the meat—which looked disgustingly, grotesquely genital-esque but smelled briny and sweet and clean—and added it to a soup of sautéed onions, chopped bacon, potatoes, and frozen corn simmered just barely covered with equal parts clam liquor (I strained the sand out of the clam-steaming water) and whole milk, with two bay leaves, salt, and pepper. The broth was thin but very flavorful, and the soup was chunky and thick. The clams were chewy and tender. I floated a bit of butter on top of each bowl and sprinkled it with chopped parsley, and that, plus a salad, was dinner.

To get to Tuckernuck from the mainland at the beginning of our three-week stay, we took the Nantucket ferry from Hyannisport on Cape Cod with Ben's car packed full of canvas bags of clothes and books, and my mother's cello. Once on Nantucket, we drove to the Stop & Shop and filled three carts with food—canned goods and staples and as much produce as we thought we could eat before it went bad—and then we went to the liquor store next door for several cartons of magnums of Junot wine, red and white, a bottle of bourbon and another of Scotch. The trunk full of food, we met old Walter Barrett with his weather-beaten boat at the Madaket dock, loaded its belly full of bags, left the car parked by the dock, clambered aboard, and chugged over to Tuckernuck.

The first glimpse of the green, low island, rising from the blue waves on the horizon, always gave me a tingle of excitement; this was the high point of my year, the vacation I dreamed about, and now it was finally here. I was never disappointed. The three weeks on Tuckernuck were like a fairy tale for me, a children's story come true in my twenties. I brought my boyfriends and best friend, Bronwen, there, and my sisters came every summer; it was the only time I got to see my family for such a long, unbroken period. It was heaven for me.

I naively thought my mother loved it there as much as I did. She seemed to, at least. She would sit on the shady breezeway in her straw hat all morning and read thick nineteenth-century novels—Tolstoy and Eliot. She practiced her cello for hours. (These, I now know, were tactics for keeping Ben at bay.) And she was so much fun there—easily the most dynamic and competitive at games, and when she won, she gleamed with hilarity and triumph. At four every afternoon, I, the self-appointed ship's mate, made a pot of Hu-Kwa tea, a smoky oolong, in the big blue-patterned china teapot with the straw handle, and served it on the breezeway with gingersnaps, which I doled out so our stores would last as long as possible. I loved teatime with my mother; she was chatty and effusive in the afternoons. We opened wine when dinner preparations got under way. I loved cooking with her in the small low-ceilinged farmhouse-style kitchen, bantering and laughing with Ben.

I also assumed naively that my mother loved Ben as much as I did. To me, he was a generous, genial, adoring stepfather, a mentor who read all my papers and stories, someone I could talk about books with for hours, a funny, charming man who felt like the father I'd never had. Not so with my mother. Her marriage to Ben was complicated and unhappy, and she was struggling to stay in it. One summer, she stayed in bed crying for several days. I couldn't understand why—here she was on an island idyll with all three of her daughters. She told me in later years that the place was a prison for her. There was literally nowhere she could go to escape her husband. He had full control over her for those three weeks.

## CHAPTER 36

## Ralph, Again

———— Meanwhile, Susan and Emily had both become raving beauties, known around Bard (where Susan was in college) and the nearby Simon's Rock early college (where Emily was in school) as "the babes of the universe." They were quite a duo, stared at and ogled and lusted after wherever they went together: two curvaceous, graceful, sultry, flowing-haired lasses with intelligence and charisma and warmth. Susan was now a modern dancer; Emily was a pianist, singer, and songwriter. They went to Dead shows and Rainbow Gatherings together. Emily was into world music and vegetarianism and smoking mullein, which she claimed was good for the lungs. She wore hippie dresses and went barefoot. Susan was alienated and solitary at Bard, which was a dark, lonely place in the early eighties. She threw herself into modern dance, went to parties, wore eyeliner and ripped sweatshirts and miniskirts with leggings and little black boots. She and Emily were both having spiritual awakenings and were questioning the way we were raised, without any religious practice or belief, by our adamantly nondogmatic, skeptical, empirically minded mother. They were both actively searching, each in her own way for her own answers, but their shared yearning allied them, made them close and bonded.

Across the country in Portland, I was busy being a writer and literary intellectual. I wore thrift-store dresses, cardigans, and cowboy boots. I listened to the Talking Heads and Joan Armatrading and Elvis Costello. I didn't drink much alcohol in college, but I loved a little bourbon every now and then. I liked ecstasy, too, which according to college legend had been invented in a Reed chem lab and was called MDA or MDMA back then, and also locally foraged psilocybin mushrooms, which were fun to take on the wild, rocky cliffs of the Oregon coast, where I lay on the spongy forest floor and laughed my head off at the hilarious gestures of the trees.

The Christmas of my junior year, my sisters came to visit me in Portland for winter break. Stephen and I lived together in a big drafty cheap old Victorian house with two other students, a ten-minute walk from campus. My sisters stayed in our housemates' rooms while they were away. Emily had become rigidly fanatical about vegetarianism and just about everything else. She openly disapproved of me—I drank straight Jim Beam, smoked Camels, ate meat, listened to unacceptable music, and wasn't spiritual or mellow in any way. I openly scoffed at what I thought of as her new-agey, fuzzy-headed crap, which naturally confirmed her view of me as uptight and unenlightened. The more we narrowed our eyes in reaction to each other, the more entrenched each of us became in our own views.

Susan, although she was of course far more aligned with Emily than she was with me in her spiritual leanings and dietary practices, managed to be neutral; she adopted the classic middle-child peacemaker role right along with Stephen, who was also a middle child. With the two of them trying to help us get along, Emily and I became increasingly polarized and hostile. One night when I was making dinner, without thinking, I took the wooden spoon out of the meat spaghetti sauce I was stirring and used it to stir the special vegetarian sauce I'd made for her. She saw me do it and refused to eat the sauce and ate plain spaghetti for dinner defiantly. I retaliated the next morning by frying an entire package of bacon for breakfast, filling the house with the smell of pig fat, eating a few pieces lasciviously, saying "yum!" with didactic fervor. Emily retreated out onto the front porch and sat on the railing in the cold, wrapped in her Mexican handmade sweater and Guatemalan scarf, smoking her mullein. I went out in my leather coat and sat on the couch on the other side of the porch, not speaking to her, and lit up a Camel and very ostentatiously blew the smoke away from her.

We were so much alike, I always believed, underneath all our differences. Fighting with her made me sad; this was the same sister I'd raced home from first grade to read to and hug and haul around the backyard. And now she thought I was the devil, or something like it. And I thought she was self-righteous and full of herself.

That winter, my sisters and I rented a car and drove down to San Francisco together to look up our father. We hadn't seen him since our trip to drop Susan off in San Francisco five years before. This time, Emily and I fought so vehemently during the entire trip, Susan had to stop the car in the middle of the street and threaten to put us both out onto the sidewalk if we didn't cool it. We cooled it, just barely.

When we called our father and told him we were in town, he asked us to come to lunch at his place on Telegraph Hill. We drove there from the friend's house where we were staying, parked, and climbed steep stairs to his front door. He opened the door and ushered us in. He was living like an ascetic Boy Scout in his bare-bones law office, sleeping on his desk. From a pot on a hot plate, he served us bowls of something he called Lebanese pea soup. He seemed proud of this concoction, but I think he might have opened some cans. Seeing him this time was as weird, intense, and charged as our lunch with him five years earlier had been, and just as unfulfilling. We all drove away subdued and shaken. Emily and I didn't clash again for days; we were all deeply allied in our bewildered sadness about this strange, compelling, complicated man who had fathered us.

Back in Portland, Susan and Emily and I performed at a Reed coffeehouse in the student union. We sang all the three-part songs we knew, among them "Star of the County Down," "Moonshiner," Emily's arrangement of a Langston Hughes poem called "This House in Taos," and a medieval drinking song I'd learned in France. We sang on and on until, I'm sure, the audience had had more than enough of us, and then Emily sang, solo, a Bengali folk song, accompanying herself on guitar. I sat with Susan at the side of the stage and watched the audience watch her. I thought then, not for the first time, that she would be famous someday soon.

I was wrong. At the end of that school year, in the spring of 1985, Emily got her A.A. degree from Simon's Rock. Although she had applied to Wesleyan, she didn't get in, probably because she hadn't taken enough academic courses at Simon's Rock; she had immersed herself in music to the exclusion of everything else except her spiritual pursuits. Without any plans for the future, she lived that summer in a hut in the woods near Simon's Rock before she went to the Rainbow Gathering in Missouri. There, as she sat playing the piano in a field, a man approached her and put his hand on her shoulder and looked into her eyes. "God means us to be together," he said. Emily, by now a born-again Christian, accepted this as her destiny and spent the next decade living with him on his remote farm in New Zealand. They got married in Fiji, sailing there and back as crew on a yacht, because Emily was underage and my mother wouldn't give her consent.

His name was Claus. He was twelve years older than she was, the son of a former Nazi. He called her Flower; he had messianic delusions. Emily developed a German accent and became submissive and meek. They lived alone in the remote Bay of Islands, tending the livestock, working in the gardens, and driving the produce to market in the farm truck to sell. Emily played music still, but only for God now, in the rustic local church, and the only songs she sang were Christian hymns.

During my senior year at Reed, I was almost too distraught and heartbroken over losing my sister to care much about school anymore. I wrote her long letters, begging her to come home. She wrote back with superior condescension, telling me I was blind and lost and sinful, and that she had found the true path. She capitalized words that had no business being capitalized. Her diction became Germanic and unfamiliar. I wrote back and tried to argue and reason with her, but she had finally won our battle: the fanatical, righteous believer always vanquishes the skeptic. And she had gone to the other side of the world.

I wrote a letter to Ralph just before Easter, finally expressing my anger at him for being such a negligent father, for abandoning us. "We would have been such good daughters for you," I wrote, fury sparking off my pen. I mailed the letter, not expecting to hear back from him. But he wrote back right away, offering me a plane ticket to come and visit him in the Bay Area for Easter, saying he'd like to spend some time together. This was so unexpected, so out of the blue, I didn't know how to respond. I felt shy, unable to imagine actually visiting my father, walking off the plane and seeing him there at the gate, staying in his law office with him and no doubt sleeping on the floor in a sleeping bag, talking to him over our makeshift breakfast on his desk. It all seemed impossible, too little, too late. I wrote back that I was too busy to leave Reed. I mailed the letter and felt nothing but relief.

## CHAPTER 37

## Roxy Hearts World Diner

During my senior year, I'd applied for permission to do a creative thesis, which was no small matter at an academic stronghold like Reed. For my thesis, I wrote a collection of four short stories called "In a Small City."

Halfway through that year, I broke up with Stephen and moved out of the cozy, airy apartment we shared and into a depressing studio on SE Division Street. I had gone home for Christmas, to my mother and Ben's house in Barrytown, near Bard College, and while I was there, I woke up in the middle of the night one night and realized I wasn't in love with him anymore. We had almost completely stopped having sex. He was like a sibling, a twin. We were best friends, and we spent all our time together and never fought; meanwhile, I had begun a strange sort of dalliance with a weird, semidisturbed guy who skulked around campus in a leather jacket. I hadn't slept with him yet, and I didn't want to, and I had the feeling that if I stayed with Stephen, I would.

I came back to school in January, announced to Stephen that it was over and I was moving out, found an apartment, and moved. It all happened within three days, leaving Stephen totally shocked and heartbroken and all our friends confused. But I felt a deep relief, as if I were coming back to life again. My new apartment was in a run-down old building far from campus, but the place was warm, cheap, comfortable, and all mine. Our friend Henry took my room in my old apartment, so Stephen wasn't stuck with the whole rent, and he didn't have to live alone. A few of our friends shunned me for a while, but I was too relieved to care. I worked on my thesis and rode my bike to and from campus and kept my head down for the rest of my senior year.

After graduation in May 1986, having no idea what I was going to do next, I spent the summer in Portland in my dump of an apartment. My friends Bronwen and Henry shared a place that summer; I spent a lot of time over there, listening to NPR and eating home-cooked meals. We all talked a lot about our plans for the future: we had none beyond staying in Portland for a while.

For my graduation present, my mother and stepfather gave me enough money so I could take the summer off and fly back east to go to Tuckernuck. In late August, I left the East Coast and flew back to Portland to find a job.

During the following winter, I quit my horrible job at Waldenbooks and took a job as a short-order cook at Roxy Hearts World Diner, a silver-chrome-and-red-Naughahyde, vintage-movie-poster-decorated little place on Burnside Street, in the Pearl District, the rough part of town where the bums lived, near the seedy gay bars, the seedy straight bars. My friend Henry and I worked the night shift, so we handled the rush when the bars closed between 3:00 and 4:00 in the morning and the entire male gay population of Portland showed up drunk, spangled, howling, cruising, and hungry for omelets, burgers, sandwiches, and French toast. Henry and I threw garnishes at each other midrush, singing operatically, laughing, cursing, punchy.

Henry was a willowy, dark-haired, blue-eyed, pale-skinned English boy by way of the San Fernando Valley, funny and sensitive, arch, with a charming mean streak. Back then, at twenty-one, he was just coming out. We were two lovelorn sensitive plants nostalgic for Reed, wondering what to do next with our lives. We were both pining for hot, unavailable younger boys who were still in college: I had reignited my unaccountable attraction to Kip, the pot-smoking physics major from California. On our days off, Henry and I decked ourselves out and headed over to campus to cruise around the student union steps, the café, the library, and the Great Lawn, hoping to "run into" one or both of them. We had nothing better to do. Before I started working with Henry, I was struggling to pay my rent ($165 a month) working fifteen hours a week at the Waldenbooks in the mall downtown, augmenting my tiny minimum-wage paychecks with government cheese and food stamps and an occasional babysitting job for my former thesis adviser.

Compared to me, Henry made pretty good money cooking at Roxy Hearts. He also worked much harder, twelve-hour shifts, but he always had money to go out drinking, and he was generous with it. When the other night cook quit, or was fired, Henry recommended me to take his place, probably so I could afford to buy my own damn cocktails. By that point, I felt that if I had to unbox and shelve one more load of slippery, glitzy romance paperbacks or help one more smarmy yuppie find a self-help book, I very well might kill someone, probably myself. I was ecstatic to get the job at Roxy Hearts.

Only once did Henry and I miss a shift. On what was supposed to have been a day trip to the Oregon coast, on the way back to Portland for our shift, Henry's van skidded and slid into the guardrail and he broke his hand, gripping the steering wheel so hard the bones were crushed. The van was towed by AAA to a local mechanic's. There was no public transportation to Portland that late in the day, and we couldn't rent a car, because I had no license and Henry was on painkillers and couldn't drive with a broken hand.

With no way to get to Roxy Hearts that night, we had to call Keith, the gay, tough, black day cook, and get him to cover for us. He was a clean-and-sober ex-alcoholic ex-junkie who later died of AIDS (as did our favorite waiter, the tiny, doe-eyed Joey, who batted his Bambi lashes at Henry and swanned around the place as if he were an heiress on a cruise ship instead of a waiter schlepping heavy plates of food). Keith had tattoos from when he was in the Navy, he was covered in scars, his nose had been broken in fights, he was a battered guy who'd seen it all, and here we were whining about a fucked-up transmission and a broken hand. Because of our ineptitude, he now had to work the kitchen all night alone after working there all day. He very understandably sighed and acted put-upon, but he didn't fire us, and he didn't get mad. He was a saint about it, and we felt like bratty little pussies.

After the van was towed away, we spent a few hours in the nearby hospital. With Henry's hand in a cast, we walked along the highway from the hospital to a convenience store and a liquor store, then holed up for the night in a nearby motel, eating Doritos and smoking and drinking cheap vodka with orange juice and watching made-for-TV movies. We stayed up all night; we felt too guilty about missing our shift to sleep. We called Keith at six in the morning, after we knew the rush was over and the place was empty and he was sitting around smoking cigarettes and drinking coffee, and told him (our voices slurred, on the verge of alcohol-inspired tears) that we loved him. He told us to shut the fuck up and get our asses back to town, now.

We got the first bus back to Portland and went straight to Roxy Hearts, contrite and pale. We told Keith to go home, we'd finish his shift. Henry's hand was broken, of course, so I did most of the cooking and let him do the setups and garnishes. We worked the rest of that day and all night. After we hosed down the grease-covered rubber mats, bagged and took out the trash, prepped for Keith's shift, scrubbed the countertops and degreased the grills, we said a bleary hello to Keith and went out into the drizzling gray early morning and walked to Pioneer Courthouse Square and got a bus back to Southeast Portland.

We were feeling too sad, brokenhearted, and codependent to sleep by ourselves in our own apartments, so we both went to Henry's, where he loaned me a pair of pajamas and a clean toothbrush. After we took showers, Henry pulled down his Murphy bed and made up a comfy foam pad for me on the floor. We slept all day, a whole eight-hour stretch, then woke up feeling groggy and seasick and took the bus back to Roxy Hearts to eat a big breakfast and drink as much coffee as we could before our shift.

That spring, my mother and Ben began inquiring, whenever we talked on the phone, about my plans for the coming year, by which they meant school year, by which they meant graduate school. I told them I didn't really know; maybe I'd move to San Francisco and get a job as a cocktail waitress. That was what I was doing now in Portland, serving drinks in a blues bar called the Last Hurrah, making more money than I'd ever made before. This seemed like a viable option to me, but they both, on different extensions, made it clear that they felt strongly that I should at least apply somewhere for something.

So I took the GREs and used two stories from my Reed senior thesis, since I hadn't written anything since then, to apply to the Iowa Writers' Workshop. Then I forgot all about it and started thinking about moving to San Francisco. When I got the acceptance letter from Iowa, I was already despairing about how hard it would be to start over, alone, not really knowing the city at all, since we'd left the Bay Area before I turned eight. I carried the letter across the Reed campus, rereading it, stunned and ablaze. Then I got another letter informing me that I had been awarded a research assistantship, which paid four hundred dollars a month, enough to live on. I was also thereby qualified to pay in-state tuition, most of which I could take out loans to cover. My mother and Ben offered to help with tuition as well.

At the end of that summer, in late August 1987, Kip (who had just graduated, and who no doubt saw me as the perfect means to postpone having to figure out what to do with his own life) and I bought a VW hatchback and put all our things in it and moved to Iowa City together.

## CHAPTER 38

## The Workshop

———— Iowa City was a flat little town filled with sorority girls with bleached perms and fake tans; burly frat boys in Hawkeye football jerseys; and a substratum of dark, gothy kids with tattoos, dyed-black hair, and motorcycle boots. Wide, straight, tree-lined streets paralleled the Iowa River and were bisected by others in neat lines. All the restaurants in town were terrible. There was one I liked called the Hamburg Inn, a classic American greasy spoon that served good eggs and hash browns for breakfast and good hamburgers and fries for dinner, but that was about it.

The Writers' Workshop itself was terrifying, chilly, and competitive. It was housed on the third floor of a gigantic Soviet-bloc-era–like building called EPB, the English-Philosophy Building, that overlooked the river, a gloomy gray bulwark with oblong-porthole windows. The hallways were bleak and cold, the classrooms modern and drab. Being in a roomful of other ambitious, dedicated writers felt like being in a zoo, stared at by all the other zoo animals. I'd always hated being watched, preferred being the observer, but now I felt the eyes of people just like me on me, observing the same sorts of things I was observing about them. It was disconcerting and unpleasant. Walking into a workshop felt like stepping into a minefield. I had heart palpitations, stage fright. Workshop parties were no better. I was even afraid to go to readings.

Kip and I rented the ground-floor apartment of an old house on Davenport Street near campus for $425 a month. The only bathroom was downstairs at the very end of the basement, and there was no bedroom. Kip built us a bed, which we installed next to the built-in dining room hutch. We ate in the kitchen, and I wrote in the living room. I went to my weekly workshop with Frank Conroy, whose first year as program director this was, and to my contemporary short-story class, while Kip looked for a carpentry job, scouring want ads and bulletin boards. At night, we sat at our kitchen table and furrowed our brows at each other, both of us wondering what we were doing here.

Then I made two friends—first Sally, a brilliant, hilarious, wild-blond-haired Czech girl from Missouri who had lived in New York for years and was worldly and sophisticated and wore a lot of black lacy things, but who also was a Christian fundamentalist who believed fervently in God and lived in a cabin outside town and decorated her one big room with bare branches. Her writing was wildly gorgeous, exalted and original. Then Gretchen befriended me one day after workshop in the hallway by giving me a sideways high five. She was a wry, sultry, kind, tough-minded poet from Oklahoma who'd gone to a women's college and wore hot-pink glasses and wrote clear-sighted, discursive, passionate poetry. Gretchen and Sally were my sources of love and support at that scary place. Sally and I sat in the student union café all afternoon over salads and iced tea, having pensive, exalted, speculative conversations about love and writing. We took walks along the Iowa River and described our childhoods to each other. Gretchen called me up late at night after I was asleep, and announced that I'd better get dressed because she was picking me up in ten minutes and we were going to a truck stop on the highway to eat breakfast and play jukebox country songs and flirt with truckers. She and I went to country auctions and bid on dish towels

and knickknacks; I developed a crush on the walleyed auction-
eer. All three of us talked about men, constantly: we couldn't
figure them out. But it seemed urgent that we do so as soon as
possible.

Kip, meanwhile, arranged to audit a physics class and got
a minimum-wage job working for a taciturn carpenter who
seemed to hate him. He left the house before dawn every morning and came home exhausted and despondent. For dinners,
we generally made variations on *Moosewood Cookbook* hippie
food, three-bean chili or pasta with vegetable tomato sauce or
chickpea mush; we were equally ascetic and low maintenance
about food. We invited friends over sometimes or went to their
houses. Kip's and my dinner parties often devolved, alas, into
sing-alongs, when Kip got out his guitar and folk songbook, but
everyone was very nice about it and chimed in on "A fox went
out on a chilly night" without protest.

One late fall night, at another dinner party, a fellow fiction
writer named Ann Packer served a rice dish of spicy sausages
and shrimp and chicken all together. She called it jambalaya.
It was amazing, and I had never heard of it before. Cajun food
hadn't caught on yet. She'd cut the recipe out of a food magazine, she told me, and it was easy to make and she'd be happy
to share it. In that midwestern college town of pizza and bad
Mexican food and cheeseburgers, that meal was a bright spot of
sustenance, a spark of inspiration I saved in the back of my mind
for later on, someday, when I once again returned to food.

Kip lasted with me until winter, and then he got fed up
with his crappy job, the horrible weather, and the podunk university town. He moved back to Palo Alto and instantly got
a great job renovating someone's house. I was sad and lonely
without him. I pined for him, called him all the time, wrote
him letters. When summer came, I went out to the Bay Area
to live with him. His father hired us to install an oak floor in

his kitchen; we house-sat and took care of pets for a number of people Kip knew in Palo Alto and La Honda. I was churlish and anxious all summer. I knew perfectly well that Kip wasn't in love with me, wasn't even particularly attracted to me, but I could not accept this as the final verdict. I kept thinking that if I did something differently, better, if I broke through his sweetly opaque, maddeningly unavailable facade . . .

I saw my father again that summer. I called him to let him know I was there. He instantly said that we should get together. One evening, he drove from San Francisco out to Half Moon Bay, where Kip's family lived, and picked me up and took me to dinner at a seafood restaurant nearby on the water. I ordered something cheap and had just one glass of wine, since I wasn't sure how much money my father had. As always, he was impersonally affable, mildly interested in my life, distant, and hard to connect with. I was shy and itchy with him. I had no idea what to say to him, and by now it had begun to dawn on me that it wasn't all up to me to try to break through to this man. Naturally, I didn't make any sort of leap of association to my current romantic relationship, which was limping along, leaning heavily on my one-sided, blind adoration.

"I saw your half sister Thea a little while ago," my father told me. "She came to the Bay Area and looked me up, just like you did. About a month ago."

"Thea!" I said. I had always wanted to know my half sisters. "What does she look like?"

"She looks like us," he said. "Like a Johansen."

At the end of the meal, my father was abruptly rude to the waitress. I was, daughterlike, mortified at his brusqueness. It was the most real, honest, nonfraught thing I'd felt with him since I was a little girl. I felt a quick intimation of what it might have been like if he'd been willing and able to be a real father to me, the complicated, interesting, bone-deep luxury of being embarrassed by him. I might have told him he'd been rude. He might have teased me for being critical. I might have laughed and told him to be nicer. And so forth.

Instead, my father dropped me off back at Kip's. We hugged good-bye stiffly, and then he drove off, and I never saw him again.

A week or so later, as Kip and I were finishing up the floor at his father's house, I got a phone call from an editor in New York City. "I'm calling from *Mademoiselle* magazine," she said. "We've been trying to track you down for weeks! Finally!"

"You have?" I asked blankly.

I had won their fiction contest, which meant a prize of one thousand dollars and the publication of my story, "Bowling with the Barracudas," in their magazine. A writer named Michael Chabon had won it the year before; I'd liked his story, so on a whim I'd entered the contest with an autobiographical story I'd written about a cocktail waitress in Portland who witnesses the stabbing of a young gay man in the street. I'd forgotten all about it. Frank Conroy hadn't thought much of my story—had disliked it very much, in fact—so I didn't expect anything to come of it.

This windfall came at just the right time. I was anxiously broke, trying to figure out how to get back to Iowa at the end of the summer, and how to pay September rent on my new apartment. And now I'd be published; the thrill of that took a while to sink in and disappeared as soon as it happened, when I realized that publishing my work opened me to an entire new world of scary exposure.

My story, now renamed "Temptations" and severely edited by three imperious New York women, ran that fall, when I was back at the workshop. Shortly afterward, I was having a drink with my friends Gretchen and Ned at the Fox Head, the workshop hangout. Ned's girlfriend, Mary, a severely plain, relent-lessly self-important poetess, turned to me.

"I saw your story in the magazine," she said. She had never paid attention to me before.

"Oh," I said, immediately nervous and flattered and hopeful.

"Yeah," she said, "I tried to read it."

Then she ignored me again.

## CHAPTER 39

## Black's Gaslight Village

During the first semester of my second year at Iowa, I took a workshop class with Allan Gurganus, who immediately became my favorite teacher there. He was dapper and ebullient and always wore a different tie to each workshop. He was also a warm, inspired teacher, opinionated, brilliant, funny; he loved real writing, hated pretentiousness. He encouraged visceral emotion, humor, real old-fashioned storytelling, rolled his eyes at cerebral formal coldness, egotistical displays of technique. He didn't care what the literary trends and fashions were. He cared about what was good.

At our end-of-semester conference, when we were invited one by one to his house to sit in front of his fireplace in armchairs and discuss our progress, or lack thereof, through the past semester, I sat in his living room by the fire and burst into tears and choked out that I couldn't write. My boyfriend, Kip, whom I so madly and irrationally loved, had just broken up with me. He'd moved home to the Bay Area the year before, of course, but I had kept hoping I'd join him there after the workshop ended. I had hoped we'd get married and have babies. However, Kip had recently told me, during an excruciating late-night phone call that had lasted more than two hours because I was crying and refused to let him hang up until he changed his mind, which he couldn't do, that he had fallen in love with his best friend's girlfriend, a nineteen-year-old blond

California girl who was the same age as most of my Intro to Literature students. Apparently, Kip's best friend was just as upset
as I was by this, but Kip didn't seem overly concerned about
either of us. In fact, he had sounded unemotional at first, and
finally impatient with my inability to comprehend this until
he had repeated it many times: he did not intend to marry me,
ever, and our relationship was really over.

A week later, I was still in a state of raw, disbelieving,
heartsick, choking shock. I hadn't seen it coming. I hadn't let
myself, hadn't been able to face it, and so I'd been caught off
guard. I had loved him since my freshman year of college, this
lithe, funny, golden, nerdy, earnest, selfish, unattainable boy.
Now that he was lost to me forever, I constantly felt like throwing up.

"Trust me," Allan said. "Heartbreak doesn't matter in the
end. What matters is that you keep writing. You've got to get
back to work." He laughed. "Always remember: getting famous
is the best revenge."

Somehow, hearing this, I felt a very small but very deep
jolt of hope. Not at the idea of being famous but at the fact that
Allan seemed to understand heartbreak; it was obvious to me
that he spoke from experience. He had survived it, and so I
could, too. He made me feel as if we belonged to a small, hardy
tribe of people who kept writing, no matter what, and thereby
triumphed over adversity. I left feeling heartened and cheered.

That year, I lived in the legendary Black's Gaslight Village on the edge of town, a romantic, picturesque cluster of
haunted, tumbledown buildings set back from the hilly street
in a copse of large old tattered trees. It was the former home
of many literary luminaries and the site of former drug and
alcohol abuse, scandalous affairs, and outrageous behavior. I
tamely, quietly occupied a second-floor apartment in the back
of the rambling old main house, a recently built addition without character, charm, or romantic history. My friend Sally

called it "the double-wide." My friend Gretchen crinkled her nose at it.

I loved it: it was a big, rectangular box, one big room plus a galley kitchen and bathroom at one end, exactly the size, shape and general ambience of a trailer, with wood paneling, a thick rat-colored carpet, huge windows that overlooked the back parking lot, and a pink little bathtub I spent hours in, sipping Jim Beam and reading detective novels, when I wasn't playing solitaire on my bed, screening my calls, or standing in the tiny kitchen making bean burritos with boiled frozen peas on the side, which seemed to be all I ate that year.

I had become addicted to detective novels. In many ways, they were the adult version of children's adventure stories—instead of going off on adventures in giant peaches or in boats or inside the wardrobe, there was a crime to be solved. Like Huck Finn and Pippi Longstocking, a fictional detective was no decent, responsible citizen; he was a loner, sealed off with no-goodniks and perps in a shadowy underworld of lawless derring-do, tracking the murderer by trying to think like one. Often a former cop who'd been kicked off the force for breaking the rules and flaunting protocol one too many times, often picking up the pieces of a failed marriage, the detective was courageous and intrepid but flawed, self-destructive, prickly, hard drinking, at odds with everything.

And almost all fictional detectives knew how to eat. Marlowe armed himself for stakeouts with ham-and-cheese sandwiches and a bottle of whiskey; V. I. Warshawski escaped danger and made a beeline for a Hungarian goulash at the Golden Glow; Kinsey Millhone girded her loins for trouble by slapping together a peanut butter and pickle sandwich. Robert B. Parker's Spencer ate as grandly as he spouted half-pretentious literary allusions, and I loved him for it; I hated his psychotherapist girlfriend, however, because she nibbled at a lettuce leaf and called it a meal. Smugly self-denying asceticism was a character flaw that seemed to me akin to meanness or hypocrisy. If I had one criticism of Dick Francis, it was that his narrators, being jockeys who had to make weight, were therefore career anorectics; there was never enough food in his novels, although his heroes often craved it, which endeared them to me somewhat.

Often, as I sat in my bathtub in Black's Gaslight Village, my fridge almost empty and my stomach rumbling, I daydreamed about my own detective alter ego's stakeout provisions. She would take a loaf of rye bread, a package of pastrami, a package of sliced Swiss cheese, a jar of mayonnaise, and a jar of mustard, and slap together three thick, hearty sandwiches oozing with mayo and wrap them in wax paper, put them in a big paper sack with a large bag of potato chips, a small pack of chocolate doughnuts, an apple, and a bottle of rye whiskey; and then, on the way to the address in question, she'd stop for a large Styrofoam cup of strong, black coffee, add whiskey to it, and drink it and eat the doughnuts on the way to the perp's address.

And by she, of course, I meant me. In the front seat of my 1974 Chevy Nova, at 11:00 p.m., without taking my eyes off the suspect's darkened windows, I'd eat one of the sandwiches, alternating bites with handfuls of potato chips and sips of whiskey. I would repeat this at 4:00 a.m. At 7:45 a.m., I'd eat the third sandwich and the rest of the potato chips and finish whatever was left of the whiskey. When the suspect appeared in his doorway at 8:27 and headed for his 1972 Camaro, I'd throw the apple out the window, put my car in gear, and tail him.

While my passion for food in literature ran wild, I believed back then that if I allowed myself to indulge it in real life at all, even a little, it would quickly balloon out of control. I had not forgotten being "husky," which I associated with depression, homesickness, drudgery, loneliness, adolescence, and lack of control over my own life. If I couldn't feel at ease in my surroundings, if I couldn't leapfrog myself into my compelling fantasy of my future life as a successful writer living in New York, at least I could eat stringently.

So I lived like a mouse hiding from a stalking cat. The longer I stayed at the workshop, the more morbidly terrified I felt there. Mary's reaction to my story was all too typical; except for my group of friends, the workshop was not a friendly place. The director, Frank Conroy, did not acknowledge female writers at all except to dismiss our writing as "little coming-of-age novels" (which was true; that's exactly what most of us were writing, but somehow it never occurred to me that of course his own first book, *Stop-Time*, had been a little coming-of-age novel). He palled around with the guys. They played pool together, they got drunk together, they lavishly praised one another's writing; it was a man's world, a boy's network.

Meanwhile, Frank wouldn't look women in the eye. It was as if we were invisible to him, except in workshop, where he tore us down. And the playing field wasn't level: there were the big men and women on campus who had published and were from New York and had connections and agents, and then there were those of us who had come from nowhere and were just beginning to write and wondered if we'd ever catch up.

In the wake of Kip's rejection of me, probably due to the combination of bleak, daunting midwestern weather and the bleak, daunting workshop weather inside EPB, by my fourth and last semester, I had fallen into a deep depression. I was hardly going to workshop or class at all, avoiding parties and the Fox Head, hardly leaving my apartment except to teach my English class or to see Gretchen or Sally or my new, terrible, sexy boyfriend, Adam.

After Kip had dumped me, I had instantly moved on to the next self-annihilating source of heartbreak and pain, like a homing pigeon seeking the familiar. Adam was a fellow writer in the workshop. He had already slept with Gretchen and Sally, both of whom had his number and didn't much care for it, but their eye-rolling disapprobation naturally didn't deter me from him. He knew how to make sushi. He rode a motorcycle. He was sad-eyed and Irish-Jewish and handsome in a skinny, feline way, and he had been a biochemist before he became a writer. He had a tragic family history. Most important, he seemed to think very little of me and to enjoy putting me in my place. This last quality was catnip to me and a clarion call to arms: I was determined to win his respect, to prove to him how worthy I was, to break through his impenetrably dense self-involvement. Also, he confirmed my worst opinions of myself, which satisfied my deep self-loathing.

From our first encounter, we became embroiled in a psychodramatic welter of dissonance and incompatibility and thermonuclearly hot sex. Whenever we felt a schism between us, which was constantly, he informed me I had problems with men, and therefore it was all my fault; he compared me, constantly and unfavorably, to his past girlfriend, Sherri, who'd broken his heart and with whom he was still madly in love. He told me I was elitist. He disparaged my writing and was self-important about his own. My journal from that last semester at the Iowa Writers' Workshop, which was the only thing I wrote the entire time, is filled with entries in which I tied myself into convoluted psychic knots, trying to understand why he hurt me so much, why I let him, why it mattered.

During a late spring thunderstorm with bolts of lightning so close, the air smelled of ozone and flashed all around us, we lay naked on my white couch and sucked each other's toes slowly, one by one. On Valentine's Day, not caring how clichéd it was, I bought strawberry-flavored edible massage oil and slutty lingerie and went to his apartment; we stayed up all night long doing everything we could think of to each other. He let himself into my apartment when he was drunk and got into bed with me and fucked me while I was sleeping; I awoke to find him there, and instead of yelling "rape" and kicking him out, I responded with melting ardor. I ignored the fact that he had slept with half the women in Iowa City and could very well give me some kind of disease. This was intense, this was real. I couldn't get enough of it; this kind of sex was addictive—it was half hateful, half desperate, and to me, it felt dangerous and thrilling, which I mistook for love.

One warm night in May, Sally cooked a Thanksgiving dinner, a roasted turkey with all the trimmings, including pumpkin and apple pie, for about ten of us, our group of friends. I relaxed my guard that night and allowed myself to eat as much as I wanted. We all sat around her long table, glutted and happy and drunk on red wine. Our friend Jim Hynes read a Wallace Stevens poem aloud, "The Rabbit as King of the Ghosts." There was a silence when he finished. It was a strangely perfect moment, spooky and calm. Outside, a full moon blazed. The workshop was almost over; we'd all survived it.

Despite my playing hooky at the end, I somehow, for reasons I've never understood, graduated from the workshop with a 4.0 grade point average. I didn't officially get my M.F.A., though, having to do with some tuition payment I never got around to making until many years later.

That August, Ben and Susan and I found ourselves alone at Tuckernuck, all of us heartbroken and obsessing and spinning in our separate hells: my mother had finally left Ben for good that year, and Susan and I were both pining for our exboyfriends; Adam and I had broken up when I left Iowa City. The weather was chilly and rainy and windy the whole time we were there. Susan and I sat at the little yellow kitchen table and listened to Portuguese music and weather reports on the New Bedford radio station and played gin rummy. Ben read through his next semester's syllabus in his wingback chair in the library, waggling his foot, letting out great, gusty sighs all day. We cooked lackluster little meals, mostly soups. Nobody had much appetite, and nobody felt like drinking much wine, either. We hadn't shopped wisely at the beginning and kept running out of things: butter, rice, carrots, cornmeal. There were no fresh-caught fish, no quahog chowder, no long hot afternoons on the beach with picnic lunches and bracing swims in the cold surf, no sunset cocktail croquet games with gleeful shouts from my mother when she whacked an opponent's ball into the tick-infested shrubbery. I kept up the four p.m. Hu-Kwa teatime, but only as a formality and source of warmth. We were like three damp, chilly dogs, skulking around, making high keening noises.

---

## BEAN BURRITO

Open a can of refried beans. Spread ⅓ of the can in an oblong shape on a gigantic flour tortilla. Grate as much cheddar cheese as you want and pack it into the refried beans. Add a layer of pickled sliced jalapeños from a jar. Roll the burrito up by tucking in the outer edges and then rolling it like a joint so the flaps are underneath it. Fry it flap-side down in plenty of oil in a hot skillet on medium-low heat. When it's brown and crisp on that side, flip it and do the same to the other. Smother it in hot sauce and salsa and, if you want a vegetable, serve it with a side of hot, buttered peas. Serves one.

---

## SPINACH PIE

*I made this savory, cheesy pie, which I found in Mollie Katzen's* Moosewood Cookbook *and adapted slightly, as often as I could through the years when I was living in Spencertown with my mother and Emily, and then as a college and graduate school student. It's cheap and quick and filling, and very nourishing and warming on a freezing cold winter night. It's also incredibly good.*

Sauté a minced onion in plenty of olive oil. Add one thawed 10-ounce package of chopped spinach with a dash each of cayenne pepper, basil, and nutmeg and plenty of salt and black pepper.

In a bowl, beat together a pound of ricotta cheese, ¾ cup of grated cheddar, and 4 eggs. Add the spinach and onion mixture and stir.

Turn into a pie shell, store bought or homemade, and bake for 40–45 minutes at 375 degrees, until golden brown on top.

# PART SEVEN

# New York

## CHAPTER 40

## In the Drink

On September 1, just after I turned twenty-seven, I moved to New York to start my life as a writer. My first apartment in New York was a share on St. Marks Place between Third and Fourth Avenues, a bleak, scruffy, unnamed neighborhood between downtown Brooklyn and Park Slope. It was a long, spacious place with a kitchen and sitting room at one end and a large living room at the other, and two bathrooms and three bedrooms off a very long hallway. As the newcomer, I got the bedroom in the middle, which had no windows, but it did have an electric ceiling fan, and it was absolutely quiet in there at night, sheltered from all the street noise, the salsa music blaring from cars, the yelling and honking and occasional gunfire. I furnished my bedroom piecemeal, mostly with stuff I dragged in off the street: milk crates, a futon frame, a beat-up blue bureau. I didn't care that it was a dark little hole: it was mine.

My roommates were two women, Sam and Anne, whom I had barely known at Reed. They had been in New York much longer than I had and were now my lifelines to a social world. Sam was a painter who worked as an assistant to other, more famous painters, and Anne was a copy editor at *Spy* magazine. They had boyfriends, sort of, or girlfriends, sort of. They knew how to talk to the guys who played cards at a folding table in front of the corner bodega when they ran in to buy cigarettes, cans of Café Bustelo, and milk. They knew where to get the best Vietnamese *pho* in the city, how to shop for fish and vegetables in Chinatown. They brought home pink plastic bags of wondrous things—bok choy, squid, whole fish, rice noodles, and bottles of dark, exotic sauces.

Anne was elegant, chic, and understated; Sam was wild and urchinlike. They both had short blond hair. Anne's was cut in a fetching new-wave pixie; Sam's was self-inflicted with nail scissors and sometimes dyed neon orange or green. Anne invited me to snarky, intimidating writers' shindigs; Sam took me to druggy downtown loft parties.

They struck me as knowing and arrived. I tagged along with them and watched their behavior, squirreling it away into a storehouse of knowledge I was trying to amass. Anne was cool and arch and ironic; I was much closer to Sam. She and I sometimes stayed up all night, talking and drinking and smoking together. After she went to sleep at nearly dawn, I wrote unintentionally hilarious journal entries, the pages of which are now crinkly with spilled vodka, barely legible, describing what it felt like to be totally shit faced. I was so transparently hungry for experience, extremes, Life with a capital *L*. I was young enough to think that other people were the answer, that I couldn't find what I was looking for unless I opened myself up to people who knew more than I did and allowed them to define and influence and impress themselves upon me.

I met James early on at a downtown party that Sam took me to. She instantly disliked him. He was four years older than I was, a Choate- and Georgetown-educated aspiring screenwriter from Connecticut who had moved to New York in the early eighties and liked to reminisce about the "old days," back when New York was cool, exciting, happening. It made me feel as if I'd missed the whole party. But I hadn't, I knew; it was still in full swing.

When we met, James happened to be living with his ex-girlfriend, although I wasn't so sure about the "ex" part, since she wasn't supposed to know about me. It should have been a red flag (there were many), but I was too young and naive to pay much attention. He was helping me get over Adam, since we'd broken up when I moved to New York. And I felt a sense of camaraderie with James. We were both frustrated young writers who thought we were much smarter than we were, which engendered a kind of chaotic melancholy that needed blotting out. Consequently, we drank—a lot. After drinking only beer on weekends in high school, almost nothing in college, and one glass of Jim Beam at a time in grad school, I started getting soused and blotto on a regular, almost nightly, basis.

One night, I chugged a whole bottle of Jameson in a stall in the ladies' room of some club in midtown at some show, it could have been the Fall, it could have been Richard Thompson, it could have been the Mekons. I saw almost everyone perform live at least once back then. James constantly won free tickets to shows from radio stations by being the fourth or ninth or eleventh caller and giving a different name every time. He possessed an uncanny genius for speed-dialing. The first show he took me to, the Jayhawks on Ludlow Street, I recognized that I hated hearing music in bars. I preferred to listen to recorded music in a quiet room where I could actually hear it. Bar music was too loud, distorted, and raw—I hated having to make conversation while a band was playing, hated feeling deaf for hours afterward. But I kept saying yes whenever James asked me to go.

That whole year, and for several years to come, my life consisted of loud music and a lot of booze, and then impersonal, physically demanding sex afterward with more booze, and then I'd go on the subway to my mindless job the next day. At my desk at work, I'd call the deli downstairs and order my favorite postbender breakfast: a Western omelet sandwich on toasted rye with extra ketchup. With it, I'd drink an enormous, sweet, milky cup of coffee, and get on with my day, and then I'd walk down Broadway after work through streets crammed with people and shop windows and noises and traffic and smells and do it all again that night.

Somehow, all this drinking seemed to have no effect on my physical health, at least not in any way I could feel. Despite my poor eating habits and excessive drinking and smoking, I rarely got sick. Hangovers were almost unknown to me except as a pleasant, muzzy state with life's edges blunted—almost a better reason to drink than getting drunk the night before. Luckily, I never blacked out; unluckily, this meant I usually remembered much of the night. I was a terrible drunk, in that I acted outrageously and stupidly; I imagine I was a pain in the ass, but I was too drunk to know it. I thought I was witty and carefree and madcap, oh dear.

I drank excessively out of my chronic and ongoing sense of self-loathing, to escape myself, to flee the annoying chirpiness of my too clear, too verbal brain, so recently educated, so freshly imbued with the powers of literary analysis and writerly dogma. I had never been bad in my life before; I'd always been the responsible firstborn daughter of a single mother, and as a kid I worried that, if I didn't keep it together, it might all fall apart. In my late twenties, I finally realized that I didn't have to pretend I could help anyone by being good anymore. I realized I had no control over anything at all, even my own fate, and so I let myself totally lose control for the first time in my life.

My first job, shortly after I arrived in New York, was as an editorial assistant at William Morrow on Twenty-eighth and Madison for a starting salary of $17,500 a year. I got hired thanks to strings pulled by my stepfather, Ben, who'd been an editor in New York for many years before he started teaching at Bard. I had an hour-long commute to work every morning, when I took the 4 or 5 train from the Atlantic Avenue station and switched to the 6 at Fourteenth Street. Sometimes my boss, a tiny, brilliant, doe-eyed editor named Susan, asked me to stay late, but only rarely. Usually, I left the office at five sharp and took the elevator down to the street. On the sidewalk, I put on my Walkman and headed down Broadway, the spine of Manhattan, to catch the subway to Brooklyn from South Ferry at the tip of Manhattan Island. I pressed Play and flooded my head with music, my own personal soundtrack to my nightly walk through Madison Square Park, the carpet district, Union Square, the East Village, and SoHo, then across Canal to the windy, empty, trash-blown streets of Tribeca, and finally the deserted, tiny, crooked streets of the Financial District, with its sheer-sided skyscrapers and old churches, all the way down to New York Harbor.

I loved this time of day. Leaving work meant shucking off my office persona, whatever that was, and returning to my daydreamy, solitary, observant, anxious, arrogant self. It was a glittering, colorful, dramatic walk every day. I never got tired of it. It was all new to me, this city, this life I had chosen for myself and embarked upon. I had no history here yet; it was all mine for the making. I was thin and aerodynamic, streamlined. I knifed along the sidewalk, impatiently skirting slower walkers and darting through traffic, away from my work life and toward whatever adventures lay ahead that night. I listened to my favorite tape, the same one every day: "Flying Cowboys," by Rickie Lee Jones. Walking down Broadway day after day, I tried to wear a groove, make a physical mark of some kind on the city, while "Flying Cowboys" made a parallel groove in my head of jazzy, ethereal, hopeful music. When I got to the station at South Ferry, I took off my Walkman—the train lurched and screeched its way under the river—and both Broadway and music closed themselves to me like something disappearing underwater, slipping back into itself, untouched by me and not mine to keep.

Although I'd supported myself, of course with some tuition and other help from my mother, for the past eleven years, working at William Morrow felt like my first real job. For the first time, I had a taxable salary and benefits, a nine-to-five, five-day-a-week schedule. As work went, it was easy and undemanding. Susan was a generous, fair, uncritical boss, which was a lucky thing for me because, to put it mildly, I was a lackluster editorial assistant, which is to say, my heart was not in it. My only real usefulness to Susan was that I had a great knack for quickly reading and articulately rejecting manuscripts. Her office was crammed full of boxes and boxes of these labored-over, sweat-stained, treasured would-be books. I saw it as my Sisyphean mission to get rid of these boxes as fast as I could, but of course their supply refilled as quickly as I could empty them.

Susan seemed to have an excellent life, a career it might have done me well to aspire to if I hadn't had other, more egotistical and less practical ideas. She arrived at 10:00 or so every morning on the train from Larchmont, made a lot of phone calls, worked on editing and writing jacket copy, wrote letters, and then, at noon, went out to have lunch in restaurants I had never set foot in and wouldn't dream of venturing into. I made reservations for her there, and found myself imagining the food as I waited on hold for the French-accented, vaguely snooty person who would write down her name and the time; Periyali was the one that most caught my imagination. Every time I called them, I sat with visions of grilled octopus, which I had never eaten, dancing in my head: stuffed grape leaves, grilled sardines, roasted potatoes. . . . I might have become an editor if the entire job had consisted of going out to lunch.

But it didn't matter to me whether or not I succeeded as an editorial assistant. I was just biding my time here. As soon as

I really started to write, as soon as I shook the earnest dust of the M.F.A. program out of my brain and "found my voice," as everyone was so fond of saying at Iowa, I wouldn't need it anymore. I looked at the towering stacks of manuscripts in Susan's office and thought, *I'll be better than all of them.*

If I had known that my first novel wouldn't be published for another ten years, I might have jumped out the window.

## CHAPTER 41

## The Countess

———— The following fall, when our lease was up, Sam and Anne and I disbanded our household and found our own apartments. Anne moved to Cobble Hill, and Sam and I both moved north to Williamsburg. I lived on Graham Avenue just off Metropolitan, above a Laundromat, in a small one-bedroom apartment with a skylight in the tiled bathroom, a parquet floor, and a roof deck outside my bedroom door. It cost $350 a month. I had hardly any furniture; the kitchen had no refrigerator, so I only bought whatever food I could eat immediately. It never occurred to me that refrigerators were cheap and that you could have one delivered; everything was so provisional and tentative for me back then. I never planted anything on the roof deck.

I had no money because I was profligate and careless with my paychecks, so I was consequently often late with my rent. My landlord was a ginger-haired, irascible, borderline-psychotic guy who looked like a stupid Vincent van Gogh. He owned the Laundromat and was always there. When I came in to give him my week-late rent in cash (he no longer accepted checks from me), I had to walk past the rows of washers and dryers, all the people sitting in the plastic molded chairs or standing at tables folding laundry. No one ever said a word in there; every pair of eyes tracked my hangdog progress to the little office in the back. It was my own version of the Walk of Shame.

Back in those days, Williamsburg was old-world Brooklyn, a profoundly local place. Italian guys sat in lawn chairs, smoking cigars and drinking Peroni; black-haired women in cotton housedresses carried bulging shopping bags along the sidewalks. I felt very safe in that part of Williamsburg; all local crime was in the hands of the professionals—but I didn't belong there. I was a stranger in a strange land on Graham Avenue. When I came up out of the L station, I was very obviously the only person to get off at my stop who hadn't been born and raised within a ten-block radius. Graham Avenue felt very far from Manhattan.

There was an Italian deli on the corner between the L stop and my apartment. Because I had no fridge, I did little cooking; and so, on many weekday nights, on my way home from work, I stopped in to the deli to get a sub, some chips, and a few cold bottles of Peroni. The subs were insanely good. I sometimes salivated like a dog, watching the guy build mine. I always asked for everything except tomatoes, since raw tomatoes on a sandwich are cold and wet and unpleasant unless it's the height of summer and they're warm from the sun and perfectly ripe. On a foot-long Italian loaf, soft and white and spongy, he slathered about half a jar each of mustard and mayo and then piled a mound of shredded iceberg, greasy rounds of salami and ham, hot green pepperoncini, and rectangular slabs of provolone. At the end, he squirted oil and vinegar from plastic bottles, sprinkled it with black pepper and salt, folded it closed, rolled it in white paper and taped it shut and cut it in half, then slid it into a paper sack between the beer and the chips. I took my dinner straight home. In warm months, I sat outside on my bare tar roof deck, staring at the sky. I always ate and drank every drop and scrap. Later, I went inside to my hot little apartment to lie in bed with my brain in a snarl of worry and wonderment. I had no idea how my life was going to go, but I knew that no one was going to help me; it was all up to me.

I had left William Morrow after nine months to work as the personal secretary of a countess who lived on Sixty-eighth off Park Avenue in a formidably elegant apartment she referred to as her pied-à-terre even though as far as I could tell, she lived there year-round. I worked five days a week from one to six p.m. for eighteen dollars an hour. Her former secretary, a fellow writer I'd met at a party, had recommended me for the job. The countess, an American native who had been born in Pearl River, NY, had married a Spanish count in the 1940s; they'd met when she worked for the OSS as a decoder in Madrid during World War II. She had an expense account at Balenciaga (she had been a fashion model for Hattie Carnegie before she was recruited); and, after her day in the office, decoding, she went to parties and kept an ear out for useful information. The count was the richest man in Spain. By the time I came to work for her, he was long dead, and she was alone. She wrote nonfiction "spy" novels, purported memoirs of her years working for the OSS.

The countess was tall and narrow hipped and elegant, and she had a magnificent pair of boobs and tailored designer clothes to show off her beautifully maintained figure. She was in her late sixties and she looked like a photoshopped, airbrushed fiftysomething. She was rich, Republican, chic, raven haired, impeccable. She was friends with the likes of Carolina Herrera, Imelda Marcos, Betsy Bloomingdale, and Nancy Reagan. Her books were *New York Times* best sellers, and she was invited to every high-society shindig in New York, Long Island, and Newport, but she often seemed unsure of herself. She screeched at me like a bat out of hell: "Kate! I cannot find my reading glasses! That's three pairs this week! You must be more careful of my things!" or "Kate! I was awake all night thinking of eight things you never did that I had asked you to do, and now I cannot remember what they were! You must *pay more attention*!" She reminded me of the teacher I had lived with in high school, Mary, who had yelled at me constantly and for similar infractions: selfishness, laziness, inattention to detail. The one old sin the countess couldn't fault me on was gluttony: I ate almost nothing all day until after work, and my clothes hung on me. They were terrible clothes, makeshift and hemmed with Scotch tape, but they fit me perfectly in that New York coat-hanger way: I was sharp and angular as a scalpel.

We were both crazy, and we were possibly more alike than either of us wanted to admit, but we intensely disliked each other and deeply disapproved of each other. Nonetheless, the countess and I spent all day alone together, buried in the gold braid and red brocade of her apartment, the dim sunlight refracted off the courtyard walls outside, the acidic, antiseptic smell of the place, the marble floor and urns of branches in her marble, mirrored foyer. She strode around her apartment like a flightless bird, flapping and cawing at me, then in a mad rush of feathers she was gone for a few hours, leaving me to dazedly decipher her scrawled instructions, to run her life when I could not in any way run my own. I was so unsuited to this job it was ludicrous. She only kept me on because I was helping her write her next book, as her previous secretaries had worked on the others. Even when I sent letters to the wrong addresses, screwed up her accounting, and wore unpresentable outfits, I was indispensable to her now, the little church-mouse Rumpelstiltskin who spun her reminiscences ("Let's say there's an accident in the car, maybe someone tampered with the brakes! And later on, the tent falls in because the peg's been cut, right before the king of Morocco comes!") into something like fool's gold. Helping her write her book was the only fun part of my job, the only thing I was remotely good at.

Every day, I left at six after storing my little rolling desk with the laptop under the counter in her pantry with papers, letters, checkbooks, ledger, and calendar stowed away in their places, a neat pile of phone messages and letters to sign left for her inspection on the kitchen table. Being away from the countess's apartment, walking through the normal streets of the city like any other person entitled to breathe the air, I felt like a prisoner whose sentence was served only during afternoon hours and commuted at night, when I was free to roam at will until the next day's incarceration.

On the days she came in, Miguelina, the countess's South American maid, made suppers for the countess, leaving a covered plate of food warming in the oven for her which she would eat alone at her little kitchen table before she went out for the night: a poached chicken breast, broccoli florets with lemon, a baked potato. Otherwise, the countess stuck a frozen lasagna or Lean Cuisine dinner into the oven and ate that. She disparaged Miguelina's Spanish, her "awful South American accent, the way they talk down there is so common and low-class," and accused her, behind her back, to me, of stealing from her. Miguelina spoke no English; I had forgotten most of my high school Spanish, but we formed a quiet alliance of two lackeys. Every now and then, we would exchange a look. That was as far as it went, but I was cheered by the small display of solidarity.

I lasted a year and a half with the countess, long enough to finish writing her book, help usher it to publication and a glowing *New York Times* review with a boxed excerpt of my own writing, and also to endure enough petty humiliations and insults to fuel my determination to succeed for the rest of my life.

Meanwhile, I had left Brooklyn when my lease was up and moved in with James and his ex-girlfriend, into a crappy apartment above a dry cleaners on the Upper West Side of Manhattan. It was a spectacularly demented ménage that had all our friends puzzled on our behalf. In fact, none of my family or friends could stand James. I supposed I could see why objectively, although I felt compelled to defend him, to assure them that there was more to him than it appeared, that he wasn't like that all the time. They all thought he was supercilious, unpleasant, and not at all nice to me or anyone else.

When we fought, it was almost always about money. He disapproved of my profligacy; he took me to task for it, and of course he was right. And he was punitive about it. During the entire time we were together, although he had no debt, a trust fund, and a comfortable if small source of income, reading scripts for HBO, that allowed him to work at home or anywhere he wanted, he never treated me to dinner, except once, on my birthday, but I felt too guilty to order anything but a bowl of chowder. We always, from beginning to end, split everything to the penny: the gas bill, the Early Bird Special at BBQ, the two or three bottles of wine we drank at home every night, the expense of car rentals whenever we went camping or drove anywhere. He paid all his bills the instant they arrived and never bought something he couldn't afford; my debt, which reached about ten thousand dollars at its worst, shocked and dismayed him. I thought nothing of treating a friend to drinks even if I was broke or of buying Christmas presents I couldn't afford, most of them for James. That, I thought, was what my Visa was for. I yearned to have money so I could be as generous and free with it as I wanted and needed to be. James was very good at living within his means, but I didn't see that this made him any happier, so his example failed to rub off on me.

James thought my stories and journal entries (which he read without my permission) were jejune, self-conscious, clichéd, and immature, whereas his work was the real thing, because in his mind he was the genius of our duo, he was an auteur of cinema, he knew how to tell a story with narrative arc. Consequently, he never once took my advice on how to edit his screenplays. He was openly dubious about my ability to make anything of myself, ever. Being unsure of myself, and nowhere near savvy and aware enough to protest, I took it.

As I had with Adam, I wrote long, involved, obsessive journal entries that laid bare every aspect of my life I was unhappy with, cataloged and parsed out and acknowledged what was wrong with me, with everything. This illusion of analytical self-loathing self-awareness gave me a weird, emotionally starved pleasure, similar to the one I got physically from my extreme thinness, denying myself food. It allowed me to feel some modicum of control over my out-of-control life: if I could analyze my situation clearly, I wasn't completely lost. If I didn't eat too much, it proved that I had discipline. Consequently, I became very good at both wallowing and starving.

At twenty-nine, I was like a street dog: undernourished, skittish, unsure of how to behave, wild, afraid to trust, and most comfortable on the street. I'd been in New York for more than two years and had never had a nice meal in a good restaurant. I ate most dinners alone at home—takeout like mu shu vegetables or slices of broccoli pizza with extra Parmesan and hot red pepper flakes, as well as the few odd little things I cooked for myself—squid with rice or steamed vegetables with baked potatoes. On other nights when I didn't feel like cooking, I went to the Puerto Rican takeout place and ordered a big aluminum dish of rice and beans with chicken and extra hot sauce. From the deli next door, I bought a six-pack of Bass Ale, trying and failing not to haggle obnoxiously with the deli guy over the price. I also failed to convince him that his prices were criminal; I bought it anyway. I brought this feast home, took off my shoes, ate everything alone at my rickety little table with bottles of cold beer. I wriggled my feet and shivered with hard-won happiness.

But real, fancy, gourmet food was so far out of my reach, I couldn't imagine ever getting to have it. I walked by French bistros and elegant Italian places and peered furtively inside, dying for anything on the menu—but even if I'd had enough money to eat there, I didn't think they'd let me in. Some childish part of me believed that good restaurants were for other people, real adults who knew how to order properly.

In the fall of 1991, I got a job as the receptionist at yet another Waldorf school, the Rudolf Steiner high school on the Upper East Side. It was there that I started my first real novel, *In the Drink*. It was, of course, semiautobiographical, about a personal secretary and ghostwriter who works for a thinly veiled countess. I spent my lunch hours inside at my desk, writing my novel on a borrowed word processor I brought every day from home, and eating chicken noodle soup with packets of saltines from the deli on Lexington Avenue. It was the only thing I ever ate for lunch on workdays—the broth, salty and rich and golden, the noodles, slippery and filling and warm, the tender chunks of chicken and carrot that gave pleasantly between my teeth, and the saltines, the perfect accompaniment, crunchy and as salty as the broth. I enjoyed this lunch as much as a medieval lord might have enjoyed a plate of perfectly roasted pheasant or duck. And indeed I felt lordly, eating my cardboard vat of hot, savory soup, letting the noodles slide luxuriantly down my gullet, slurping the broth, opening a fifth packet of crackers.

## CHAPTER 42

## East Village Rathole

During the time I started *In the Drink*, I began seeing a therapist, as many people do in New York, and this therapist was very interested in excavating any buried anger at my mother I might have had, as therapists generally are. He didn't have to dig very deeply to find a well of long-suppressed bubbling molten oil. He stuck a pipe in it and tapped it, and it gushed freely forth for the first time in my life. Soon, I was lying awake every night, drunk, my head stuck in a vise of seemingly bottomless anger, my guts roiling. I lay there like a live bug pinned to a corkboard, paralyzed and flailing at the same time. Finally, in my late twenties, I was experiencing what so-called normal adolescents are generally able to go through before they leave home. The timing was unfortunate, but then, I was a late bloomer, and this was my lot.

My mother was now living alone in a big-windowed cabin with a woodstove on a mountainside in Woodstock, and she had started a private psychotherapy practice in Red Hook that was becoming increasingly successful. She was free of Ben finally, after six years of marriage. I wasn't in touch with him these days: his new girlfriend was two years younger than I was, and she was deeply threatened by my sister Susan's and my presence in his life. She had forced him to choose between her and us. Of course, he chose her. This was a hard loss for me;

Ben and I had been close, and whatever problems my mother had had with him, he had been like a real father to me.

Since leaving Ben, my mother had begun calling me too often for my liking, in need of advice, reassurance, and support. I knew that if I didn't call her back soon enough, she would be resentful and hurt, but sometimes I didn't feel like talking to her until several days after I got her message. The needier she got with me, the angrier I got at her: how, I wondered, could she possibly feel entitled to demand anything from me when she had been emotionally unavailable as a mother since I'd hit puberty? I didn't care now what she was going through herself in the wake of her divorce or that she was suffering deeply from the long-delayed effects of the hardships and her own lack of mothering she endured as a child. These things no longer concerned me. I had empathized with her all my life, taken care of her as much as I could, denied my own feelings in order to protect her, and tried never to upset or worry her. Now I was grown up, and so was she—for the first time in my life, I let myself feel all the things I hadn't been able to when I was younger.

Finally, after a particularly guilt-inducing message on my answering machine, I boiled over and wrote her a letter, hard, angry, and forceful: I was her daughter, not her mother. I was done being her caretaker, and she had no right to demand that I give her anything at all. All my life, I'd tried never to ask anything of her emotionally, never to be needy myself. I was sick of feeling guilty and inadequate for not giving her enough support.

I sent it off, a ticking grenade in an envelope. My mother never responded to my letter, which must have exploded in her face, out of nowhere, although these feelings had been building in me for many years. She could have pointed out that she had helped pay for the therapy that had unleashed my rage at her, and that she had never asked me to be self-abnegating with her. I had intuited as a small child a need and hunger in her for the unconditional support she'd always lacked, and had tried to supply it of my own volition. My mother would in fact have done anything to be close to me, and she had always tried to give me whatever I needed, even when it meant she had to go without herself. But I forgot all that now and sank into a burning, twisting black hole of pure and powerful rage.

Stubbornly I refused to contact her until she wrote or called me first. Months went by, and then a year. Just like that, we weren't speaking to each other. This was a relief to me, in a low-down blackhearted sort of way.

Meanwhile, James and I had moved into a minuscule roach-infested studio apartment in the East Village whose rent was only $300 a month. Its two windows looked out onto a fire escape and dim airshaft. Its so-called kitchen was wedged into the tiny foyer: a cube refrigerator, a two-burner stove set into a counter with a tiny corner sink, and a battered set of metal shelves. On one wall were built-in shelves that held our TV, stereo, books, and opposite there was a futon couch that folded down at night. Next to the kitchenette was a small table with two chairs. The floor was covered with a ratty, stained beige carpet when we rented it. While James was away, I spent several nights after work ripping the carpet out and hand-sanding and polyurethaning the hardwood floor. I installed green and white linoleum in the tiny kitchen area and painted the walls a clean, warm off-white.

James was almost never there; his millionaire uncle owned a house in Rhode Island, and it stood empty most of the time, so James decamped up there as often as he could to work on his screenplays, and I stayed behind to eke out my living, half of which went to pay off my credit card debts and student loans, the other half of which went toward rent, food, and alcohol. Whenever I could, I took the train up to Rhode Island for the weekend, a few days, as long as I could afford to stay. Instantly, as soon as I got there, I was relaxed and happy. I loved New England and never wanted to go back to New York—I longed to live there full-time in a little cottage near the ocean and write and take long walks and breathe sea air and eat fresh fish, and never go back to the dirty, noisy, crowded, expensive city again. I loved the wild warmth of the North Atlantic, the deep shaggy woods, the wry sense of humor of the people up there, and the feel of the air by the ocean—clean and briny, fresh and bracing.

We ate well in Rhode Island; it was the only time I allowed myself to cook and eat lavishly and really enjoy food. We bought fresh vegetables from the nearby farm stand, and peppery, oily smoked mackerel and fresh seafood from the fish place in Newport, and *vinho verde* from the Portuguese market in New Bedford. We sat on the wide, shady porch of James's uncle's house and drank bottle after bottle of the light, cold, slightly fizzy wine. We started with smoked mackerel with a baguette, then ate steamed corn and new potatoes, salads of pea shoots and tender butter lettuce and radishes, scallops poached in lemon juice, white wine, fresh herbs, and butter, and a fruit salad of strawberries and peaches. Sometimes we steamed a heap of clams, and sometimes we splurged and bought lobsters.

For a few years in a row, we went to the Cajun and Blue-grass festival in the middle of Rhode Island and saw Vassar Clements and a young Alison Krauss. For the second time in my life, I had jambalaya and remembered the first time I'd eaten it, at Ann's dinner party in Iowa City. We drank big jars of lemonade with bourbon and passed the days in a pleasant haze of great music and gumbo, barbecued ribs, and crawfish. It was the most fun James and I ever had together.

Toward the end of 1992, my sister Susan and I stopped talking to each other. We were both living in the East Village, only ten or so blocks apart. She was dancing professionally with two modern dance companies and waitressing in SoHo. She lived in a cheap, comfortable, sunny walk-up with her long-time filmmaker boyfriend and their two cats. She was thriving, making plenty of money, touring with her dance companies to Eastern Europe and India, and hanging out on her boyfriend's film sets. She seemed, to me anyway, to have her shit together in a way that I profoundly didn't. Whenever my sister and I had dinner together or ran into each other at a party, I could feel how disappointed she was in me, how much my current life of drunken flailing annoyed her, how embarrassed she was by my frank and unstoppable downslide. And she was angry at me for my anger at our mother. She tried to be supportive and understanding when I explained to her why our long silence had come about, but it was clear that she was unhappy about yet another rift in our splintering family and that she blamed me for inflicting more pain on our mother. And without me as a buffer, she had taken my place as our mother's comforter and confidante.

Susan and I had some minor sisterly spat one day over a lunch of pierogies and borscht at a Polish place on Second Avenue, but it was the catalyst we needed to make official what had been happening for years in a subterranean way. We didn't contact each other for so long after that, it became clear to me that we were not speaking to each other now, either. About a year later, I passed her on the street. I saw her, and she saw me, but neither of us said a word. It felt necessary and inevitable. It was, like my silence with my mother, a strange kind of relief for me.

By then, I had long since left my job at the Steiner School (or rather, after I was fired from it, or rather, after I was not asked to return the following year) and had started doing secretarial work through temp agencies around Manhattan for seventeen or eighteen dollars an hour. Temping was freeing and pleasant at first: I loved not having a set schedule and working for temporary bosses who had a transient presence wherever I went. Every morning at home, and during my downtime at work, I worked on my novel. For the first time since junior high, it seemed to me, I was writing in my own voice, the same voice I'd used in eighth grade to make Kenny, my brown-eyed, pudgy crush, laugh in social studies class. Gone was the earnest Iowa Writers' Workshop attempt to be Faulkner, to be Great. I didn't care, suddenly, that I lived in a three-hundred-square-foot studio apartment with a cold, depressive, barely there boyfriend. I was having pure, subversive fun.

Very early, before I had to go to work, I would leap out of bed, having lain awake much of the night on a hamster wheel of panic and inspiration. I made myself strong tea in a large porcelain pot I'd bought in Chinatown, and sat at my little table and drank cup after cup as I read what I'd already written, despaired, edited, chewed my cuticles, and finally wrote another new page, then another. I was sure there must be some secret method, something all the other writers knew, some key to the kingdom I'd find if I only worked hard enough. I burned to write this novel. I *had* to get published. My thirtieth birthday had come and gone, and I hadn't achieved anything. I was afraid I would soon explode in a white-hot burst of frustration.

Sometimes I felt electric with joy at the words that came from my fingers, but most of the time it was agonizing and terrifying. I was driven and frenzied and melodramatically manic-depressive—desperately sure one day that I'd never figure it out, clutching my head and hyperventilating, and the next day, laughing out loud as I wrote and walking through the city afterward feeling exalted.

All day at whatever job I had to go to, I took any opportunity I could get to write edits and ideas as they came to me in the big hardbound notebook I always kept with me. At night after work, I read novel after novel in the bathtub, my brain on fire with Edith Wharton, Penelope Fitzgerald, Muriel Spark, Evelyn Waugh. I collected new words, looked them up in the dictionary, made lists of them: "adamantine," "cloacal," "hieratic"; each new word I acquired and used felt like a nugget of nourishment for the novel. I satirized ideas about things that had always flummoxed me, because I didn't like them and wanted to articulate why—Freudian theory, *The Wasteland*, Easter. As inspiring good-luck touchstones, I held both *Jane Eyre* and the Kingsley Amis novel *Lucky Jim* in my head at all times.

My narrator, Claudia, whose circumstances were not altogether different from my own, but who was fictional and invented rather than autobiographical, was a helpful, comforting embodiment and extension of my own troubles; I made her problems much worse than my own, and so I was able to subsume my fears, channel them into my work. Like Claudia, I was completely alone in the world, severed from my family, almost friendless, a hermit, essentially single since my boyfriend was in Rhode Island (sleeping with some other woman, I found out later). And maybe because I was so free and alone, because absolutely no one was watching, I was now truly writing, and writing well, for the first time in my life. I was discovering how good it feels to invent characters and set them in motion, how the parts of my life that were messiest and most difficult to fix could be wrangled, shaped, and made useful, artful, fictional. My novel was like a live thing in my mind that demanded to be fed and tended to and nurtured constantly. Its needs eclipsed everything else. And no one else was going to do this for me. I was luckily naturally suited for this sort of stubborn, solitary, obsessive work, but there was never any guarantee of payoff, and the idea of failure gave me cold sweats in the middle of the night.

## CHAPTER 43

## The Boy Next Door

In 1994, I was making a lot of money at a full-time corporate job, working on the fiftieth floor of the World Trade Center as the secretary for the legal department of DKB Financial Products, the swaps-and-derivatives subsidiary of Dai-Ichi Kangyo Bank. I was finally paying off my debts, and I spent my downtime at my job working on the second draft of *In the Drink* at my desk, looking out over New York Harbor, high up in the air.

I had also, at long last, broken up with James. In our last conversation, shortly after we'd broken up, he told me that reading *In the Drink* was "like having a sharp stick shoved up my sphincter." I knew enough by then, had gained enough confidence, never to speak to him again after that.

For $450 a month, I lived alone in Greenpoint, in a huge, high-ceilinged, beautiful place on North Henry Street just off Norman Avenue, way up near McGolrick Park and the sewage treatment plant. Finally, I could afford to buy furniture and dishes for my apartment, clothes and food for myself. Finally, I was taking proper care of myself; I even had health benefits now, which I hadn't had since I'd worked at William Morrow five years earlier.

My favorite postwork supper in those days was an icy, dry vodka martini with olives, along with two cut-up raw red peppers, cold, dipped in Paul Newman's hot salsa. I sat at the table in my dining room with music on and candles lit and slowly, happily ate the red pepper and salsa and drank the martini. While I ate, I wrote in my journal and occasionally sighed with contentment. I loved this apartment, loved living alone.

On my long hike home from the L train after work, I passed the Busy Bee supermarket, a Polish grocery. I did much of my shopping there. The shelves were full of beer, hot mustard, pickled beets, herring in jars, canned meats, and sauerkraut. Behind the cash register were heaps of uncut loaves of fresh Polish rye bread. The register was next to a deli case piled high with cured meats, blocks of cheese, kielbasa, and cold salads. The cashier and the deli guy were one and the same person; the entire line had to wait while he sliced each customer's bread, meat, and cheese. The inefficiency of this system drove me a little batty with impatience, but it also afforded me a certain amount of entertainment. It was easy to tell who was from the neighborhood and who wasn't by the degree of irritation versus resignation they exhibited.

I had a new boyfriend, a musician and painter who lived down in Williamsburg in a huge industrial loft on Metropolitan and Wythe. I'd met him through our mutual friend Dan. I sang backup and played viola in Dan's band, and Jon had gone to high school with him. Jon came to all our gigs and often tried to talk to me afterward. He had a girlfriend and I had a boyfriend, so I didn't pay much attention to him, but he persisted. Then he broke up with his girlfriend and asked me on a date, with Dan as chaperone, since I was still technically with James, even though he'd been gone for months and we were in the throes of prebreakup doldrums. The three of us went to Coney Island to ride the Cyclone, then to Brighton Beach to eat Russian food and drink vodka on the boardwalk. I was extremely attracted to Jon, who was strong, handsome, tough, straightforward, and sweet. I also felt totally comfortable with him, and I trusted him completely, right from the start.

Unlike me, Jon understood that restaurants were democratic, open to anyone who could fork over the money it cost to eat there. It was the mid-nineties, a golden time, financially speaking. He was raking it in as a building contractor, renovating Upper East Side apartments, building shoe stores and designers' showrooms. We met on weeknights after work and took turns treating each other to dinner—one night, he paid; the next night, I paid. We were equally generous and free with money, equally happy to buy presents for each other, to pay for things. There was never one moment's tension with him about money, partly because we both usually had enough, and partly because we shared a happy insouciance about it. We chose to live as if we would always have enough.

Jon taught me to eat in restaurants, how to enjoy food without guilt or remorse or puritanism. He took me to fantastic, wonderful places, the kind I used to stand outside and look at with longing. He ordered for both of us: steak frites, artichokes, frisée salads with lardons and a poached egg, steak tartare, raw oysters, asparagus. He took me to Coney Island for raw clams at Ruby's, then over to Brighton Beach for lamb soup, pelmeni with sour cream, applesauce, and sautéed onions, and blini with caviar. We went to the Savoy for roast chicken, to La Lunchonette for beef bourguignon, to a tiny Italian place on Jane Street where the owner made his own wine and came out to pour it for us; we ordered his excellent venison and fresh pastas. We ate at a homey old Italian place in Williamsburg called Milo's whose owners, an ancient Italian couple, tottered around serving two-dollar beers and rustic red wine along with mounded plates of cheap, homemade spaghetti with meatballs; we always dared each other to order the half goat's head, but we never did. I inhaled all this food; I would have rolled around in it if such a thing had been possible.

One day after work when I had just arrived at home, Jon called me and told me he had put a chicken in the oven and asked if I wanted to come over. I stuck whatever supper I'd been making into the fridge for the next night and walked the mile or so down to his loft. When I showed up, "A Love Supreme" was playing and his floor was freshly mopped and he'd opened a bottle of red wine. We sat at his table and ate the chicken, which was juicy inside and crisp outside—he was a far, far better cook than I was in those days—with roasted rosemary red potatoes and steamed asparagus dipped in lemon mayonnaise. That night, as we lay in his bed together, our arms wrapped around each other, breathing quietly, on the verge of sleep, I felt completely safe with him. He felt so familiar to me, as if we had known each other since we were kids, as if we'd grown up next door to each other.

I thought, out of nowhere, "I must never betray this trust." Then I felt a little chill, a premonition of sorts.

Jon came from a big Jewish family, almost all of whom lived in Pittsburgh. His views on family, which he got from his father's parents, were that you never estranged yourself from anyone you were related to no matter what; you stayed close and helped them in any way you could and did your duty, whatever that was—showing up at bar mitzvahs and weddings and funerals, giving them money if they needed it, and offering advice and moral support. When I told him I wasn't speaking to anyone in mine, he immediately said, worried, "You have to get back in touch with them. You need them, and they need you."

Shortly after this conversation, my sister Susan left a message on my answering machine, telling me that our mother had just been diagnosed with uterine cancer. Instantly, I called my mother, then Susan; hearing their voices again brought back all the complicated, unresolved things I still felt about them, but the fact that my mother had a potentially fatal disease made it all fall away. None of it mattered. They were my family.

My mother told me that my sister Emily had recently left Claus after a decade on the farm with him. She was now in Australia, living with a religious community in Sydney, and she had recently contacted our mother after a long period of silence. She was back now, too.

After I hung up, I sat alone in my apartment, weeping.

---

### MINESTRONE

*Back when I lived alone in the East Village, I would throw this quick, cheap, easy soup together on cold nights after I got home from my temp job. There was generally enough for three nights, and every night after I made it, it tasted even better. I have never been a fan of pasta in soup because it tends to get slimy and fall apart; this recipe contains none, therefore, but feel free to add a handful of macaroni if you like.*

In plenty of olive oil in a soup pot over medium heat, sauté as many chopped cloves of garlic as you want, plus an onion, 2 carrots, and 1 rib of celery, all diced. Throw in some chopped sausage if you like; a mixture of sweet and spicy Italian sausage is best. Season with basil, oregano, black pepper, and salt. When everything is soft and fragrant, add a can of diced tomatoes and a good glug of red wine. Stir well, add a quart or more of good chicken broth, and bring to a simmer. Meanwhile, dice any vegetables you happen to have around the house, and add enough of those to make a thick, chunky soup: any combination of green beans, zucchini, peas, spinach, yellow squash, chard, kale, cabbage, broccoli. Rinse a can or two of beans and add those—garbanzo, kidney, and cannellini all work well, but I've also used black beans without any untoward consequences. Taste the broth, add whatever seasoning it needs. Let the soup simmer until everything is cooked. Serve with hot red pepper flakes and grated Parmesan.

## BACON-CHEDDAR BISCUITS

*I made these for breakfast one morning at the beginning of my courtship with Jon when his loft was full of musician friends from Philly who were crashing there while they all made a record together. I packed a sack of them for Jon to take to south Brooklyn and share with everyone at the studio. The sound engineer, a burly white guy from Kentucky, took one bite and said to Jon, "Your girlfriend cooks like a black woman. Is she black?" This might be the greatest compliment I've ever gotten for my cooking.*

Preheat the oven to 350 degrees. Separate 1½ pounds of thick, fatty bacon onto a cookie sheet and bake at 450 degrees until crisp and brown, about 20 minutes. Meanwhile, to 2 cups of all-purpose flour, add 4 teaspoons baking powder, 1 teaspoon salt, and ½ teaspoon sugar. Mix these dry ingredients well with a whisk. Cut a stick of butter into the dry ingredients and, with your bare hands, quickly massage the butter into the flour until the flour is yellowed and grainy and uniform, but no longer. Make a well in the flour-butter mixture and pour in about 1 cup of milk or buttermilk, then add ½ cup of shredded sharp cheddar. Mix the dough quickly and lightly with bare, floured hands into a firm, sticky ball. Turn out onto a floured board and roll it or press it with your hands into a 1-inch-thick layer. Take a 2-inch-diameter water glass and cut rounds until only scraps are left. Mold the scraps into a 1-inch-thick layer and cut biscuits. Repeat till all the dough is used. Bake on a cookie sheet for 15–20 minutes, until tall and golden.

Cut each biscuit in half and make a bacon sandwich with as much bacon as you want.

# PART EIGHT

# Williamsburg and Greenpoint

## CHAPTER 44

## Tornado Warnings

———— After my mother's radical hysterectomy, she was now cancer-free and didn't have to undergo chemo or radiation. She and Susan met Jon and me at an Italian restaurant in the East Village to reunite, celebrate her recovery, and give my mother and sister a chance to vet my new boyfriend. It was an easy, comfortable meal, despite our recent history. Jon's presence made it feel warm and uncomplicated; he charmed them both and openly showed them how much he loved me.

That spring, we all went to Australia to see Emily. After such a good reunion among ourselves, we couldn't wait to see Emily again. Also her divorce from Claus was now final, and she was planning to marry a man she'd met in the community, and we wanted to look him over. I invited Jon to come with us; I wanted Emily to look him over, too.

When we arrived in Sydney, Jon and I found out that, because we weren't married, Emily's community wanted us to sleep apart in their single men's and women's dorms in bunk beds, which was not an option for us. So we got to stay in a hotel room with a balcony in King's Cross while my mother and Susan shared the big guest room in the community house, a sprawling Victorian minimansion in a suburb just outside the city.

The group, which evidently existed in communities all

over the world, was called the Twelve Tribes. They lived the way they imagined the first-century Christians had lived, sharing all their possessions, celebrating Shabbat, meeting at dawn and dusk for intensive group prayer sessions. The women wore their hair in braids down their backs and dressed modestly in long-sleeved blouses and long skirts; the men all had beards and ponytails and wore loose pants and smocklike shirts. They obeyed the literal words of the Bible, as interpreted for them by their prophet, a former carnival barker from Tennessee named Elbert Eugene Spriggs who'd rechristened himself Yoneq. His followers believed that they would bring about the second coming of Christ once all Yoneq's edicts were fulfilled. Everyone who joined got a new name: Emily was now Ishah, and Campbell, Emily's fiancé, was called Yotham.

"They're a cult," said Jon when we got back to our hotel. "They give me the creeps."

I suspected that he was right, but even so, it was a joy and a relief to see Emily again. She had been a painfully missing piece of my life for ten years. But she had changed drastically from the headstrong, opinionated girl I'd known. She had become meek, humble, obedient, and devout. All the women and children in the group were. The women worked hard together from dawn to dusk, were never allowed to be alone, and rarely saw their husbands, except at night, in bed, to procreate. I later learned that they were required to hit their children with balloon sticks to make them behave, starting when they were six months old. Children were hit for asking for seconds at the table, hit for playing make-believe games that would distract them from recognizing Christ (Yashua) when he returned, hit for questioning authority, hit for any mischief or disobedience. Meanwhile, at the twice-daily prayer meetings, people informed on one another, Stasi-like, and were punished.

But we didn't know most of this at the time. And they certainly weren't starving in the Twelve Tribes. The women seemed to be perpetually preparing feasts of fresh vegetables, meat, homemade bread, and rich desserts which they ate communally, of course, at long tables in their large, airy dining room or under the trees in the yard when the men returned from their carpentry jobs in the city.

Although all the men in the group seemed self-righteous and intense, we loved Campbell right away. He was completely different from Claus—dynamic, smart, charming, and seemingly in touch with reality. And he clearly adored Emily. All in all, Emily seemed healthy and happy and surrounded by friends, much better off than she'd been with Claus in New Zealand, and so we tried not to worry too much about her, although something in the back of my mind warned me that she had not returned to our family, not really: this group, whatever its true nature, dictated her actions and behavior. In any case, she wanted to stay where she was, and that was her choice.

A few months after we got back, on my thirty-fourth birthday, Jon proposed to me at the same place he'd taken me for our first date, an outdoor restaurant on the Brighton Beach boardwalk called the Cafe Moscow. I accepted in tears. On November 8, 1996, we had the official part of our wedding at my mother's house in Woodstock on her back deck, under a chuppah Jon had made. We found a conservative rabbi willing to marry us in a Jewish ceremony, even though I wasn't Jewish, because I was planning at the time to convert. My mother graciously opened her house to Jon's family, none of whom she'd ever met; she hired a photographer and a caterer. I had a dress made by an Ecuadorean seamstress I'd found by asking around—she had rushed it, and it wasn't finished with the row of seed-pearl buttons up the back she'd planned, but it was satiny and formfitting and a glowing, ethereal ivory, and I felt beautiful in it.

Only our immediate families were there. Susan was my maid of honor; Jon's father was his best man. My mother walked me down the flower-strewn aisle, both of us on the verge of tears. It was November but warm, windy, and dark; there were tornado warnings that day. Standing next to Jon under the chuppah, looking into his eyes, I trembled so visibly, everyone could see. As the rabbi said the prayers invoking God, the chuppah roof whipped up and down in sudden strong gusts. As he pronounced us husband and wife, a flock of blackbirds rose like one thing from the tossing trees into the stormy sky. It strikes me now as a perfectly accurate omen.

After the ceremony, we all drove down the mountain for a feast at a cozy streamside restaurant my mother had rented for the night. We had filet mignon and red wine, and afterward, champagne and a wedding cake the restaurant owners, a married couple, had made us. The next day, we all drove down to Brooklyn for a huge party in an old bank on Grand Street in Williamsburg with Mexican food, a wild klezmer band, an ocean of booze, and a roomful of people we loved.

## CHAPTER 45

## Food-Inspired Rush of Love

The transition from dreamy, passionate court-ship to fraught, contentious marriage was immediate and shocking. For our honeymoon, Jon and I had decided to take a three-week road trip to New Orleans and back in a rented car. It was not a romantic trip, to put it mildly.

"Which way do I go?" Jon barked at me as we approached the end of the Verrazano Narrows Bridge on our way out of New York, headed toward New Orleans. For the two years we'd been together, he had never raised his voice with me, ever, even a little.

"Which way?" I repeated, dazed; I had no driver's license and no concept of New York's highways or any highways, for that matter. Before we'd left, he had asked me to look at the map because he wasn't sure where we were going; I had failed to figure it out in time.

"Look at the map!" he shouted. "Quick! Which way do I go?"

Cringing, I unfolded the map, turned it right side up and looked ineffectually at it while Jon swept past our exit.

He pulled the car over. "Look," he said, jabbing the map with his forefinger. "We're right here. Don't you know how to read a map?"

"Yes!" I lied. "But not if you yell at me."

Of course, this was not really about my map-reading abilities, or lack thereof. We were both freaking out. How were we going to navigate this new marriage together? Was I going to ride along while Jon did all the work? Was he going to blow up whenever I didn't hop to fast enough? We sat there for a moment, trying to get our bearings, internal and external. Yes, we had missed our exit. But worse, now that we were married, we'd suddenly turned into two strangers. It was as if an evil fairy-tale witch had cast a spell on us and turned us into clichés, a dithering, smoldering wife, a hot-tempered, critical husband.

Luckily, we had decided to bring Jane and Michael Stern's *Roadfood* with us. Although we fought constantly the entire trip, what could have been a disaster turned into a culinary orgy of American regional classics. On our first night, in Baltimore, at the Lexington Market, we glutted ourselves on crab cakes, clam chowder, and raw oysters. In Nashville, we ate pulled pork and drank bourbon and danced drunkenly to live bands. Just off the interstate, somewhere in Alabama, we found a barbecue shack with pulled pork so tender and good we moaned as we ate the sandwiches, our chins and wrists running with sauce. In Mobile, we had dozens of big, briny, fresh raw Gulf oysters for lunch, dinner, breakfast, and lunch, despite headlines warning of red tide. In New Orleans, we ate muffulettas from Central Grocery and jambalaya, red beans and rice, and fried chicken at Coop's Place. In Memphis, we ate all the barbecue we could stuff in our pieholes. On our way north, we stopped in Missouri for the famous throwed rolls and unlimited free sides at Lambert's.

All this food distracted me from my dawning realization that we might have made a mistake. And this set the tone for our entire marriage. Food and drink, which had been so central to our courtship, our shared passions, and the things that had brought us together and cemented our romance, now sustained us. When we were unable to connect any other way, when the distance between us felt too wide to cross, we could always share a table, a meal. Filling our bellies, tipsy, we could say the things we needed to say to each other, cry and laugh, and feel temporarily bonded again, in love again. We had a joke about this: we called the phenomenon a "food-inspired rush of love."

Before heading back to New York at the end of our honeymoon, we made a stop in St. Louis for one night to visit Jon's grandmother Fan; she and I had loved each other from the instant we'd met almost two years before. She had severe emphysema after a lifetime of heavy smoking, and her health was declining. She was thrilled that we'd come to see her on our honeymoon, almost beside herself with happiness. That night, we ate our first home-cooked meal since before our wedding: Jon cooked a roast chicken with mashed potatoes, I made a salad, and we opened the wine we'd brought. The three of us stayed up into the early hours of the morning, and Fan talked about her life. She had traveled a lot with her husband, Jon's grandfather—to the Far East, to Europe and South America—and her tiny apartment was crammed full of the things they'd brought back. She looked around her little living room, pointing at a mask, a carved mahogany table, a piece of embroidered cloth on the wall, telling the story of where it had come from, how they'd found it.

The next morning, Fan was so tired she could hardly get up to see us off. As we drove away, I said with sad certainty, "That's the last time we'll see her."

She died a few months later. After that, there seemed to be an unending stream of deaths. My aunt Aillinn was next, of a rare, aggressive form of breast cancer, and then my grandmother Ruth of complications from the flu at ninety-three. Two close, longtime friends of Jon's died, one of esophageal cancer, one of a heroin overdose. Then, horribly, Jon's younger brother, Mathew, was diagnosed with ALS. Taking turns with the rest of his family, Jon and I nursed him in his Idaho cabin near the Canadian border through a painful, terrible three years, until he died. Meanwhile, Jon's beloved stepfather, Richard, succumbed to colon cancer. Then September 11 happened; the towers fell. I had a breakdown. Shortly after that, Jon's father, who had been sick for years, died of lung cancer and complications of diabetes.

But I'm getting ahead of myself.

When we got back from our honeymoon, I left my big, cheap, beautiful apartment in Greenpoint and moved into Jon's loft on Metropolitan and Wythe in Williamsburg. It was a huge, low-ceilinged industrial space he'd carved into rooms, with a big studio where his improvised industrial-noise band rehearsed and where he painted. There were interior windows and exposed brick painted white, a bathtub on a plywood platform to hide the plumbing, a small outdoor deck built over the tiny one-story garage next door, which we got to by climbing out our big bedroom window, and a kitchen he'd built himself with things he'd scavenged from construction jobs—orange metal overhead cabinets, a little gas stove that had once belonged to Rudy Giuliani, a table whose top was the smooth, sanded slate from an old pool table, and a porcelain farmhouse sink. We had a very comfortable long red couch and a less comfortable pink-brown armchair where we watched TV late at night.

Unfortunately, we lived right on the main truck route in an industrial neighborhood, and the front of our house was a popular sleeping spot for truckers. All night, they would park below our windows and let their engines idle, spewing diesel fumes into the bedroom. Crack whores plied their trade on the sidewalk in front of our building to these truckers and the

Hasidic men who pulled up in station wagons. Our upstairs neighbor got drunk every night and wailed away on his electric guitar for hours, oblivious to his ringing phone and Jon's thumping on his door; we nicknamed him Wankin'.

In the mid-nineties, Williamsburg was just starting to become the epicenter of the known hipster universe. Back then, the streets were wide and quiet, the sky was huge over the low two- and three-story row houses with aluminum siding and the brick factory buildings that ran all the way to the waterfront. When I'd first come to the neighborhood, Bedford Avenue had no bank machines: there was one old deli, a bodega or two, the Greenpoint Tavern, which we always called the Budweiser bar, the Northside Pharmacy, the hardware store with dusty tools that appeared to have been there since the 1970s, and a Polish restaurant. Now, suddenly, ATMs sprang up, along with trendy thrift stores, little boutiques, a hip record store, and—this heralded the beginning of a new era—a minimall on the ground floor of an old loft building.

Through all this change, the food industry in Williamsburg was still run by local vendors. Although there was an odd supermarket called Tops on the Waterfront where I could get staples and produce, most of my shopping I had to do in the old style. Up on Bedford Avenue, the main drag of Williamsburg, were two butchers, the "red butcher" and the "blue butcher," so called because of the colors they were painted inside; they had official names, but no one used them. According to anyone who knew anything about the neighborhood, one of them was good and the other was bad. But I could never remember which was which. I went into one and sniffed hard, then did the same thing in the other one, hoping to ferret out the bad one by any hint of putridness or rot. I never could tell the difference; they both smelled equally of garlicky sausage and the tangy stink of fresh meat. I generally bought kielbasy in either one and felt perfectly safe in both. Until one day, I bought a piece of beef from the blue butcher which, when we cooked it, tasted gamy, and the texture was sinisterly stringy but tender. I was convinced it was horsemeat, and from then on, I went exclusively to the red butcher. A few years later it closed, and a bubble tea emporium opened in its place.

## CHAPTER 46

## Mermaids and Vampires

Every summer, Jon and I went to the Mermaid Parade out at Coney Island along with tens of thousands of other New Yorkers. The first year I went, in 1993, the year before Jon's and my first date, I gyrated and lip-synched in a blond wig, aquamarine spandex minidress, and fishnets on the back of my band's friend Larry's pickup truck with the other Sporkettes, who were similarly sluttily attired, as was everyone else at the Mermaid Parade, male or female, gay or straight. We won Best Musical Group that year, and the next time I marched as well, with Jon's band, the Hungry March Band, a rotating group of about twenty-five musicians who played Latin and Balkan songs on horns, winds, and drums.

We fueled ourselves on Nathan's hot dogs before the parade, then hung out with all the other mermaids before we strutted down the boardwalk, sardine packed with paraders and spectators. Most of Williamsburg and the East Village turned out with all due pale tattooed pierced flesh, black leather bustiers, and Doc Martens lace-up boots. The nautically themed costumes and floats were beautiful, funny, and inventive—sea creatures, underwater gardens, schools of fish, squid puppets, floating plankton, dolphins. There were little girls in glitter and mermaid costumes dressed just like their mothers, green-painted skinny algae men in Speedos, body makeup melting in the heat, dogs on leashes, music, cheering, the background noise wash of rides and games.

Every year, the Hungry March Band ended their parade by walking off the boardwalk down the steps onto the wide, crowded beach, through the sand and crowds on towels, and straight into the ocean, gathering followers as they went. There, we splashed around thigh-deep in the shallow, foamy waves in a bacchanalian, decked-out, ragtag bunch and didn't once think about hepatitis or E. coli or floating syringes. When it was time to disperse, we drifted in clumps back up the beach to Ruby's, the bar on the boardwalk, which had a food stand in front with raw clams and deep-fried everything. There was always a half-hour wait in line for the bathroom. The bartenders were witty and frantic. All of us were tipsy and happy and sunburned.

Afterward, a group of us walked a mile or so down the boardwalk over to Brighton Beach to watch the sun set and eat Russian food and drink vodka at the Winter Garden. There always seemed to be a table outside big enough to accommodate us, and there was always a group we knew at the next table, so we expanded to include them. From the beautiful, mock-scornful, playfully sneering waitresses, we ordered pelmeni, oysters, blini with caviar and sour cream, broiled whole fish, shrimp cocktails, octopus and crab salads with mayonnaise dressing, and beakers of vodka.

This was the serious part of the night. It was a Saturday, which meant Shabbat was ending, so the Russian Jews came out to celebrate after sunset. It was a whole new parade on the boardwalk, and we were the spectators this time. Just as we had all known one another at the Mermaid Parade, they all greeted one another, kibitzed in Yiddish and Russian, caught up, moved on to the next group of friends—the older men dapper in white suits, the younger ones fashionably urbane in tight jeans and loose shirts, women of all ages just as sluttily dressed, in their way, as the Mermaid Parade marchers—slippery sexy short summer dresses, perfume that wafted behind them on the warm air, movie-star makeup, scalloped baby-doll hair.

This rite of passage into summer was my ritual for many years. Then Coney Island got bought out in the early oughts and the parade turned corporate, and we old regulars started complaining and gradually stopped showing up.

On Halloween, the Hungry March Band always marched in the Greenwich Village Halloween Parade. The men went in drag, dressed as aliens or cowboys, or wore rubber masks. We women dressed in our sluttiest, fishnetiest attire, a cabal of blood-red-lipped medieval serving wenches, Mad Maxine dystopian sci-fi wet dreams, and Morticia-Vampiras in satiny black slip dresses with glow-in-the-dark fangs, my own preferred costume. The parade thronged through lower Manhattan, so densely packed it was impossible to tell who was marching and who was spectating. It didn't matter. It was a big, decadent, wild, loud, raucous party.

My life in those days felt like a protracted adolescence or postcollegiate idyll. Jon and I went out constantly to lavish dinners, wild loft parties, live music, underground clubs, rooftop barbecues, and all-night binges. We ran in a big, loose crowd of local painters and musicians, many of whom were Jon's old classmates from Bennington.

For the most part, except for my writer's group, which I'd joined the year I met Jon, I kept away from other writers. It was mostly out of fear, as I always expected the same kind of cold competitiveness from my fellow writers that I had found at Iowa. But I did have a close writer friend, Cathi. She lived on the Upper West Side with her husband, Dan, who was also a writer, and their baby daughter. Theirs was a grown-up world of schools and restaurants and baby carriages and enormous, proper apartment buildings with awnings, far removed from the scruffy, low-lying warehouses, dive bars, and messy artist lofts of Williamsburg. I took the subway to Broadway and West

Ninety-sixth. Cathi and I would meet at Empire Sushi, where we sat for hours over spicy tuna rolls, California rolls, and miso soup, talking and laughing and exchanging news about our lives. She was a breath of "real" life, as I thought of it, the life I hoped Jon and I were headed for, soon.

By that time, I had a finished manuscript of *In the Drink*, and Cathi helped me find an agent for it. Over the next year and a half, at least twenty-seven different editors rejected it. Many flat-out hated the book. One of them wrote to my agent that she literally threw it across the room. Others tried to find a more delicate way of expressing their dislike for poor Claudia—she was the problem, not the writing, which they all grudgingly admitted was not bad. But Claudia was too drunk, too much of a loser, and too pathetic; worst of all, she didn't seem to want to help herself. She didn't fit the mold of the scrappy, decent, charming heroine who pulls herself up by the proverbial bootstraps. Her problems were all entirely her own fault. It was hard to root for her, hard to care about her when all she did was screw up. Unfortunately, that was the point of the novel.

During this constant influx of disheartening, depressing rejections, Jon never flagged, never lost heart on my behalf. Right after our honeymoon, he'd convinced me to quit my job and offered to support me until I sold my novel. It was the first time in my adult life that anybody had ever done that for me; I felt a complex brew of intense gratitude, guilt, pressure to succeed, and safety. Jon read every draft of the book, believed fervently in my writing, and encouraged me to keep going. He built us a new bedroom so I could have his old one for a writing studio, soundproofed his music studio so his band's late-night practicing wouldn't bother me, refurbished the deck outside our bedroom window for a garden and a place to have cookouts. At one point, when I felt almost suicidal, he took me out to our favorite restaurant and spent the whole evening comforting and reassuring me. "It will sell," he said for the ten-thousandth time. "I promise. Just wait."

He was right. My agent finally managed to finagle a two-book deal with a determined, persistent, brilliant young associate editor at Doubleday. The higher-ups weren't wild about *In the Drink*, apparently, but she'd convinced them to take a chance on me, and they wanted to see what I'd do next. They liked my writing, at least.

In 1999, when I was almost thirty-seven years old, *In the Drink* was published. It was then promptly swallowed up in the first wave of "chick lit" that came crashing onto these shores from Bridget Jones's England. It was a mixed blessing, like so many other things.

## CHAPTER 47

## Baby Lust

Sometime in 1998, Susan announced to us that she was marrying Alan, our ex-stepfather Ben's nephew. I was overjoyed, if slightly bemused: I'd always thought of Alan as our stepcousin. But it made sense. As teenagers meeting for the first time on Tuckernuck, they had been instantly attracted to each other but had lost touch for many years afterward. Then, the summer before they got married, they reunited at Tuckernuck, then went off to Paris and had a fantastically romantic fling. When Susan got pregnant, they decided to get married, and she moved to Holland, where Alan, who was Dutch, lived.

Although I knew Susan was dying to settle down, I was worried about her, in an annoying older sister sort of way. She had a seemingly wonderful life as a trained masseuse and yoga teacher in Northern California. Now she would be living in dark little Holland, where she didn't speak the language, didn't have a job or any friends, with a baby on the way, married to a man she barely knew. Of course, our mother had taught us all how to start over, to land on our feet, and to make the best of any circumstance. And Alan was a kind and loving man, and I had no doubt he would make an excellent father.

A few days before the actual ceremony, Jon and I flew to Amsterdam to hang out with my other stepcousins, Christian, Daniel, Liesje, and Jason. We ate *bitterballen* and *fritjes* and drank *pils* in various cozy little Amsterdam pubs while Susan and Alan, who was loyally staying by her side, remained at home. It never occurred to me that it might be hard for Susan to be left out while Jon and I had fun with our cousins, her new in-laws.

The ceremony was at Alan's family house in southern Holland, an old converted mill in the countryside. Their legal ceremony had already taken place at the town hall. For the wedding itself, they had asked Daniel to marry them, and me to read "The Owl and the Pussycat." For some reason, I balked at this, and insisted, in prima-donna-like fashion, on reading an excerpt from "Song of Songs" instead. I also insisted on marrying them along with Daniel, to which they acquiesced wearily in resigned second-born fashion. Then I proceeded, cluelessly, to show up wearing an off-white cocktail dress to the ceremony. I did manage to have a black sweater and a colored scarf over it, but what sort of sister does that? Susan, of course, had thoughtfully worn black to my wedding. In fact, she had been an impeccably selfless maid of honor. I was apparently incapable of that.

Despite my knuckleheaded behavior, the ceremony was beautiful and moving. Susan seemed to float down the aisle on our mother's arm, a crown of flowers in her hair, heartstoppingly gorgeous in a velvety, skintight ivory dress that hugged her swelling belly. Daniel and I stood with Alan and his parents at the altar, our backs to a burbling stream. Daniel and I read the biblical vows, taking turns asking them if they promised to love, cherish, honor, and obey each other. I looked Alan fiercely in the eye as if to say, "This is my sister, dammit. You'd better love her, or I'll kill you." He looked back at me with steady tenderness and responded in a voice that held no doubt. I was so choked up I could hardly get the words out.

The bride's and groom's siblings all gave toasts. When it was Jon's turn, he stood up and raised his glass and looked them each in the eye. "Watch out," he said with a smile. "You're really in for it now. Marriage is incredibly hard. And, Alan, good luck being married to a Christensen."

Everyone laughed except Susan and Alan, who both looked at Jon with solemn, dazed relief. Susan later told me that they had loved his toast the most. They hadn't realized he was joking. They were grateful that amid all the congratulations, romantic wishes, and jokes, here was someone willing to tell the truth.

The truth about our marriage was that, despite the undeniable fact that we had a lot of fun together, gave each other mutual support and comfort, and were close friends and loved each other deeply, we could not stop fighting. Through the early years of our marriage, we fought and fought and fought; neither of us was capable of giving in or folding. We fought about small things and big ones: fingernail clippings or a clogged sink drain, his intensely stressful road rage or my bursts of sharp meanness. After these fights, we sometimes didn't speak to each other for a week. We were too proud to show any weakness to each other and too stubborn to admit we were scared.

At the beginning, before we got married, when our dual fiery natures were still a source of friction and sexual energy and excitement in the relationship, we used to joke about what hotheads we both were. Now, in the settled routine of a marriage, things were different. It didn't help that, in our thirties, we were both fairly set in our ways. When Jon complained about something I did, I would say, "But I've always been like this." When I attacked him for something that was driving me crazy, he'd lash back with, "This is how I am." I hated myself as a wife: I'd become nagging, demanding, and critical. I was as hard on Jon as I was on myself.

My anger at Jon often took the form of tipsy late-night half rants during which I listed all the things I wished he'd do that he wasn't doing. He vented his own rage on other things: errant power tools, slow drivers, long lines, people who betrayed him or took him for granted. But his anger, whenever it exploded, flat-out terrified me. When he threw an electric drill against a wall in the next room or went ballistic when the car ahead of us went too slowly and made him miss a light, the traumatic memory of my father's violent outbursts flared up instantly in my lizard brain. I started hyperventilating with panic; all I could do was hunch over and close my eyes.

Jon tried to assure me that he was not my father, that he would never hurt or assault anyone, especially not me. I tried not to take his rages personally, but just as he couldn't control his temper, I couldn't control my reaction to it. Consequently, I spent much of our marriage trying to fend off his anger at anything but me while, ironically, frequently feeling enraged at him. It was a harmful and unhealthy dynamic, a toxic emotional Möbius strip that was both unsustainable and chronic, and neither one of us had any control over it.

I often woke up in the middle of the night with Jon asleep next to me. I lay there, breathing the exhaust fumes from the idling trucks outside, the woodsmoke from a neighbor's chimney, thinking to myself "What the hell have I done?" Whenever I walked by my old, high-ceilinged, beautiful apartment in Greenpoint, I mourned the autonomous, contented life I'd had there.

Jon worked late in his studio every night; he had rented and renovated a raw space in Bushwick where he now painted, practiced his horn, and developed his photographs. On most nights, we ate together when he got home, at nine or ten or sometimes even eleven. But once in a while, I called to tell him not to hurry. He never complained: this meant he could stay as late as he wanted.

I was happy, too, because I preferred to eat earlier, and I loved going out by myself to restaurants. On those nights, I headed out early, at seven or so. Back in the late nineties, new restaurants were opening here and there, but the old tried-and-true ones still thrived, hadn't been driven out yet by exploding rents.

My favorite place to go for "bachelorette nights," as I called them, was a place called the L Café, on Bedford just off North Seventh, near the L stop, owned and run by three people Jon had gone to Bennington with; it was definitely "new Williamsburg," and it was funky and quietly glamorous, but it wasn't achingly hip—that was a few years away, the relentless self-consciousness that infected the neighborhood.

The L was in a narrow, long storefront. There was a garden out back with wrought-iron tables and wooden booths. The interior had the dark wood wainscoting, tin ceiling, and linoleum floors of classic North Brooklyn decor.

I walked in and was instantly enveloped in moody indie music and a warm breeze from the kitchen. Strings of tiny white lights twinkled behind the bar. I always sat at a small table in the back and ordered a plateful of something homey like yellow rice and red beans and roast chicken, or lamb stew with chickpeas and root vegetables. While I ate and drank wine, literally wriggling my toes with the deep happiness of autonomous solitude, I would write by hand—in those days, I still kept a journal I wrote in almost daily, like finger exercises for a musician. And I annotated the printouts of my current novel in progress with a pen.

I always had a second glass of wine but never a third. I stayed there at that table for two or even three hours in a self-contained bubble of words and food and wine. People came and went and talked at the tables all around me; I didn't look at anyone. I eavesdropped a little but only in a desultory because-it-was-there sort of way, without any real purpose. If someone I knew came in and greeted me, I said hello back with the borderline-rude brusqueness of a night watchman, guarding the factory. The whole point of these nights out was to be alone in public with a plate of food and some wine and my writing.

These nights afforded me immense happiness, more, I think, than any dinner party or one-on-one dinner with Jon or a friend, in those days. I have always felt loneliest in the presence of other people—people I can't connect with, people I feel unseen by, people who make me feel insincere or uncomfortable. For me, loneliness comes from a sense of missing something. I never miss anything when I'm alone.

During the year following Susan and Alan's wedding, I turned thirty-seven. I was more than ready to have kids by this time. *In the Drink* had just been published. Jon and I had been married for three years. I wanted to have two of them, so time was running out fast.

When I announced this to Jon, expecting him to agree, expecting us to unite in shared excitement over this next phase of our life together, he told me that actually he didn't want them, not yet, and maybe not ever. He was still enjoying our fun freewheeling life too much and didn't want to give it up.

This hit me like a sucker punch to the gut. Here was another, new source of painful contention between us, the worst we'd ever been through. It turned out that we wanted radically different things. I wanted a conventional life, a real house, which I'd never had as a kid, and Jon was still rebelling against his own conventional upbringing. He'd married me in part because he loved my wild side, and I'd married him in part because I loved his stable, conventional side. He saw me as exciting and a little crazy, and I saw him as deeply trustworthy and solid. Unfortunately, these were the qualities in ourselves we most wanted to leave behind. I wanted to live in a clean, renovated Victorian house full of books, not a rough-hewn, unfinished industrial loft. I wanted to raise bright, good kids, to write bright, good novels in a quiet study, to cook wholesome meals and listen to Bach. He wanted to play loud amplified music, sleep late, drink tequila, and travel. It seemed to me that we didn't want to be the people we'd married each other for.

At first, I refused to believe this. For the next year or more, I begged Jon to have a baby with me, pleaded with him, often crying, to trust me, that he'd never regret it, that this was the most important and wonderful thing we could do. But he remained firm. We were having so much fun. Why wreck it? Why clutter up our loft with bottles and diapers and cribs? He was right, in a way—we were having a golden time of it in those days, going to parties and concerts, traveling, exploring far-flung outer-borough restaurants. None of the closest friends we shared as a couple had kids. It was premature in that sense, and I could see his point, but I was in my late thirties, and I felt like now was the time: now or never. I had always thought I would have kids. I had always assumed my husband would acquiesce when I was ready, or even share my excitement. This deep, sudden schism between Jon and me was terrifying.

Meanwhile, my best friend, Cathi, and my sister Susan were both pregnant. I imagined how great it would be if we all had kids around the same age. My longing for a baby, dormant for my whole life until now, had become the most powerful, overriding urge I'd ever felt. I could feel a solid, warm, nestling little body in my arms sometimes, a hallucinatory desire so strong it made me dizzy.

As time went on and Jon refused to give in, I finally realized that I had to accept this or leave him. But I didn't want to leave; how could I admit failure after only a few years of marriage? And I loved him, in spite of our differences. So I accepted his decision sadly, but my heart was broken. As our life went on, as I felt increasingly stuck, stymied, powerfully disappointed, my ability to put a good face on things, which I'd inherited from my grandmother and mother, began to be my most useful attribute. As far as everyone knew, I was perfectly happy, and I made myself believe it, too.

## CHAPTER 48

## The Heartbreak Hotel

After *In the Drink* was published, I finished my second novel, *Jeremy Thrane*, a love song to New York City narrated by a gay man in his thirties, with food as its leitmotif, its bass line. In it, I wrote frankly and without fictionalization about my father. It was the first and only time I had done so. This was my most autobiographical novel, with me disguised as a gay man.

In the weeks after it was published, *Jeremy Thrane* disappeared. September 11 devastated us and our whole circle of friends. In the months following the fall of the World Trade Center, where I had worked during the two years of Jon's and my happy courtship, I underwent a kind of internal, shell-shocked, nerve-racked breakdown, and I was not, by a long shot, the only New Yorker in this condition.

I found that I couldn't write in our loft anymore, so I rented a room in a falling-down nineteenth-century house in Greenpoint, down by the river, nicknamed the Shady Rest and the Heartbreak Hotel. It was a sort of SRO for sad-sack men who lived on public assistance and sat all day in their shirtsleeves, smoking and waiting for their Meals on Wheels to arrive. My landlady, Nancy, was Italian, born and raised in Bensonhurst. Her dad had been a mobster, and so had her dead husband. She was frank, smart, a born raconteur with a round, impish face and a hoarse smoker's chuckle that always made me laugh.

Nancy lived in the cozy, renovated basement apartment and rented the two or three empty, uninhabited upstairs rooms, cheap, to writers and artists—first to my old Iowa friend Sally, who had recommended me to Nancy when I was looking for a studio, and then, on my recommendation, to Jon's photographer friend Hal, who almost got kicked out for having a nude model in his studio who hung out the front window, smoking. He frantically explained to Nancy that there was nothing pornographic going on—this was art. She grudgingly, good-heartedly went against her own better judgment and accepted this explanation and let him stay. Soon she was his greatest fan.

I paid two hundred dollars a month for the large room on the top floor at the back of the house. My two windows faced north and looked out over flat tar paper roofs, old brick warehouses, backyards, and treetops all the way to the green, shining Citicorp tower in Queens. The room had a linoleum floor, a boarded-up fireplace, and a falling-down plaster ceiling; the roof leaked, there was no heat, and I shared the place with a noticeable but not intolerable population of mice. I warmed the room up with plants, Jon's paintings, and a large old rose-colored flower-patterned wool rug. I brought a small coffeemaker and a radio. In the cold months, I worked in my hat, scarf, and coat.

Every day, I packed myself a lunch—a sandwich of sardines and mustard on rye, roasted nuts and dried fruit, a Styrofoam container of instant black-bean or lentil soup to which I later added hot water from the coffeemaker's carafe—and walked the mile and a half from our loft in Williamsburg over to Greenpoint, along the waterfront's angled, industrial streets with astoundingly beautiful views of Manhattan and the sky above it. In my workroom, I sat at my grandfather's old desk—an old door on two heavy wooden filing cabinets. It was there that I began writing what would become my third novel, *The Epicure's Lament*.

That winter, it was too cold to write in my unheated north-facing room, so I moved my desk into a smaller room at the front of the house that was filled with warm sunlight on clear days. Just outside my new window was a huge old chestnut tree whose bare branches were inhabited by a plump-chested, medium-sized brown bird. There only seemed to be one of him; if he had a mate, or any friends, they were nowhere around. He would cock his head and stare back at me through the window that separated us, which made me feel that he was as aware of me as I was of him.

One day, the tree and the bird found their way into the novel I was writing and became a sort of fulcrum between the fictional, imagined world of the novel and my real life, a symbolic hinge that joined the two together. I named the bird Erasmus, since he seemed to have a philosophically stalwart cast of mind. All winter long, he watched me write while I watched him going about his birdly business.

*The Epicure's Lament* is narrated by a forty-year-old hermit and failed writer, Hugo Whittier, who's simultaneously smoking himself to death in his ancestral mansion on the Hudson River and cooking a lot of old-fashioned, comforting, hearty food for the very people he professes to want to get away from. I found that, for reasons I couldn't articulate at the time, writing about the things Hugo chose to make—ham with holiday sauce and spaghetti puttanesca—eased my terrible, gnawing depression. So did cooking and eating them myself. After the day's work was done, I went home and made dinners that were inspired by Hugo's culinary repertoire.

When I was about halfway through the novel, my bad state of mind worsened, and I couldn't write anymore. I stopped going to my room at Nancy's, stopped working on the novel, stopped doing much of anything. Soon, I found I couldn't get out of bed, couldn't stop crying.

To pull myself out of this depression, I decided to run the New York City Marathon. For many years, I had stood on the sidelines cheering the marathoners on, and I always found myself in tears at the grit and camaraderie of the runners thronging the streets. Now, I wanted to join them instead of watching from the curb.

Although I had never run before, or rather, I hadn't run since I'd been on the track team in junior high, I was sure I could do it. That summer, it was unusually hot, so I started training on the treadmill at the air-conditioned gym up near Kellogg's Diner on Metropolitan Avenue. My gym was .65 mile from my house; the jog there and back counted toward my daily quota (training for a marathon involves doing more math on a daily basis than I had ever expected). I had decided that I wanted to finish the marathon in less than four hours, and was following an intermediate training schedule I'd found online. The beginning one didn't seem ambitious or dreadful enough. This foolish decision landed me in the emergency room with hyponatremia, a dangerous and often fatal sodium deficiency. As soon as I was released from my weekend at Beth Israel, I resumed training right where I'd left off, only now I drank Gatorade instead of water.

In August 2002, Jon and I took a trip to Glacier National Park for my fortieth birthday. We stayed in a motel near the lodge and hiked during the day. Every night, after our long hikes, we went to the lodge for dinner and drank wine or tequila cocktails and ate bison burgers, venison steaks, or roast wild game birds.

Glacier National Park is full of trails through fields of wild-flowers to aquamarine glacial lakes and up mountainsides to windswept glaciers and peaks, but I wasn't thinking about the stupendously beautiful scenery, or rather, I wasn't concentrating on it. I was counting the miles, timing our walking speed, pushing us to go as fast as we could so that I could count these hikes as part of my daily training mileage. I was determined not to fall behind; it was almost autumn already, and I was in the thick of it.

Maybe at least partially because of my unswerving, single-minded drive, Jon pulled his ankle on our third hike and was down for the count. Instead of taking the next day off and keeping him company in our cabin, as any thoughtful spouse would do, I assembled a lunch for us both from whatever I could find at the general store attached to the motel, made sure he was supplied with ice and whatever else he needed, filled my water bottles, and stuffed a sweater into my day pack.

"I'll be back in less than five hours," I said. "Promise me you won't worry till then."

"I can't promise that," he said with his usual stubborn solicitousness.

And so I set off for a 13-mile round-trip hike up to the Continental Divide and back. I was glad to be able to do it alone. I'd been anxious all summer, trying to run my daily miles, that I'd never be able to do 26.2 of them, all at one go. This hike was my test.

For the first few miles, I wound over streams, through lush meadows, blooming and bright. Eventually, the trail turned vertical, running on a narrow cutout up the mountainside. I charged up it, passing two people on horseback admiring the view, not bothering to look at it myself.

Up and up I climbed, my muscles working well, my breathing even and steady. I was walking, not running, but my pace was extremely fast, and I wasn't winded. This hike was half the length of the marathon; New York City is pretty flat. If I could keep up this pace, I told myself, I'd do all right on November 3.

I had already run the Staten Island half marathon in well under two hours, after all.

Feeling cocky, I left the vegetation behind and scurried across a bare, rubbled mountain face and continued up and up, winding through a gravelly moonscape. The wind had picked up, but I wasn't cold, I was sweating and exhilarated. For miles, I had the place to myself, until a park ranger appeared coming down the trail toward me.

"Hello!" he said. "You're the first person I've seen in a while. Be careful around Devil's Elbow, there's a hailstorm going on up there."

He tipped his hat and continued down. Not surprisingly, Devil's Elbow turned out to be a narrow section of the rocky path that jutted out and around a cliff face. Down below, the green valley looked very far away. I was getting pelted by hail and the wind was trying to blow me off the mountainside, as if I were a bug. For the first time, I was really spooked. I caught a glimpse of the mountain range I was in, stretching away, dizzyingly far. I was up very high.

After Devil's Elbow, the trail started climbing steeply again. The higher I went, the colder and windier and more desolate it became. I passed the glacier field near the top and stopped to add my own rock to a hikers' cairn, and then there I was, on the roof of the world. I crouched in the howling wind, shivering in my sweater, and ate my lunch as fast as I could, shoving it into my mouth with both hands—two hummus sandwiches, an apple, two carrots, and a chocolate bar. I drank all my water. I was still hungry and thirsty, but that was all I'd brought. A black storm was boiling up on the other side of the mountain. Two weather systems were about to collide right where I sat.

In a hurry to get back down now, I almost ran past the glacier, across Devil's Elbow, and down the mountainside. An hour later, I realized that I was exhausted. My feet were heavy, my back was sore, my teeth were clenched, my breathing was shallow, my foot was cramping, and I couldn't stop shaking. I wasn't even into the valley yet. I had miles left to go.

I thought of Jon waiting for me in the motel room, trying to keep his mind on his book, with only a radio for company. I knew if I were one minute late, he would feel compelled to come and find me, and he was in no condition to do that. I kept going, faster than I thought I could, but my mind was in charge now, not my body. I forced myself to forget I had a body at all, much less a depleted one. I came to the verdant valley. It was filled with hikers in the late afternoon sun, groups of school-children and couples out for a little adventure. I stomped past them, as single-mindedly set on my goal as ever. The valley was shockingly gorgeous, but I had no time for it.

Then, with two miles to go, beyond hunger and thirst, I experienced a strange, unexpected thing: I recharged. Out of the blue, I was given a surge of energy, as if my body had held it back to spur me at the end, to reward my persistence. My feet were light again. My muscles worked again. I charged along, amazed and grateful.

When I flew into our motel room, Jon looked up from his book with a furrowed brow and a relieved smile. "In five minutes I was going to go out there and find you," he said.

I helped him gimp into the lodge to dinner. There, we ordered venison steaks with extra potatoes, and drank all the red wine we wanted while I looked out at the lake and surrounding mountains, replaying in my memory all the views I'd missed that day.

## CHAPTER 49

## I Cannot Live on Bread at All

I discovered that I was gluten intolerant in 2003, the summer after I ran the marathon, reluctantly, with the help of a naturopath and an elimination diet. It was simple. When I stopped eating gluten, my symptoms went away. If I ate just one crumb of bread or strand of spaghetti, they came back.

I hadn't known it yet, but I had been extremely gluten intolerant while I trained for, and ran, the marathon. I had managed to run the marathon in just under four hours, albeit with tremendous difficulty in the final six miles, but the doubt has always stayed with me—what if I'd trained without gluten? I was eating a lot of carbohydrates, which meant pasta and bread, far more than I normally would have.

All that wheat had intensified my symptoms which, to make matters worse, were all the things my training had been intended to eradicate: an ongoing crushing sense of doom; hot-headed irascibility; bloat (especially depressing when you're exercising constantly—I gained ten pounds of water weight in my stomach and hips and had permanent water bags under my eyes); fizzing insomnia; fast, fluttering pulse; and cloudy, foggy brain.

For many years, in fact, I had accepted the fact that I was a depressive, an agoraphobic, a hothead, and a space cadet, but now I finally learned that these mental problems all had the same actual, preventable cause. Still, I was embarrassed by my own condition. I had always been impervious to any food-related weakness; I was a culinary Viking, a swashbuckling food adventurer. Eating in restaurants with Jon had been a grand pastime for me. I ate everything with gluttonous enthusiasm, as irrationally proud of my ironclad stomach as I was of my high tolerance for booze, my open-minded willingness to indulge myself in anything high or low, be it White Castle jalapeño sliders made of questionable meat, fresh Costa Rican turtle, ethnic food made with the hottest chilies or spices, raw oysters and steak tartare, or raw clams on the Coney Island boardwalk.

Of course, now I knew what true food-related danger was, and it was not fun at all. But back then, in those old, carefree days, I'd smugly, secretly believed that anyone with a food-related restriction of any kind, self-imposed or otherwise, was a wimp: vegetarians were limp-wristed and self-righteous, vegans loony and sickly, the eating-disordered crazy and pathetic, and the allergic a bunch of hypochondriacal hothouse flowers.

I had so far to fall. Now I was hobbled by a constant obsessive-compulsive fear that mimicked an eating disorder, even if it didn't precisely constitute one. The things I couldn't have were legion, insidious, and ubiquitous. Forget pizza, pasta, and bread, they were child's play. I also had to keep a constant eye out for malt, barley, rye, oats, spelt, couscous, bulgur, and sprouted wheat. I had to avoid any food fried in oil used to fry wheat-containing food, most sauces, corn tortillas or chips with hidden wheat in them, certain ice creams, canned chicken broths, and anything containing added gluten or modified food starch, which is to say, almost all processed foods. Maybe the worst blow of all was that almost every brand of soy sauce contains wheat; and because of this, most Asian restaurants, which should be a haven for the gluten intolerant, were now death traps.

I began to dread being handed an unfamiliar restaurant

menu in a place where they didn't know me, and I was suddenly timid and full of mistrust in the restaurants where they did. "I'm severely allergic to wheat and gluten," I now found myself saying, with an edge of apologetic desperation, to the waiter or waitress the instant he or she appeared with pad in hand. I looked them dead in the eye to underscore the importance of this, to make sure they'd heard me and would take action on my behalf. Maybe I imagined the look of jaded forbearance on many waiters' faces when they realized that I'd need special attention—back in those days, gluten wasn't on many restaurant workers' radars yet; no one had heard of celiac, let alone gluten intolerance. But I soon had sufficient experience with not being assertive enough—not, for example, asking the waiter to double-check with the chef about the ingredients of a particular dish, no matter how sure he was that it was gluten-free—to know that it was better to be demanding and annoying than to inadvertently eat hidden gluten, which I began to call "getting wheated." Almost instantly, I would become horribly bloated, in a black mood for the rest of the night; and then I would lie awake, thirsty and insomniacal, with a rapidly pounding heart and a percolating brain, cursing to myself. The next day, I was short-tempered and depressed. It took about twenty-four hours to return to normal after one crumb of gluten; I got more and more insistent on avoiding it.

But I desperately missed the savory, eggy, bacony silkiness of spaghetti carbonara, the rich crustiness of hot fresh-baked bread slathered in butter, and chewy thin-crust pizza with tangy sauce, laden with artichoke hearts, sausage, and mushrooms, straight out of a brick oven. Knowing I couldn't have any of it ever again was like losing the steadfast, stalwart, adoring man you didn't realize you loved till he was gone forever. I missed waffles drenched in butter and syrup. And flour-tortilla burritos stuffed with black beans and spicy chicken, cheese and cilantro. And tart, springy lemon–poppy seed muffins washed down with sweet, milky coffee; the luxurious crumble of hazelnut cookies; anything in flaky, buttery, light phyllo dough—spinach and ricotta or nuts and honey, it didn't matter. I tried to nip my sadness in the bud whenever possible by forcibly redirecting my cravings to the things I could actually eat, polenta and potatoes and corn tortillas and risotto, but I could have wept over the permanent loss of pelmeni, those nuggety, hot, slippery little Russian meat dumplings served with sour cream, fried onions, and applesauce.

Over time, to my surprise and relief, the cravings faded as I replaced these things with other, gluten-free things. But it took years before the yearning ceased entirely.

In the late winter of 2003, Jon and I bought an old row house on Calyer Street, two blocks up from my former workroom in the Heartbreak Hotel. We spent the following nine months renovating it. We, meaning Jon, with me as his part-time, incompetent, subpar assistant, ripped out drop ceilings and bad partitions, crappy carpeting, linoleum, paneling, ugly fixtures, an upstairs kitchen, and several walls, filling an enormous rented Dumpster with trash. We hired a guy to refinish the original pine floors. We scraped and plaster-washed and repaired the plaster, upstairs and down, scraped and repainted the bedroom shutters, installed a kitchen and a half bath, refinished the upstairs bathroom, and renovated the basement to create a separate rental apartment, including laying an oak floor over the old dirt one down there. We created a grassy backyard bordered by flower beds, with a flourishing grapevine and cedar tree, from a pile of rocks, oyster shells, trash, and cinder blocks. Every day, we awoke in our old loft on Metropolitan Avenue, put on our dust-caked, sweaty work clothes from the day before, and drove together with cups of coffee to the job site, as we thought of our new house, saying little, both of us exhausted and grim, to spend another day yoked together. None of our friends understood how miserable we were; in their minds we were impossibly lucky for owning a nineteenth-century Greenpoint house, which was true, but my guilty understanding of their inability to understand our misery just made me feel lonelier. We were sealed in a bubble by ourselves, a bubble in which I screwed up and Jon lost his temper, I collapsed with tiredness and he kept working, I knocked off early and he went on until almost midnight, doggedly. "I'm building you a house," he would say to me, only half joking.

Little by little, over the months, we returned our little 1875 house to a semblance of its original beauty. As the renovation neared completion, we had the second big blowout fight of our marriage. It was over the living room walls. I scraped off all the old wallpaper, leaving streaks of old pink glue the color of Pepto-Bismol over the streaky green and brown plaster walls. It was a gorgeous long narrow room with an original plaster medallion in the high ceiling, a fireplace we'd had restored, French doors opening to the foyer, pocket doors opening to the dining room, plaster moldings, and big front windows. "What color should we paint the living room?" I wondered aloud to Jon, looking at the depressing, ugly, fucked-up old walls I'd revealed with my scraper and then screwed plaster washers into. In one spot, the plaster had fallen away to reveal the old lath.

"I don't want to paint these walls," said Jon. "They're beautiful. I want to leave them exactly as they are."

I had already agreed to paint the living room and dining room ceilings black; Jon had begged me just to try it, it was Victorian, it would look cool. They did look cool, because, I reasoned, they would be lightened up by crisp, beautiful, pale walls.

"No way," I said, "these walls are hideous! I can't live with them! No way!"

"I won't paint them," he said. "Once they're covered over, they're gone forever."

And here it was again: our fundamental difference. I wanted an uncluttered, light-filled, traditional house; he seemed to want a dark, baroque, artsy Bywater shotgun shack. We started fighting about the walls loudly, sometimes at the tops of our lungs. Once, I stood at the top of the stairs, Jon stood at the bottom, shouting at each other, like a reverse Romeo and Juliet, locked in passionate discord, our faces contorted.

In the end, the walls stayed exactly as they were. Jon exacted a promise from me to give it one year, and then, if I still didn't like them, we could paint them. I backed down; this was a battle I could not win now but might win eventually. But then, although I still hated them as much as ever when the year was up, Jon refused to paint them. Those walls clearly represented something very deep to him. I could have painted them myself, in defiance, of course. But I didn't. I couldn't go against something he so strongly felt, even though I felt just as strongly.

The kitchen, however, was beautiful. Jon built it in a former bedroom on the first floor, the long narrow room at the back of the house. He installed old wrought-iron casement windows that looked out on our tangled, green little yard. He built a deck off the back door, big enough for a small table and two chairs, with stairs leading down to a little bluestone patio where we kept our gas grill. He installed an old Chambers stove we'd found at a salvage place in Queens for a hundred dollars, in perfect condition. The walls were a cheery, perfectly ordinary butter yellow; the cabinets had opaque glass doors. It felt like a kitchen in a French country house—high-ceilinged, airy, hodgepodge, filled with beautiful things—a graceful wooden table that acted as a counter island and stood underneath the enormous multipaned window, a porcelain farmhouse sink, an old framed line drawing of a pig. It was a joy to cook in.

After we moved into our house, since Jon didn't get home

most nights until very late, I took over most of the food buying and menu planning and cooking. Over the course of our marriage, guided by his feedback and encouragement, I had become a better cook; then a pretty good cook; and then a confident, adept, occasionally strike-of-lightning cook. Now I had an ongoing subscription to *Cook's* magazine and read every issue cover to cover; I tried out many of their recipes and many others from our good, always growing cookbook collection.

I rarely relinquished the kitchen anymore, but there were still certain things that Jon always cooked as a matter of course. For Passover, he made matzo ball soup using his grandmother's recipe, which involved throwing out the first round of vegetables with the bones and cartilage and starting over with fresh peeled carrots in the second phase. I made the haroset and chopped liver and was told every year by Jon's family that I cooked like a Jewish grandmother. At Thanksgiving at Jon's mother's house in Pittsburgh, he made the mashed potatoes, and they were the best anyone had ever had.

Neither of us had ever fully understood that ancient rule that women cook and men grill, but we also never questioned it. Even in the bone-chilling dead of winter, with a drift of snow outside, Jon put on his hat and coat if the menu called for grilled meat, took his drink and cigarettes with him, and stayed out on the patio by the gas grill until the meat was done while I sat in the warm dining room, entertaining the guests.

In recent years, Jon had finally come around to wanting kids. But by this time, after everything we'd been through, I wasn't sure I wanted them anymore. This, however, wasn't a dramatic impasse: in general, we'd struck a genuinely loving détente in our marriage, having mutually and implicitly decided we'd rather stay married and accept our inherent, insurmountable schisms and differences than fight constantly or, even more unthinkably, leave each other. And so we co-existed in a state of hard-won tranquillity, even though I no longer felt the passionate hope for true connection with Jon I'd had at the beginning of our marriage, despite all the fighting and strife. His adamant, yearlong refusal to have children with me had broken all of that in me, and irrational though it may have been for me to feel this way, it couldn't be fixed.

But I gave in now, on the theory that I'd probably be happy once the baby arrived. We tried on and off for the next couple of years to get pregnant, but evidently my biological window had closed, or my body sensed my own ambivalence. In my early forties, we looked into adoption. This, too, came to nothing, also probably because my heart was never entirely in it.

Finally, in the summer of 2005, we adopted a trembling, formerly homeless, possibly abused young street dog. We named him Dingo, because that's what he looked like—a skinny, wild, intelligent, aboriginal canine with enormous bat ears and almond-shaped brown eyes that bugged out slightly like a Chihuahua's and an earnest furrow between his brows. In the South, he would have been called a yaller dog. When he came to live with us, he weighed a skeletal twenty-seven pounds and was not housebroken and spoke no English and appeared to be unfamiliar with stairs, puddles, furniture, and domestic life in general. After he graduated from obedience school, we kept training him on our own. He was so eager to learn and so easy to teach, we figured he was a doggy genius, until it dawned on us that he would do anything—anything we asked of him—for food.

He was passionately, single-mindedly food obsessed. He had no sense of humor about food. He was not one of those hilariously antic, clowning dogs who entertain for treats, nor did he beg with seductive whines and cute, obsequious expressions. He was quiveringly aware of everything that happened in the kitchen. He knew his rights and exercised them without overstepping: he licked the beaten egg bowl, for example, and was always on hand to do so, but he wasn't allowed to chew on chicken bones, so he never asked, even though they were the thing he loved most in the world. Maybe because he grew up on the street, he wouldn't go near anything toxic: he had no interest in raisins, chocolate, onions, or avocado, even if they fell on the floor near him.

Dingo understood from the start that he was supposed to lie at our feet while we ate, but sometimes, when it was a meal he loved, especially chicken, he forgot himself. His nose nudged my thigh and I'd look down to see him sitting right next to me, looking up at my plate, his face alight with quasireligious exaltation. But he was not begging, exactly. His feelings about food were so similar to mine, I couldn't help feeling that there was some sort of essential kinship at work there.

---

## PERSIMMON PUDDING

*A few years after we got married, when the Internet was just coming into full swing, Jon urged me to find my half sisters. We found Thea, living in St. Paul; she was married, but she'd kept her maiden name. I wrote to her, and she wrote back. That winter, I met her and her twin sister Caddie, and ever since, we have been family to each other.*

*Thea, who is an amazing cook, sent me the following old-fashioned, excellent recipe, which she typed verbatim from an old index card in her recipe box. I made it one cold late fall day from very ripe persimmons. The insides of 3 of them whizzed in the blender yielded exactly 1 cup of golden pulp. I steamed the pudding for the full 2 hours, as instructed. It was so good, I wolfed down 2 slices of it before it had even cooled.*

1 cup sugar
1 cup flour
1 teaspoon baking powder

1 teaspoon baking soda
1 teaspoon cinnamon
½ teaspoon salt
¼ cup milk
1 cup persimmon pulp
2 tablespoons melted butter
1 teaspoon vanilla
1 egg
sprinkle of nuts

Mix all ingredients except nuts. Pour batter into a greased mold or coffee can or metal mixing bowl (I used a Bundt pan). Sprinkle nuts on top (I used a combination of pine nuts and chopped walnuts because that's what I had on hand). Set mold on a trivet in a large kettle, and pour water in the kettle to a depth of 2 inches. Cover the kettle and steam the pudding for 2 hours. Freezes well. Resteam for ½ hour to reheat before serving. Serve with hard sauce, as follows:

½ cup soft butter
1½ cups sifted confectioners' sugar
1 teaspoon vanilla extract or 2 tablespoons rum or brandy

Cream butter with confectioners' sugar until light and fluffy. Stir in vanilla extract or rum or brandy.

---

### HOPPIN' JOHN

*Jon's and my favorite holiday tradition together was our annual New Year's Day party, the good luck hoppin' John hangover cure. We invited every single person we knew and made a huge spread. We started cooking on the morning of New Year's Day after we'd had some coffee. Jon always made two roasts and a glazed ham, and then, when they were in the oven, he made pitchers of Bloody Mary mix, and meanwhile, I made the sides: a huge pot of hoppin' John—spicy black-eyed peas* with long-grain rice and andouille; two trays of oozing mac and cheese with a crusty top; collard greens stewed in cider vinegar and lardons; and jalapeño cornbread with a honey glaze. On the table in the kitchen, we set out stacks of paper plates and plastic forks; on the dining room table, shrimp cocktail, cornichons, bread, cheese, olives, crackers, salami; and on the sideboard, the ice bucket, stacks of plastic cups, the pitchers of Bloody Marys, bottles of various kinds of booze and wine, cut-up lemons and limes, and seltzer.

Starting at four o'clock, our house began to fill with people and music and cigarette smoke; someone always lit a fire in the living room fireplace. People brought desserts, liquor, interesting presents. Often, later on, we all danced. Dingo circulated with his snout to the ground, inhaling whatever he could find; he was always sluggish for a day or two after the party, but there was no stopping him.

For the quasivegetarians in the crowd, I used organic turkey andouille instead of pork sausage in the hoppin' John, and for speed, I used canned black-eyed peas.

Sauté 1 chopped onion; 2 ribs celery; 1 each green and red pepper, chopped; and many cloves of minced garlic in plenty of olive oil. Add while it's all cooking generous dashes of cumin, paprika, salt, pepper, thyme, as well as 2 chopped jalapeño peppers and a bay leaf. Add 2 chopped turkey andouille sausages and sauté until everything is fragrant and soft. Add 2 cups of chicken broth, a can of diced tomatoes, several shots of Tabasco, 2–3 cans of rinsed black-eyed peas, and ½ cup long-grained white rice. Make sure there's enough liquid to cook the rice and have it wind up just a tiny bit on the soupy, rather than dry, side. Taste—adjust seasonings—cook until rice is soft. Serve with Tabasco.

# PART NINE

# Monitor Street

## CHAPTER 50

## Hunters Point

—— Once the question of having kids was completely moot, our marriage began to run aground. We retreated to separate wells of misery and lost each other. Food, which had always sustained and protected our bond, could no longer fill the emptiness, and our once-joyful, decadent drinking became numbing and solitary.

During recent years, I had wallowed in a series of crushes on other men, as a way of trying to find some respite from the grief and strife Jon and I were going through. I was a terrible flirt, but I never even remotely crossed a line into actual adultery. Now, as our marriage disintegrated even further, as Jon and I shut each other out and buried ourselves in work and alcohol and threw an affectionate gloss over the big hole in our marriage, I became unhinged, unmoored, ungrounded. I did something that had terrible consequences, something that changed the course of my life.

In August 2006, I had an affair with possibly the worst person I could have chosen. He was Jon's old college friend; his wife had briefly been Jon's girlfriend in college. They lived in our neighborhood with their two kids. Nathan and I were both starving and lonely, and had been for many years. We found each other, recognized each other, and didn't even try to resist. We were both far too desperate to be rational or cautious or good.

Our affair was very short, as well as euphoric, druglike, and vertiginous. Nathan was a poet, a songwriter, a romantic; he was sensitive, dreamy, quiet, soothing, calm. I sincerely believed I'd found my soul mate, my true love. He felt exactly the same way about me, or at least he told me so, that I was the woman he'd always hoped to find. And so we plunged into a free-fall swoon of ecstatic communion. Neither of us tried to stop it or slow it down.

Actually, my lovesick dementia was so far gone, I couldn't imagine that anything bad could ever come of something that felt so purely right, so urgently necessary, so destined. Somehow, I imagined that when our love came to light, the world would rejoice with us, including his wife and two kids, including Jon. Obviously, I was out of my mind, beyond all rational thought; extramarital affairs are said to mimic the effects of crack on the brain, and this strikes me as totally true in my own case. To justify and augment my complete severance from reality, I fantasized that we were living inside a poem, that this love between us was foreordained and unstoppable.

But one afternoon, I brought him a picnic—cheese, olives, artichoke hearts, figs, chocolate, wine. He looked at this spread, which I had laid out before him with anticipation of the happiness it would give him, and said flatly, as if he didn't care at all about it, "yummy." And then he paid no attention to it. I should have known then that our so-called true love was illusory: he didn't care about food. A small alarm bell went off in my head then. But I ignored it. To pay attention to it would have forced me to face this terrible thing I was doing, would have introduced a jot of reality and sober truth into our folie à deux. So I pushed it aside and went on telling myself that this was the perfect love I'd always wanted.

The end came ten days into our affair, when we fell off the cliff and decided that we had to be together for real and blow up our marriages. That night, Nathan told his wife that he wanted to leave her to be with me. The next day, when he told me, we both panicked; here was the dose of reality we'd needed to make us see things as they were.

"You can't leave your marriage," I said. "Mine is over, but you can't leave, at least not for me. You have kids."

"You're right," he said. It was agonizing and unthinkable to us in our current state, but we agreed to end our affair. He would stay in his marriage, and I would leave mine, and this thing between us was over. We left the hotel and said good-bye and went our separate ways.

The next morning, Nathan's wife went into his e-mail account and read an e-mail he'd just sent to me, in which he said he was going back on our agreement and asked if we could meet that afternoon. I wrote back to say yes. Immediately, his wife called me to beg me to leave him alone. Properly mortified finally, and horrified at myself, I assured her I would let him go and that the affair was really over. And after that, except for the letter I wrote him to say good-bye, a letter his wife intercepted and read, I did not talk to or contact Nathan ever again. He went back to his marriage, and the waters closed over our love affair, whatever it had been.

That day, in tears but resolute, I told Jon that I was leaving him and that our marriage was over. I told him that I'd fallen in love with Nathan, but it was over. When he asked if we'd had an affair, I had to tell him the truth. I could not allow him to hear it from anyone else, but part of me wanted to tell him, to make the marriage irreparable. It was a means of escaping, of shattering everything so that he'd force me to leave.

Of course, he was devastated, hurt and furious. But he also said instantly that he knew he had been neglecting me, taking me for granted. He vowed to win me back. He asked if I'd see a therapist with him. I told him I didn't think there was any hope for our marriage, but therapy might help us end it.

A few days later, I moved into the basement apartment

of an old house behind a French restaurant in Hunters Point, Queens. It was one big room with stone walls, an old fireplace, small high-up windows, a beamed wooden ceiling, and a door out to a back garden. It was half dungeon, half French country cottage, the perfect place to go crazy in.

Technically, I shared a kitchen with the couple who lived upstairs, my landlords, but I never used it; I didn't feel like interrupting their twosome. They were strangers, and I was feeling low and antisocial. They fought a lot late at night, drunkenly shouting at each other overhead. I found this immensely soothing as I lay awake. It was good to hear voices in my deep dungeon solitude. It was good to know that other marriages were fucked up.

I spent every morning at my desk, drinking coffee and writing my fourth novel, *The Great Man*, while cooks and busboys came out to smoke by the Dumpsters in the courtyard. I watched their feet through the window above me. For breakfast every morning, I ate thick, sweet gluten-free bread with peanut butter. After I finished my day's work, in the early afternoon, I walked over the Pulaski Bridge to my old house. Dingo had stayed with Jon in Greenpoint, since my new landlord didn't accept pets. He barked at me despairingly, questioningly every time I arrived. Jon had already left for the day; the agreement was that he did the morning and bedtime walks, and I did the long afternoon ones. Dingo and I roamed through the parks and the streets of north Brooklyn every day, sometimes for hours. Every evening, I took him home and fed him, and on most nights I left him there and walked back to my self-imposed exile in Queens, wishing I could bring him with me.

Because I had no kitchen of my own, I ate in the unfamiliar restaurants of Hunters Point. I had no close friends during this time, or rather, I had allowed myself to drift away from my friends because I was too deeply immersed in the knotty problem of my own life to be good company, so I ate alone.

Afterward, I went back to my underground burrow and stayed up reading as late as I could. Finally, when my eyes started to cross, I went to bed to lie awake and wait for daylight, wondering whether a person could literally go mad and die from loneliness.

The abrupt, forced end of my just-begun love affair, just when hormones and feelings and mania were surging as high as they could go, was weirdly and extremely traumatic, like a psychic amputation in whose aftermath the phantom pain from the missing limb was almost unendurable. To make things worse, facing my part in the end of my marriage and the suffering I'd caused Jon would have been adequate punishment, but Nathan's wife had told the two biggest gossips in our group of friends about the affair. Soon, everyone knew. I might as well have worn a scarlet *A* on my chest when I walked Dingo through north Brooklyn. Although I knew I had no right to expect a speck of sympathy from a single person and received none, the fallout caused me a shocking amount of pain. I felt like I was in a waking nightmare.

My mother had told me, when I was much younger, that an extramarital affair is never a good idea; it's really about problems in the marriage, and involving another person never ends well for anyone. It's always better to end a marriage on its own terms. Of course, she had been right. And of course, I had ignored her advice. But she didn't say "I told you so." She came to visit me. She listened without giving advice. She was stalwart and kind, and she didn't judge me. She was worried about me, but she treated me as if I'd be okay, as if what I'd done was really no big deal, and this was just a little bump I'd get over. This was exactly what I most needed. I didn't tell her how heartbroken and crazy I felt. I didn't want to; it would only have upset her and exacerbated the pain I was in. So we talked very little about what had happened. Instead, we walked Dingo together, drank wine in the evenings, and talked about books, about Susan's kids, about my mother's happy new life as a retiree back in Arizona, in a town called Oracle outside Tucson. By the time she left, I felt comforted, but the instant she was gone, all the demons came back again howling.

Cathi, who had been my best friend since before my marriage, tried very hard to empathize with and understand this sudden, alarming turn of events in my life, even though it had shocked her that I'd suddenly had an affair and left Jon, since I'd convinced us both that I was happy in my marriage. But try as she might, she could not respond to me in a way that I could tolerate. Whatever she said, I felt judged, which made me agitated, defensive, and hurt. I told her I needed her to listen; I knew I'd fucked up. No one could be harder on me right now than I was being on myself. She told me she loved and supported me unconditionally, but she couldn't help worrying about me and trying to help me do the right thing; it was human nature, it was what friends were for. I got more and more angry at her, until she finally told me she couldn't help me, and she needed a break. Her reaction was visceral, instinctive, and honest. I felt as if I'd lost her, and she felt the same way about me.

There were three things that saved me during that time. The first was the unquestioned, unswerving love of Dingo, and the second was the Thai place near my new apartment, Tuk Tuk. It became my regular hangout in the evenings. Its vegetable green curry was good and cheap, and the waitstaff was friendly and kind. I loved the simple warmth of the routine—a glass or two of white wine and a vegetable green curry every night. The third thing was the mathematically conceived structure of the novel I was working on, which I stole loosely from *A Midsummer Night's Dream*, and which comforted me with its orderly precision.

As with my other novels, I wrote *The Great Man* in a state of dire loneliness, and possibly because of this, food serves an important purpose in the book. Eating and cooking bring the novel's solitary characters together, and, in writing about the meals they ate, my own loneliness lifted, just a little.

A few evenings a week, after I walked Dingo and brought him back to Jon's house, Jon came home from his studio early to meet me. We went out to dinner together, and then back to Calyer Street so I could say good night to Dingo. Whenever Jon tried to kiss and hug me good-bye, I panicked; I hyperventilated, and my brain started to go dark. I went back to my basement dungeon to lie awake all night twisting in agony. I wanted desperately to go back to my marriage, but I also couldn't bear the thought of it.

And then, one day, back in my old neighborhood, I ran into my former writing-studio landlady, Nancy. She knew Jon and liked him.

"Kate!" she said to me. "How's it goin'? I haven't seen you around lately."

"I moved to Queens," I said. "I separated from Jon."

"Are you nuts?" she said. "Does he beat you? Is he a drug addict? No? Then why the hell did you leave him?"

I had no easy answer to this.

When my three-month lease was up in Hunters Point, after Dingo's body had stopped making blood platelets and he'd literally almost died of a broken heart and had to go on prednisone for six months, after Jon and I had both come undone because of our own broken hearts, I moved back into the Calyer Street house.

## CHAPTER 51

# Trouble

—— Over the course of the next two years, Jon and I saw two marital therapists: one very bad who told us to just break up already because we were obviously incompatible, one very good who did her best to help us stay together because she could see how much we wanted to. *The Great Man* was published; I went on a book tour. Then it won the 2008 PEN/Faulkner Award. Gradually, the terrible pain from the aftermath of my affair lessened until I could sleep again. I never contacted or spoke to Nathan again, although I sometimes saw his wife driving by or on the sidewalk. She always glared at me as if she wanted to kill me, which no doubt she did, but she never said a word to me.

Slowly Jon and I began to drop our guards and talk to each other. I worked to regain his trust. He worked to regain my passion. After therapy with the good therapist, whom we saw for a year and a half, we went out to eat and drink together, always at the same place, an Italian bistro in Park Slope. This routine, somehow even more than the therapy itself, comforted and steadied me. I always ordered the sausage frittata with a salad, always drank Orvieto. We hunkered down at our table and smiled at each other over our food. This was what we were best at, the thing we knew how to do together to connect. I began to take heart. Maybe things would be all right.

Then one night, about a year after I had moved back, I had

too much to drink at a Christmas party. When I came home and got into bed with Jon, out of nowhere, I saw the violent breakfast scene from my early childhood as if it were happening right in front of me, all over again. There it was, on my brain's screen in living Technicolor: the breakfast table, my father leaping at and pummeling my mother—the suddenness of the violence, that fierce eruption, swift and monstrous— my mother sobbing and hurt and crumpled over the table, my father a muscular tense hotheaded ball of rage, slamming out the door, leaving us there. The long-delayed reaction I hadn't let myself have as a tiny kid was now forced on me in a purely physical way. My chest seized up and constricted in choked sobs. My heart raced like a revved engine in neutral, going nowhere. My brain recoiled in a panicky bruise.

Two paramedics arrived and questioned me and reassured my terrified husband that I wasn't having a heart attack, it was a severe panic attack, and I needed to take some deep breaths and calm down, there was nothing they could do for me. They talked to him as if he were my father, as if I were a small child. I remember feeling that this made sense, somehow. I felt that I looked like a small child in that moment. I was a small child again.

This was the culmination of all the other panic attacks I'd had throughout my marriage, the recoil I'd felt early on, when Jon threw things or had road rage, the collapse into loneliness I'd felt after September 11, the instinctive paralyzed fear I'd felt when we were separated and he tried to embrace me. Coming back to this marriage had not solved anything. I could try to tell myself that everything would be all right, that I would be able to stay with Jon, but my psyche and body were telling me otherwise. They were telling me, more and more loudly and clearly, to flee.

I called my mother and told her what had happened. We both cried, me for her, and her for me. "It never occurred to me that it affected you," she said. "I'm so stupid! You were so little, but I should have known. And me, a therapist."

"You poor thing," I said. "How could he do that to you? How often did it happen?"

"It was maybe five times in seven years," she said. "Well, of course that feels like all the time in some sense. So why did I stay? I always wanted it to be different, I thought somehow magically he'd understand and stop. Also, I was crazy about him. He was always the most fun and interesting person in the room. I never stopped hoping that my leaving would wake him up and make him want us. When I was accepted at ASU, I wrote him a letter asking for permission to move out of state. I was hoping *that* would get his attention, but no. And then with his sudden appearance at our Tempe door—I finally got it, he wasn't going to ever want us."

"I carried that feeling with me for years, too," I said. "Never quite getting that he'd never want us. It was heartbreaking."

After that conversation, I realized that that scene over breakfast so long ago had haunted me all my life. I had always denied it, had always pretended to myself that I was like my father, not my mother, trying to keep my mind safe in any way I could, for as long as I could. For much of my life, I had willfully denied that part of me that was female, not realizing that, ironically, this was the source of my true power, my real identity, and my happiness.

During that winter, I wrote a novel in three months, aptly named *Trouble*. Set mostly in Mexico City, it's about two close friends, women in their midforties, who go for a week's vacation together when both their lives fall apart. In this novel, food and drink represent freedom, exotic romance. They eat chorizo tacos from the little stand outside the Cantina Tlaquepaque;

they sip tall shot glasses of tequila and *sangrita*, and then, in the mornings, hungover, they eat *chilaquiles* from the Hotel Isabel restaurant or go to the Café Popular for *pan dulce* and *café con leche*, then get a fresh pineapple juice from the juice bar across Cinco de Mayo and take their breakfast to the Zocalo to sit in the winter sunlight. Their lives are going to hell, so they eat and drink and smoke cigarettes, as if they were twenty-five, ignoring mortality, middle age, and propriety. The narrator has left her husband without any problems or seeming consequences, met a sexy younger man and embarked on an affair with him, and started a whole new life in her own apartment.

The book was, of course, sheer fantasy. I was trying to stay in my own marriage, so I let Josie do all the things I couldn't let myself do but most yearned to.

Yet as hard as I tried to ignore the gaping loneliness I still felt in my marriage, to put a good face on things in a Pollyannaish way, that lifelong habit of mine, I was still having panic attacks and crying jags. I started drinking far too much, even more than usual, and stopped eating. I became very thin. I flirted maniacally and drunkenly and indiscriminately. I was behaving like a starving animal. I felt as if I were going to explode, but I didn't know how to leave. Jon was so good to me, so loyal and kind and generous and devoted. He did not deserve to have his marriage end. So, given my inability to face myself, the only way I found to leave was to become the villain, to create chaos, rip a hole in the fabric of my life to escape through. I had to unravel, behave crazily, wreck enough of Jon's trust and respect to allow him to let me go.

In August 2008, I flew to Guadalajara to meet Jon, who had gone down a week earlier to hang his work for a group show at the Ex-Convento del Carmen. It had been curated by two Mexican artist friends, both of them named Carlos, who had a loft in the building where Jon had his studio. All the artists in the show were from Brooklyn, a Bushwick collective the Carloses had dubbed the Leonard Codex. Hundreds of people came.

Afterward, Paco, the gallery director, invited a few of us over to his beautiful, strange, dark house, where every wall and surface was crammed full of small paintings and artifacts and his own work, an assemblage of eerie, mechanical, Victorian wind-up toys and boxes. Three guinea pigs and two reeking, semisavage dogs had the run of the place. Paco played 1950s Mexican cha-cha on his old record player, and we all ate roast pork with rice and beans and drank huge amounts of tequila and danced. Jon and I sat alone, close together on the couch, and leaned our heads against each other, smiling at everyone. "You two are so in love," said the smart, serious Dutch girlfriend of one of the Carloses. I felt a lurch in my chest.

The next morning, Jon and I rented a car and drove to Cuyutlán, a tiny town on the Pacific coast, for two nights. It was the off-season. We were the only guests in the huge, crumbling, formerly super-mod hotel that must have been very swank about forty years earlier. It was like *The Shining* set in Brasilia, a long-gone architect's modernistic sci-fi dream, rooms built around the inner wall of a huge curving shell, the lobby set within, with internal freestanding rooms, the now-closed bar, restaurant, and dance floor as grand as an MGM movie-musical set, now all falling to pieces, with chunks of concrete breaking off and plaster sconces detaching from walls. We were given the room on the top floor at the very end; we perched up in the furthermost corner in a little box with a tiled balcony that looked out over the black volcanic beach and the ocean. Except for the two of us, all seventy or so rooms were empty.

The main street felt like a movie set, too, waiters standing idle, music playing futilely, a hot ocean wind blowing across empty chairs and tables, ruffling place mats and nap-kins. Everyone eyed us with hopeful yearning as we strolled up and down the street, studying menus and consulting each other. We finally chose the restaurant directly across from our hotel. As we seated ourselves in the centermost of the empty tables, we could feel a collective sigh around us. Our waitress was a young girl, all merry smiles at having been the lucky win-ner of our business. She encouraged us to order the fish special, and so, of course, we did. We were served plates of well-fried whole sea fish with heads and tails intact, alongside yellow rice and a limp salad.

Although we had been passionate fellow eaters from our first date all through our fourteen years together, neither of us had much appetite. We didn't talk about the terrible summer we'd just had, during which Jon had worked night and day in his studio to get his photographs ready for the show, and I had gone very obviously insane with grief, longing, and panic. We sat over our dinners, trying to eat our fish, making quiet, grim jokes about being the only game in town.

After dinner, we crossed the street for a drink, because there seemed to be another customer in the outdoor bar attached to the hotel, a man sitting alone, hunched over his lap-top, wearing headphones. He turned out to be the owner and local expat; he was American, and he had married the daughter of the previous owner. He was a chain-smoking, shambolic, entertaining, obsessive music buff who mixed drink after drink for us—Herradura mixed with a weirdly delicious neon-blue soda—while he played us choice, rare old R&B and jazz he'd downloaded into his computer. At about two in the morning, we got up to go. He begged us not to leave. There were so many more songs he wanted to play for us.

We crossed the street to our dark, cavernous hotel and climbed the stairs to our room. Its tiled floor was slick with condensation, and the air was stuffy and humid. We opened

the window and went to bed. I lay awake for a long time, listening to the wind blowing steadily off the ocean. Jon lay next to
me. I thought he was asleep, but then he asked out of the darkness, "Are you having an affair?"

Shocked with a strange relief I didn't understand, I burst
into tears.

"No!" I said. "I know, I've been so distant and strange. I'm
so sorry. I'm not having an affair, that's the last thing I need.
But I needed you to ask me that."

Then we had sex. It turned out to be the last time. Although
things between us were warmer and calmer for the next two
weeks, and it felt almost as if we had returned to each other,
the marriage was over. Gradually, I became manic and panic-
stricken again.

The night before he flew back down to Guadalajara to take
down his show, as we sat in our living room at opposite ends of
the long red couch, Jon looked at me with clear comprehension.

"You're out of here, aren't you," he said.

I felt the same odd shock of relief I'd felt when he had confronted me in our hotel room.

"Yes," I said, a little dazed. "I guess I am."

## CHAPTER 52

*Sweetwater*

———— Jon and I were together for a total of fourteen years; much of my grief at leaving him was that I was losing the person I trusted absolutely, whom I had so much deep history with. We were young when we got together, and now we were middle-aged. Our marriage had been good in so many ways. We were family; we supported each other, had each other's back. We went through deaths and September 11 together. He helped my mother and me plan an intervention, over the course of two or three years, which ultimately failed, to try to get Emily and her family out of the Twelve Tribes. And, thanks to Jon, I had found my older half sisters, Caddie and Thea.

We were comrades in work. He believed in me unswervingly. Likewise, I had supported and encouraged him through the ups and downs in his own work—painting, music, photography.

We traveled together to Australia, Oaxaca, Israel, Mexico City, the Yucatán and Chiapas, Costa Rica, Panama, New Orleans, Amsterdam, Paris, Guadalajara. We endured and shared a daily life, two hardheaded, hotheaded, stiff-necked, hardworking firstborns, bustling and blustering through our days in Brooklyn, fighting all the time but always, in the end, managing to make a kind of peace.

Although I am technically the asshole who behaved badly and left, I know that it was no one's fault. I feel that we were tuned to radically different frequencies. We were temperamentally incompatible. It was as if we were two entirely different species trying to coexist in one cave. It was like a hypothetical *Star Trek* episode in which a Romulan falls in love with a Klingon and they genuinely try to adapt to each other's ways and characters and then, in sorrow and heartbreak, fail.

And I could not stop yearning for some other, lighter, easier kind of connection. I craved true love with a soul mate so intensely, it felt sometimes to me as if I would die without it.

During the time it took for our marriage to officially end, which is to say, during the time I was simultaneously trying to leave and trying to stay and consequently going slowly out of my mind and breaking both our hearts, Jon and I cried a lot in restaurants. Crying in restaurants had become something of a joke between us during the years when everyone was dying— we could never eat out without one or both of us shedding at least some tears and not infrequently weeping openly. But during our breakup, our restaurant crying surpassed anything we'd done before.

We did most of it at a local place called Sweetwater, where our favorite waitress—a beautiful, elfin, madcap girl—knew our favorite drinks and brought them to us without asking and stayed by our table to banter and kibitz. We tipped her very well, of course—we always tipped all waiters and waitresses very well but her most of all. She also somehow knew to stay away from our table if one of our heads was down, especially after four or five rounds of drinks—Herradura on the rocks for him and Sancerre for me.

I was the worst offender. Sometimes I had to duck my head for fifteen minutes at a time while unstoppable tears poured down my face onto my lap. But sometimes it was Jon. He was angry at me, and I was angry at him, because we had a heavy weight of accumulated, unsolvable things between us, but most of all we were unbearably, bitterly, mutually sad.

Two years of marital therapy and determination hadn't worked. I had given this marriage my all, and I was still frustrated and lonely. In October 2008, I finally left for good after too many episodes of self-medicating alcohol abuse, severe panic attacks, manic spells, depressive spells, out-of-control behavior, and overwhelming, debilitating sickness of soul. I left because I had to, but I ran away from my good, solid, kind husband in a state of terrible panic and grief. It was the hardest decision I'd ever made.

After we separated, we agreed to share custody of Dingo as long as we could, because he was both of ours, and we both loved him. And we kept eating together: food had been our greatest bond, and we weren't ready to lose that, too. We continued to cry in restaurants, and we continued to joke about it—but now, instead of going home together to sleep in separate lonely tandem, we'd go home to our now-separate places to sleep alone.

Not once did I regret leaving—I was devastated and sad, yes, but I also felt suddenly miraculously better, as if I had been let out of a cage or freed from a spell. My psyche and soul, which I'd bent for so long to the task of staying in my marriage, sprang upright, relieved all at once of my impossible demands on them. I felt intact, autonomous, and whole—able to shape my behavior and thoughts according to my true desires and untrammeled will. I could breathe.

And I was far less lonely now that we were separated. Or rather, my loneliness took on a new quality—when I was living with Jon, it had been unacknowledged, diffuse, scattershot, and therefore dangerous to me and possibly others. Now that I was alone, I could discover safely, gingerly, and by degrees that I was sane.

## CHAPTER 53

## The Blue Hour

──── For the first five months, I sublet my friend Jami's loft a mile down the waterfront while she did a stint on the West Coast. When she returned, I moved back to Greenpoint, to a big, airy railroad apartment on Monitor and Norman, exactly one block away from the old apartment I'd lived in before I married Jon. I felt like I had come full circle, except that now my rent was $1,800 a month, and that was considered a bargain.

There's a certain time of day, after sunset, when people naturally seem to feel the urge to gather together by a fire or a stove or a hibachi or another common source of heat and food and hunker down together to eat and drink. I started thinking of the blue hour as a hump I had to get over, a period of restless bleakness during which I yearned for company. I wanted to go out and eat in a restaurant just to be around other people. Suddenly I missed Jon, missed being married. On some especially blue evenings, I almost, but never actually, wished I had a roommate. And I regretted the solitary nature of the writer's life—other people, normal working people, spent their days with coworkers, rode the subway home with a crowd, walked through thronged streets. I worked at home, all by myself. Of course, I had Dingo, but a dog just doesn't cut it in the blue hour.

Although it was preferable to eat with other people, cooking for one, that one being my own damn self, was the most effective way I had of shaking that sense of desolation. As soon as the sun went down, I went into the kitchen and started chopping things. I made just enough dinner for me, a simple and comforting and filling meal—one broiled chicken thigh, or even two, with a baked sweet potato and a side of garlicky red chard, for example; or cauliflower curry over basmati rice served with cashews, sriracha hot sauce, and cilantro; or a puttanesca with gluten-free pasta and anchovies, capers, olives, and hot red pepper flakes. I always made sure I had plenty of food in the refrigerator and cupboard; keeping the kitchen well stocked was another comforting bulwark against loneliness. And I became much neater as well. The Calyer Street house was generally messy and cluttered, dishes in the sink, laundry not put away, stuff covering the dining room table, and I didn't care and neither did Jon. In my own place, I kept everything neat and shipshape.

When the meal was ready, I heaped up a plate, sat at a table set for one, and feasted. I looked out the window at headlights and taillights streaming beneath the spangled struts of whatever bridge I was looking at; Jami's loft in South Williamsburg had a view of the Williamsburg Bridge, and my apartment on Monitor Street in Greenpoint had a view of the Kosciuszko Bridge. I found that I looked out the window a lot more often now than I had when there was someone else in the house with me, as if a view of the outside world were some instinctive way of feeling connected to other people. Sometimes I put music on. Sometimes I lit a candle. Sometimes I wolfed down the food so I could get back to my e-mail. I always drank wine.

These meals for one had a counterintuitive, resonant coziness. Eating by myself in my own apartment, single and alone again for the first time in many years, I should have felt, but did not feel, sad. Because I had taken the trouble to make myself a real dinner, I felt nurtured and cared for, if only by myself. Eating alone was freeing, too; I didn't have to make conversation,

I got to focus on my food without thinking about anyone else's needs at all, and that made it taste even better. I didn't have to share my dinner or worry about taking too much food: it was all mine. I could sing along to the music and wear pajamas and eat with my hands and drink the whole bottle of wine and lick my plate clean. Who would know or care?

Dingo lay at my feet, and little by little, as the evening went on, his company became, once again, sufficient. When I was done with my food, if there was anything left and he was allowed to have it, I gave him a scrap or two. Then he and I went out into the now-dark evening and made our rounds together, ambling along the sidewalk. I waited while he sniffed intently at tree trunks, lampposts, and bushes and deposited a squirt of pee on everything, lifting his leg as high as he could get it and often missing the thing entirely, sending his little stream out into space to land on the sidewalk or street. He squatted; I hovered behind him with a bag at the ready, scanning for the nearest trash can.

Then we went home again and spent the rest of the evening together. I read a book or wrote e-mails; he lay nearby and watched me. He always turned in before I did.

Sleeping alone was another luxurious pleasure that should have been depressing but wasn't. I got to hog the covers, sprawl across the whole mattress, use all the pillows, and move around as much as I wanted without worrying about disturbing anyone else. No one snored in my ear or talked in his sleep. No one woke me up. No one stole the covers or accidentally nudged me with his leg or got up and creaked the floorboards on the way to the bathroom. After my satisfying solitary dinner, I was the captain of my bed, the master of my sleep. But even so, I longed for a bedmate—the urge became stronger and stronger as the months went on. I became tired of the blue hour, cooking for one, eating everything all by myself, watching the cars streaming over the bridge, and daydreaming about falling in love.

## BACHELORETTE PUTTANESCA

*At the end of a hard, interminable, raw winter day, when it was too late
to schlep to the store, in need of a quick hearty feast, I invented an easy,
unorthodox cupboard-supper version of puttanesca from whatever I had
on hand.*

I opened a 24-ounce can of fire-roasted tomatoes, simmered these
with herbs and lots of red pepper flakes, a minced onion, a nice fat
dollop of red wine, 2 tins of sardines, an oversized handful each
of chopped black olives and chopped marinated artichoke hearts,
a pound of chopped spinach, and a chopped bunch of parsley.
Meanwhile, I boiled some chicken broth, whisked in some polenta and
herbs, added lots of Parmesan cheese and butter, then baked it in the
oven for 45 minutes at 350. The spicy, insouciant, brackish sluttiness
of the dish cheered me up more than I would have dreamed possible.

The above paragraphs contain not one letter "g," and I did that on
purpose to make a point—I'm fairly sure the omission is unnoticeable.
Cooking without gluten is akin to writing without a crucial letter:
it's tricky to do, but if you succeed, no one should notice or feel
deprived. It's a minor trick, and when it works, it's invisible.

## FISH IN BANANA LEAVES

*When my friend Janice and I both found ourselves single at the same
time, we cooked for each other or went out for dinner at least once
a week. She can't eat gluten, like me, and, to make things even more
complicated, she also can't eat dairy, so our meals were of necessity
limited and proscribed. When we went out together, we felt like
special-needs, high-maintenance nudniks, interrogating the waiters,
deliberating over menus, sometimes even sending things back, but when
we cooked for each other, our meals were relaxed and luxurious feeling.*

I loved going over to her top-floor walk-up apartment in the East Village and sitting at her wooden table, drinking wine and talking, while she bustled around. She put on Mexican music and set out bowls of freshly roasted pepitas with sea salt, rice crackers with rich goat cheese, pulpo in garlic sauce, and red pepper–spiced green olives. While she cooked, we drank the wine I'd brought, and then we opened another bottle to drink with dinner.

Dinner could have been fish baked in banana leaves, or fish and scallop ceviche, or pollo pipián (chicken in pumpkin sauce with green chili). Whatever it was, it was always so perfectly cooked and savory and fresh and interesting that we were temporarily, happily unaware of our irritating dietary restrictions. We dined together like normal people, like people who could eat whatever the hell we wanted.

For 2 people, buy 1 pound (2 good-sized fillets) of very fresh, firm ocean fish, such as red snapper or grouper.

Peel a head of garlic. Blend the cloves in the blender with enough olive oil, about ¼ cup, to make a thick paste.

Rub this olive oil/garlic mixture into the fish on both sides and then cover the fish with dried leaves of the Mexican herb hoja santa (available at Mexican specialty stores).

Wrap each fillet in a banana leaf and tie into a packet with cooking twine. Bake the packets on a cookie sheet in a preheated 350-degree oven until done, about 20 minutes.

Serve with basmati rice with roasted corn, and kale cooked in olive oil with garlic.

For dessert, serve chocolate or coconut goat's milk ice cream and glasses of a light dessert wine like vin santo.

# PART TEN

# New England

## CHAPTER 54

## El Quijote

One day in mid-October 2008, two weeks after I left Jon, I sprained my ankle badly. That weekend, my friend Lara, a novelist who lives in Taos, New Mexico, was in town for one night, so I gimped on crutches down to a waiting car service and went off to the West Village to meet her and a group of her friends in a bar. Later in the night, she turned to me and said, "The most beautiful man is about to walk into the bar. He's a lot younger than you, but don't let that stop you. He won't look at any woman under forty."

"I'm not ready to meet anyone yet," I said. "I just left my husband!"

Lara was fierce and vehement. "He's a classical guitarist, Kate, a documentary filmmaker, and a writer," she said. "He's on his way from Taos to live in a farmhouse in New Hampshire and write a book of poetry. He just made a documentary about Marines killing a goatherd in remote Texas. Just trust me."

My instant, private reaction was Taos? Classical guitarist? *Poet?* I expected a ponytail and a leather bracelet.

A while later, in walked a tall, lanky, graceful young man who looked like a cross between a seventeenth-century duke in modern dress and *le petit prince*, all grown up. Lara had been right: I almost laughed out loud.

"Hello," he said, having seen me looking at him. "I'm Brendan Fitzgerald." He had glinting blue eyes with thick lashes, swooping golden hair, and a warm smile. I figured that any young poet must need mentoring; there was nothing else to be done with someone so young. I found myself launching into an anti-M.F.A.-program rant.

"Well, then, maybe I won't apply to an MFA program," he said, evidently amused and not at all intimidated.

"Well, good," I said. "You're from Taos?"

"I've lived there for the past few years."

"Do you all sit by fire pits with your dream catchers, talking about past lives and drinking chardonnay?"

His eyes glinted at me. "That's *exactly* what we do there."

I asked him about his documentary. He asked me about my novels. He was warm, thoughtful, erudite, and funny; he did not seem twenty-seven or however old he was (twenty-six, it later turned out). I could have eaten him for breakfast, but it was much too soon to eat anyone for breakfast, especially a handsome young documentary-making classical guitarist poet who could laugh at himself.

I said good night at 11:30 and gimped out and hailed a cab.

As I left, Lara said to Brendan, "Isn't she great? You should run after her!"

"She wouldn't be very hard to catch on those crutches," he said.

Brendan went up to his farmhouse in the White Mountains of New Hampshire for the next six months to write, and I stayed in Brooklyn all winter and cried over my failed marriage, saw a lot of my women friends, and did not go out with anyone, if only because no one asked me on a proper date. Newly single after fourteen years, I found myself in a strange new world of hookups and sexting and online dating and IM'ing. I was good at none of those things and unwilling to try any of them. Single men my age seemed shy, as I was—or afraid of sticking their necks out, as I was. I felt as if I were at a junior high school dance again, all us single people in our forties looking fearfully at one another, either never married or just divorced, gun-shy, burned out, traumatized.

In March, I went up to visit Cathi and Dan in Northampton, where they'd moved with their two kids about a decade before. It was the first time since my affair that I'd been there. Maybe because Cathi and I are both fighters who never give up on anything, we found, to our mutual relief, that our friendship was somehow stronger than ever for having been broken. And Dan, who had maintained all during our schism that we were both insane, welcomed me back as if nothing had ever happened, still his same warm, laconic, wry self.

One night, after we'd all gorged ourselves on Cathi's and my mutual favorite dinner—baked chicken thighs, baked yams, and steamed chard with plenty of red wine for me and plenty of dessert for her—she and Dan and I sat talking after their kids had left the table. They were curious and sympathetic about my midlife dating difficulties and listed all the potential available men they knew, who were all, it seemed, divorced with two kids, all writers of one sort or another.

"They sound great," I said. "I'd love to be a stepmother. And writers are okay, whatever, I just wish someone would ask me on a damned *date*. Dinner. That would be nice."

"Describe your ideal man," said Cathi, who loves a hypothetical discussion as much as I do. "Go ahead, say everything you want."

"Okay," I said. "Here goes." And I listed a set of attributes, laughing the whole time at the sheer unlikelihood of ever finding a man with all of them, let alone enough of them. "Someone totally available, first of all. No jealous, possessive, crazy women anywhere in his life. Someone funny who challenges me—that would be good—and someone I feel totally comfortable with *and* madly attracted to, someone who doesn't bore me, someone calm and soothing, someone who has a good relationship with his work—he doesn't have to be rich or successful. But of course he should be sexy. Also handsome, intelligent, literary, musical, and physically coordinated." I looked at them and laughed again. "But, really, I'd go out with *any* of the guys you suggested. Seriously."

It hadn't occurred to me to specify the age of my ideal man. Evidently, the universe was listening, but it had a sense of humor.

A week after this conversation, Brendan e-mailed me that he was coming to town soon, and would I like to have dinner? As I found out later, Lara had told him that he'd made quite an impression on me, and he wanted to see if it was true; it was. I wrote back to tell him I'd be delighted.

It was the first date I'd been on since leaving Jon; I'd been well and truly single for six months. I got waxed and bought new lingerie, confident that we were going to sleep together— after all, what else could a guy who had just turned twenty-seven want with a forty-six-year-old woman, or any woman for that matter?

When I entered El Quijote, a tapas restaurant on West Twenty-third Street, Brendan was already sitting at the bar. I smiled, walked up to him, and dropped my keys on the floor. He laughed. It put me at ease immediately. I wanted to commandeer our menus, certain that a man in his twenties had no idea how to order anything, let alone tapas, but he took over and ordered for both of us with grace and ease. For the next five hours, we sat close together, turned toward each other on our stools, telling each other about our entirely different yet mysteriously similar lives, families, passions, and experiences. I forgot to eat, I was so interested in our conversation.

When they kicked us out at closing time, we fell into a cab together and hightailed it back to his place. Our clothes came off in a blur; there wasn't time for me to worry about our age difference. Too charged and euphoric to sleep, at one point we both started laughing together at the shock of unexpected happiness. But the next morning in the bright light of the shower with him, I freaked out, wondering what I looked like, having been up all night.

However bleary-eyed I might have been, apparently he didn't mind. At one point, he even asked me to marry him, albeit jokingly.

It turned out the joke was on us. For our second date, I took the train up from New York to Boston. Brendan picked me up and we drove north, high and floating, with loony grins on our faces. After a couple of hours of driving, we turned onto a dirt road that ran by a huge, pristine lake. Wet sunlight shone on bare mountains through charcoal clouds; the lake surface was choppy in a stiff, cold breeze. We turned into a driveway, pulled up to a barn, and walked across frozen grass to a cozy farmhouse.

Inside, Brendan opened a bottle of chilled Orvieto, pulled out a *peperonata* he'd made, wrapped cantaloupe slices in prosciutto, and assembled a *caprese*. We fell on this cold feast, eating with our hands, standing by the counter. It was still winter, but to us, it was torrid tropical spring. We drank the first bottle with the food, talking and talking in a state of intoxicated, jibbering mania, and then we drank another, sitting by the fire—and here the Victorian curtain goes down.

## CHAPTER 55

# Elaine's

—— Whenever Brendan and I stayed at my Monitor Street apartment in Greenpoint, we cooked in my old-fashioned kitchen with its pantry, the refrigerator in the hall, the 1940s cupboards, the view of the Koscuiszko Bridge. Sometimes we went out to a little French place in Williamsburg where I had almost no history. Walking through the streets of north Brooklyn with Brendan felt surreal. There was no scarlet *A* anymore: my marriage was over, and I was free to do whatever I wanted now. But the memory of that feeling, the sense of wrongdoing, persisted. I felt as if I were doing something illegal. I even skulked. When people I knew saw us together, I had an instant flash of guilt even though I knew it was irrational. I couldn't believe that no one had the power to stop me from being with him. On warm nights, we sat up in the roof garden of Juliette at a little table among total strangers and ate raw oysters and steaks with salads and drank glasses of cold Provençal rosé. Afterward, we smoked cigarettes, luxuriantly letting the smoke curl skyward. I hadn't smoked in years, but I felt that nothing could hurt me.

I had finally, for the first time in my life, found my true soul mate. It felt like a cosmic joke that he'd turned out to be almost twenty years younger than I was. Age didn't matter at all. I hadn't known this before. The most important things, at least to me, were a shared temperament and desires, a sense of effortless, joyful, almost mystical connectedness that went beyond the superficial facts of our circumstances.

However, along with our delirious, manic joy, we both felt anxious and wary. Brendan had recently been shaken by a couple of flings with unstable, needy women who were much older than he was. They had objectified him and treated him as if he weren't a serious prospect because of his youth, and he was leery of its happening again.

But I could relate to their fears. Still grieving and raw from the end of my marriage, I sometimes wondered, in a panic, if I could expect to be happier with someone so young. Even though he was ambitious and hardworking and brilliant, Brendan had no real career yet, no money. Even though he had traveled all his life, had had plenty of adventures and relationships, I still had twenty years more of life experience, during twelve of which I had been married. I was worried that I was too traumatized by the fallout from my marriage to be able to give myself fully to him, so soon after it had ended. I wondered whether I could make him happy ultimately.

Much of our talking in our first six months was about these fears. We challenged each other, tested each other, put each other through the wringer, even as we offered each other reassurance and love. We were both blown over by how quickly, fully, and precipitously we had fallen in love. Of course, we were terrified of being hurt and disappointed, of making a mistake. It was very clear from the start that this was no halfway thing, no light romance or short-lived fling. It was all or nothing with us from our first date. We'd put ourselves in each other's hands, exposed ourselves completely and absorbed each other, and so we had to be very careful. We were splayed out, completely headlong.

One night in late September, we went out to dinner with my mother's ex-husband Ben. It was about a week before Brendan and I were supposed to fly to Italy for three months to live in his grandmother's villa in Tuscany; it was being sold and therefore sat empty, waiting for a couple of mad writers in love to haunt it. After a bland meal and a couple of martinis, Ben announced that he had decided that Brendan and I could never work as a couple; it was impossible. He told us that my "whole family" was concerned that Brendan wasn't strong enough for me (my mother and Susan later scoffed at this claim). He added that, based on his own experience and knowledge of men (meaning himself), Brendan would inevitably cheat on me. And he'd leave me eventually, as soon as I got old and wrinkled; it was only a matter of time. "No man can resist young flesh," he said. Or Brendan would be too intimidated by my relative success to stick around. Either way, we were doomed.

On the way home that night, I was terror struck. Ben had hit a nerve and articulated all my worst fears. Marching along the sidewalk in a tipsy fog of defensive self-protection, I said, "Ben was right. I'm too old for you."

"I'm not Ben," said Brendan. "I will never cheat on you, I don't give a damn about 'young flesh,' and I'm not intimidated by you, and I never will be."

"How can you know that?" I said. "You can't. Things change."

"I won't change," he said. "In fact, I'll love you even more when you're wrinkled and old."

"I don't believe it," I said. "Also, it's too soon after my marriage ended. We have to end it now."

"I can't force you to change your mind," he said. "I wish I could."

I felt nothing but relief.

The next morning, we called the airline and canceled our tickets to Italy.

The relief I'd felt the night before intensified. We had to go our separate ways. My stepfather was right: this could never work.

During the next hour or so, we began disentangling our psyches, bodies, belongings. Brendan packed his things—his clothes, guitar, and books—to head back up to New Hampshire alone. I looked around at my apartment and imagined being single again for a while, free to meet a man my own age when I was ready, when I'd recovered from the end of my marriage.

Then it occurred to me that my stepfather had always had a drastic track record with women. When he was younger, he was a narcissistic charmer and serial seducer; and in his later years, after my mother left him, he was constantly getting involved with women my age or younger, affairs that always ended painfully for him when his girlfriend of the moment left him for a man her own age. He might have been projecting his own fears onto me and his own former caddish behavior onto Brendan.

The truth was that Brendan and I were ideally well suited to each other, no matter how old or young we were. We wanted and loved and valued the same things in life. He had never wanted kids, had always felt much older than his age; I was a late bloomer, young for mine. He was extremely calm, easygoing, even tempered. In fact, he was exactly the person I'd described at Cathi's: he had every single quality I'd listed, and more. If we parted ways now, I knew that this would be over, that there wouldn't be a way back in for either one of us. It hit me that if he left now, this would be the end for real.

I looked at him. Here he was—too young, too soon, too intensely, too complicatedly. But nothing was ever perfect.

If I let him leave now, I would never know what might have happened between us. This thought was more untenable, far sharper and scarier, than any of the fears Ben had named.

Cautiously, apologetically, I told Brendan that I'd made a mistake. I asked him to stop packing, to stay. I explained: Ben had been projecting his own fears onto us, I knew that he had no authority to doom us. It took a while, but finally Brendan was persuaded. He called the airlines and managed through force of will to convince the person on the other end to reinstate our tickets, free of charge.

## CHAPTER 56

## The Hermitage

—— For most of three months, from early autumn into early winter, we lived in the large stone villa where Brendan's aunt and mother had lived as schoolgirls, a former convent up in the Florentine hills. We watched the dawn on our first morning, standing out on the bedroom terrace, listening to roosters yelling all over the valley while the sky over the wooded hills turned neon pink and orange.

The place had its own vineyard and olive grove, as well as persimmon trees, rosemary and sage bushes, potted lemon trees, a few scraggly chickens, and a vegetable garden. It was olive season. The air was smoky from the olive branches burning everywhere. Nets lay under the olive trees, and men stood on ladders reaching into the branches all day. When it was time to press the olives, we went with Fabio, the villa caretaker, to the Cooperativa agricole. The huge truckload of olives was dumped onto a conveyer belt that took them into the washer and sorter; they embarked on a long, intricate journey of pressing and turning until finally, two hours later, streams of fresh golden oil poured from a spout to fill eight or nine enormous, stoppered vats. It was bitter and rich and tasted like nothing else on earth.

The wine from the villa's vineyard was thin and light and very subtle, almost like liquid Valium. Fabio filled wine bottles for us from the demijohn in the toolshed and corked them with a manual press. We drank legendary quantities of it.

Renting the apartment attached to the villa was a Botoxed, boob-jobbed, trout-lipped So-Cal fortysomething divorcée named Jennifer, who might have seen *Under the Tuscan Sun* one too many times. She held spiritual meetings for her expat friends and didn't speak any Italian although she'd been there for two years. Her lonely little son was obviously yearning to be back in L.A. with his friends. She wore a shawl and twitched it self-consciously. I was fascinated by what I took to be her hilariously cartoonlike personality.

Near the end of our time there, Jennifer invited us over for dinner. She turned out to be funny, vulnerable, and self-deprecating, impossible to dislike. I had probably looked askance at her because I was also a fortysomething divorcée. Her situation reminded me too sharply of what I'd just been through. All I wanted to do in Italy was escape.

That winter under the Tuscan rain turned out to be exactly what I needed. Living so far away from everyone and everything I knew, and my recent past, gave me perspective and clarity and a respite from this absurdly intense hothouse of emotion I'd been stuck in. Brendan and I became true friends there, engaged in a solitary, productive life in our hermitage in that beautiful but freezing-cold place that cost a small fortune to heat. We were like wacky children together, laughing and singing and babbling in various accents, wandering around in our bathrobes, cooking meals, playing Scrabble by the fireplace.

We set up small worktables in the two deep dormer windows of our bedroom, side by side against the wall opposite the big bed, separated by a trunk and an armchair. We spent our days and nights in this room, writing, listening to music, sleeping, watching movies on our computers with the heat on. We cooked meals in a huge kitchen down the stone staircase through a long tiled hallway at the other end of the house.

Safe in Italy, in the throes of new love, far from my old house and neighborhood, I began work on my sixth novel, *The Astral*. The narrator of the novel is a man in late middle age, cast out of his home like an old Adam banished by his Eve from a comfortable, domestic Eden, falsely accused by his jealous wife of having an affair with his female best friend. I shaped the book around the idea of secular paradise lost, Harry alone, humbled and brought low. His need to understand the past is intense and urgent; he's a falsely accused man hell-bent on proving his own innocence and discovering the actual perpetrator of the crime. The book was inspired in about equal parts by Joyce Cary's *The Horse's Mouth* and the convention of detective noir, in which the accused becomes the crime-solver by default, to clear his own name, and goes around interviewing anyone who can help him figure it out.

During the time I spent writing the novel, my life felt as if it were zooming simultaneously ahead toward the future and back to the past—like dual time travel. Harry took me around the neighborhood where I'd lived for the greater part of twenty years, most of my adult life, the neighborhood I had just left behind forever. While I went on with my life, he stayed in north Brooklyn for me, faced it all, grappled and wrestled with the insoluble mystery of the death of love.

Every day, at around two o'clock, Brendan and I took the same walk, a big loop that brought us along a high ridge, through vineyards, and down tiny Tuscan country roads to the village, where we often had a little coffee and bought supplies—clementines, a whole chicken, romanesco—before climbing up the steep hill through a big olive grove and home again. On the ridge, we could see Florence down below on the left and on the right, a lush terraced valley and mountains with long fingers of fog in the high gulches.

Once home, Brendan cooked us classic, simple, rustic Italian dishes he'd learned from his father: spinach *gnudi* with a butter sage sauce; roast leg of lamb with green pepper-apple-onion curry, arborio rice, and mango chutney; tender osso buco; a *peperonata* over polenta so silky it melted in our mouths; lasagna with veal Bolognese and béchamel; breaded veal cutlets, crisp and thin, with a fresh chopped garlic-tomato-and-basil sauce; a Sicilian eggplant pasta known as *alla Norma*, a pure alchemy of olive oil, garlic, eggplant, fresh basil, and *ricotta salata*, mixed well into a bowl of hot, freshly cooked penne.

He made pizza from a recipe invented by Marcella, the villa's retired cook and housekeeper. On a rolled-out rectangle of golden-white dough rubbed with olive oil, he spread chopped black olives, capers, and anchovies; thinly sliced mozzarella and prosciutto cotto; and a sauce of strained tomatoes with more olive oil, oregano, basil, and salt. Then he baked it hot and fast. It was the best pizza I had ever eaten.

One day, we went with Brendan's father to Perugia, the medieval mountain town where he and his five siblings grew up while Brendan's grandfather Robert Fitzgerald was translating *The Odyssey*. We had lunch in their old family villa, a huge, drafty, very beautiful old place with a view all the way across the valley to Assisi. It was bitterly cold that day, and the massive stone house was like a walk-in refrigerator. We all sat hunched for warmth by the kitchen hearth at a long wood table while Brendan's aunt and uncle, who lived there with their young son, served an Italian Sunday lunch—spaghetti *al pomodoro* (I gave up and ate gluten in Italy and was therefore bloated and churlish much of my time there, but it was almost worth it), then flank steaks and cauliflower—they grilled the steak on the open kitchen hearth. We drank prosecco first with olives and cheese, then Chianti with lunch, and for dessert, *vin santo* with pears poached in red wine and cinnamon and sugar, along with the pignoli cookies we'd bought in town before lunch. It was a memorable, dreamlike afternoon.

For two weeks during the holidays, we stayed in Rome in Brendan's friends' apartment, a large aerie overlooking the Piazza di San Cosimato in Trastevere. We were dog-sitting an ancient female yellow Lab. We called her Mrs. Walrus because she was portly and philosophical and possibly very dumb. A few times a day, we took her down to the piazza in the creaky old elevator and shuffled beside her as she made her lumbering but enthusiastic rounds. Her gnomic, sweet disposition struck me as something to emulate in old age.

On Christmas Eve, Brendan made a *bollito di manzo*, the traditional Italian Christmas meal, a shoulder roast boiled with vegetables and herbs. When it was done, he took the meat out and set it aside and cooked tortellini in the broth, soup to start. The meat was sliced and served with *salsa verde*—a thick, savory sauce of blended hard-boiled egg, anchovies, garlic, parsley, capers, and olive oil—and arranged on a plate with sliced boiled potatoes, tomatoes, and hard-boiled eggs.

After dinner, we walked to midnight mass at Santa Maria in Aracoeli to see the famed Gesù Bambino. It was a warm, wet, windy night. The old cobblestones were gleaming, the river was wild and rushing, and everything was lit up. In a tree by the Tiber, thousands of tiny birds crowded the branches, singing. We climbed a mountain of slippery steps to the church and sat with a crowd of yuppified, bourgeois Roman families in the pews, all of us awaiting the Bambino. After the oddly cheesy, subdued mass, he was finally released from his cabinet near the altar and grandly processed about the church. Brendan and I started giggling; he looked exactly like a dark, dried pineapple.

On New Year's Eve, because we'd forgotten to make reservations, we landed in a cynical restaurant for an overpriced meal that gave us both intense stomach pains immediately afterward—the condition of the kitchen and food-handling standards were nothing I cared to think too much about. Brendan had described the Roman New Year as a kind of Mardi Gras—wild decadence, fireworks everywhere, the city exploding with abandonment, people fucking in the streets, drunk and high and lost in pleasure. I had been understandably excited to see this, but we had to go straight to bed after that dinner; also, a thunderstorm with wild wind and rain competed with the fireworks, so being inside seemed doubly attractive. We crawled into bed, and the poor terrified Mrs. Walrus came with us. We fell asleep well before midnight, huddled together warm and snug as the thunder and fireworks blasted all around us. The next morning, we awoke fully recovered.

## CHAPTER 57

## Homecoming

During the following spring, spending most of our time back in Brendan's farmhouse together, it began to dawn on me that I had actually left New York.

I remembered one morning, a month or so before I'd fallen in love with Brendan, when I had awoken trapped in my bed, listening to clanking, roaring garbage trucks outside, choking on cigarette smoke from the apartment downstairs, sensing the seething millions of people around me, pressing on my skull. That morning, I saw the city clearly, suddenly, as if for the first time—it was loud, dirty, crowded, touristy, expensive, maddening. Had I changed or had New York? Was it me or it? It didn't matter. From that moment on, I had to leave.

In my mind, of course, I was still a New Yorker, just an expatriated one. New York was the only place I'd ever felt I belonged. Whenever I went back, I felt the startling relief of hearing my own language, and every block shimmered with a ghostly overlay of memories. But nothing made me want to live there again.

I loved the deep, total quiet of the farmhouse. I loved not seeing any lights at night, only the Milky Way arching over the sloping fields. One morning, we saw a coyote foraging for fallen crab apples; that afternoon, we walked down to the clean, wild lake as the sun set and stood on a dock listening to the spooky, theramin-like singing of the freezing surface.

On a faraway ridge, a line of shaggy old hemlocks marched along like primordial beings. The next day, a hawk landed in the meadow below the house and sat in the sun for a while, apparently daydreaming.

In July 2010, just as I finished writing *The Astral*, I heard from my mother that my sister Emily with Campbell and their four children had come out of the Twelve Tribes. They had left Australia altogether and moved in temporarily with Campbell's parents in the Bay of Plenty in New Zealand. After all these years, she was back in our family, and without any strain or strangeness; that was never Emily's way.

But, she had told our mother, it was wrenching for her to be away from the community she'd lived in for so many years, where she'd met and married her husband, where all her children had been born, where her closest friends lived. They had all raised their kids together. Emily had been the community's teacher. Now, their little family was isolated in a small, suburban New Zealand town where Emily knew no one except her in-laws, where she and Campbell had no jobs, no home of their own. She told our mother that she was having a very hard time adjusting to life outside of the group. She needed to feel close to her family again. And we needed her just as much.

My mother had been planning to spend most of December in Amsterdam with Susan and Alan and their two sons, Milo and Luca, so she offered to fly Emily there, and of course I decided to go, too.

And suddenly there we all were, the four of us, together again in Amsterdam. Everyone still looked the same. We all shared the same old jokes. We were a little rusty with Emily, and she with us, but only at first. The habits of being in a family are deep and ingrained. Over the decades, during all the rifts and schisms and confrontations and silences and offenses

and resentments, something had been at work, a strong under-
tow of love, in all of us. We sat around Susan's table on our
first night and looked at one another, smiling, hardly knowing
where to begin. All four of us were adults now, all of us were
settled in our far-flung lives: Susan in Holland, where she ran a
yoga center and was raising her two boys with Alan; me in New
England; our mother in Arizona with a huge group of friends,
a full social life, and a lot of adventures; and Emily in New
Zealand—all of us with some combination of life's natural
weight: friends, husbands, kids, dogs, houses, in-laws, work,
regrets, triumphs, and histories. It was a cold, snowy December in Holland, but we were warm, inside and out.

We took Emily shopping in Amsterdam's finest thrift stores
and bought her a whole new sexy, stylish wardrobe to replace
her community clothes. We got her hip-length chestnut-brown
hair cut into a sleek and shining mane that fell to the middle of
her back. I took her to get waxed. When she emerged from her
baggy modest dresses and heavy braid of hair and sensible sandals, she looked about the same as she had at seventeen, when
she'd left to marry Claus: willowy, curvy, beautiful, leggy, and
suddenly confident, suddenly laughing a lot more, her once-
drawn face alight again, full of fun. We went to pubs and ate
mounds of *fritjes* all afternoon, while the boys drank sodas and
we adults had beer and wine. We cooked big dinners together.
Susan, who is an ayurvedically trained vegetarian cook, made
beautiful, simple meals. I made vegetable curries and homey
soups. Emily, who isn't fond of cooking, happily chopped and
peeled whatever she was asked to. Our mother ate whatever we
put in front of her and gushed over it.

After we ate, Emily sat at the piano and Susan and I stood
around her with our glasses of prosecco or wine, and we sang
all our old three-part songs, the ones we'd performed all those
years ago at the Reed coffeehouse the year they'd visited me
in Portland, the winter Emily and I had fought so bitterly. We

sang "Moonshiner" and "Star of the County Down" and "Home in Pasadena" and Mozart's "Laudate Dominum," our mother listening on the couch and smiling with tears while the three of us fell easily into our old harmonies, our voices, older now, rusty, and sometimes even creaky (and sometimes I had to sing through a lump in my throat), blending just as naturally as they had when we were young girls. All our differences seemed to melt away—all the things we'd ever disagreed about, all the things we'd been so angry at one another for through the decades. While we sang together with our eyes on each other's faces, smiling, we were as close as we had ever been in our lives, maybe closer, for having been separated for so long.

Our family was so much bigger now than it had been when we were young. It had expanded to encompass so many other people—my six nieces and nephews; Alan and Campbell, and Jon, too, who'll always be part of my family even if our marriage is over; and Brendan; and Caddie and Thea, our half sisters, and their husbands, Pop and Vin, and Caddie's daughter, also named Thea. And now that Emily was back, the circle was well and truly complete.

After two weeks of food and wine and laughter and the occasional flash of ancient annoyance (families never change) and overwhelming, amazed, grateful joy, I flew back to New England. Brendan and Dingo picked me up in Boston, and we drove north through a dark, snowy, cold evening. I was so happy to see them again, so happy to be back home in New England where I belonged. We drove the last miles slowly along the pitch-dark, empty dirt roads back to the farmhouse. We slept deeply together in the absolute quiet and dark, woke to the morning light on the mountains, coffee with half-and-half and honey, and warm soft-boiled eggs with buttered toast.

## CHICKEN TAGINE

*I invented this recipe by describing it on the fly in the first chapter of my novel,* The Great Man, *in which a seventy-four-year-old woman half seduces a forty-year-old man with food, and then I made it in order to test my imaginative culinary instincts. There is no modest way to say this: the apricots melt into the broth and sweeten it deeply, the olives give it brine, and the almonds and cilantro and lemon bring it to life. And it contains cinnamon; it is, in a word, delicious.*

On low heat, sauté a chopped red onion and 5–6 minced garlic cloves in lots of butter (or ghee) or oil. Add coriander and cumin, about a tablespoon—yes, I said tablespoon, of each (feel free to use already ground; I like using a mortar and pestle, but some people don't)—a teaspoon of cinnamon, half a lemon's worth of grated zest, a generous pinch each of saffron and cayenne, a teaspoon of paprika, 2 bay leaves, and a thumb-sized lump of grated fresh ginger. Keep heat low, stir constantly, and make sure nothing burns or sticks; add more ghee or oil if necessary.

When it's all cooked into a commingled fragrant brown spice puddle, add a red and a yellow pepper, diced; a large carrot or 2 medium carrots, peeled and chopped small; a generous handful of cracked green olives; a handful of dried Turkish apricots, chopped small; one 15–16 ounce can of well-rinsed chickpeas; a cup of Pomì diced tomatoes; and a cup of hearty chicken broth. Bring to a gentle boil, then right down to a simmer, and cover.

Cut up 5 skinless, boneless chicken thighs and 3 breasts, more than 2 pounds of chicken in all, into big bite-size pieces—the kind you have to cut in half to really eat—and grill them in a cast-iron skillet in ghee or oil till they're brown just on the outside and still raw inside, then add them to the stew and stir everything together and gently simmer it, covered, for 4½ hours. Add more chicken broth as necessary.

Sauté and slightly brown 1 package or 2 cups couscous—or, if you're gluten intolerant, quinoa—in 2 tablespoons butter, then cook according to the directions on the packet. Serve with harissa or shug, along with bowls of chopped toasted almonds, lemon slices, and chopped fresh cilantro.

---

## ORECCHIETTE WITH BROCCOFLOWER

*In the first year of our love affair, when we were delirious and invincible and I could eat anything I wanted, Brendan made this for me with real pasta. Now, four years later, my gluten intolerance is back to normal, and we are no longer delirious or invincible, merely profoundly happy and contented, so he uses gluten-free pasta. Either way, it is a fantastic dish.*

Chop a broccoflower (a neon-green broccoli-cauliflower hybrid with dizzyingly otherworldly conical whorls that looks like a *Star Trek* vegetable and is also known as romanesco) into bite-size pieces. Bring a large pot of salted water to a boil. Add broccoflower and simmer for 5 minutes. Add 1 pound of orecchiette to the broccoflower in the water and follow directions on package for cooking, usually 11 minutes.

Meanwhile, peel 8 cloves of garlic. Chop roughly and sauté in hot olive oil in a large skillet on low heat. Add salt, pepper, and crushed red pepper flakes. Let the garlic just begin to brown—don't overcook.

Drain the pasta and broccoflower and add to the large skillet and toss with the oil and garlic. Add generous amounts of Parmesan, more salt, black pepper, and crushed red pepper flakes to taste, stir, and cook on low heat for 2 minutes. Serve hot with more cheese and pepper. This simple but luscious meal serves 2 voracious people.

## Epilogue

———— Starting over in midlife is an interesting thing. The past doesn't go away or even recede behind you; it stays with you. I didn't know that when I was young. I thought things fell away and disappeared. Now, I know otherwise. I am exactly the same person as I was when I was born, and I always will be. Everything that has ever happened to me—every meal I've ever eaten, every person I've loved or hated, every book I've read or written, every song I've heard or sung—is all still with me, magnetically adhering to my cells.

In the fall of 2011, Brendan and I bought a nineteenth-century brick house in the West End of Portland, Maine, and then we moved all our things into it and hired a contractor to renovate it. The farmhouse is just over an hour away; we go back and forth along little country roads in our Subaru with Dingo in the backseat. Our life is settled, quiet, and calm. It turns out that true happiness is a simple thing, as simple as dirt.

On St. Valentine's Day, Brendan and Dingo and I took our walk along the dirt road, then veered off down the path through the woods to the lake. We walked out onto the frozen lake and back toward home. The ice seemed thick enough, but we didn't know for sure. It made strange whale-groaning sounds far out on the lake and at one point it cracked thickly under Brendan's feet. We were a little spooked, but not enough to go sensibly back to shore, so we continued out over an inlet. Dingo, highly intelligent as always, walked far enough away from us, closer to shore, so that if we fell in, he'd be safe. Meanwhile, we humans burbled along like daring eight-year-olds, shoe-skating and light stepping and whooping with suspense. Out there on the flat, frozen surface, we had a dazzling view of the White Mountains just to the north. It was a clear day, and the far-off, snow-covered, looming Mount Washington seemed close enough to walk to.

After about a mile, we made it safely to the dock where we swam in the summertime. Although rationally we knew the danger was minimal, we were giddy from the relief of not falling into the freezing-cold lake. We climbed up through the woods and came home along the road. In the warm house, we shed our coats, out of breath.

I made us buckwheat blini with fine black mild caviar and crème fraîche. We drank *cava* with a dash of orange juice and listened to the most innocuous, elevator-music-like bossa nova in the world, and laughed at ourselves for liking it.

We ate and drank all day long. Brendan shucked fresh Maine oysters, which we ate raw on ice by the fire with shallots in white wine vinegar and a cocktail sauce of lemon juice, ketchup, Worcestershire sauce, Tabasco, and horseradish.

I dismantled two small endives and, on twinned pairs of the crisp, subtly bitter leaves, I slathered sour cream and loaded each with capers, fresh basil, and oil-packed artichoke hearts. We ate the whole plateful with a fresh batch of blini and slabs of two rather spectacular mild cheeses and some seedless purple grapes.

Then I steamed a bunch of slender asparagus spears and served them with a gobsmackingly delicious dipping sauce made of the rest of the white wine vinegar-and-shallots mixed with mayonnaise and Dijon mustard. After this, I steamed